wire art

wire art

Scott Hann and David Smith

Chilton Book Company
Radnor, Pennsylvania

Published in Radnor, Pennsylvania, by Chilton Book Company
and simultaneously in Don Mills, Ontario, Canada
by Thomas Nelson & Sons, Ltd.
Library of Congress Catalog Card No. 78-22149
ISBN 0-8019-6712-0 *hardcover*
ISBN 0-8019-6713-9 *paperback*
Manufactured in the United States of America

1 2 3 4 5 6 7 8 9 0 8 7 6 5 4 3 2 1 0 9

Contents

	Acknowledgments	vii
1	Basic Materials and Techniques	1
	Introduction	1
	Tools and Supplies	2
	Covering Backboards with Fabric	10
	Enlarging Patterns	14
	Nailing Patterns	16
	Basic Instructions for Wiring	22
2	Basic Geometric Designs	31
	Square	32
	Circle	36
	Rectangle	40
	Curve	44
	Angle	48
	Opposite Angles	52
	Various Angles	56
3	Combining Basic Geometric Designs	61
	Double Square	62
	Double Circle	66
	Rectangle and Square	70
	Circle and Angle	74
4	Using Three Layers	79
	Diamond	80

5	Abstract Designs	85
	Snowflake	86
	Extended Diamond	90
	Continuous Curve	94
	Wave	98
	Boxes	102
6	Ships	107
	Hull Making	108
	Two-Masted Schooner	110
	Skipjack	114
	Spinnaker	118
7	Advanced Projects	123
	The Crisscross Method	123
	Clipper Ship	124
	Antique Roadster	132
	Valentine	136
	Balloon	140
	Spiral	144
	Motorcycle	148
	Hummingbird	152
	Fluffy Egret	156
	Groundhog	160
	Kangaroo	164
	Runner	168
	Figure Skater	172

Acknowledgments

Special thanks to Scott Hann from David Smith for his extensive work on this manuscript.

Thanks, also, to the manufacturers past and present for whom we have designed wire art and to the Hobby Association of America at whose trade show we met our editor, Lydia M. Driscoll.

Our gratitude to Robert McLean, our good friend and associate, for losing the first draft in Houston. This copy is much better anyway, Bob.

The following people deserve special mention for their patient moral support and help on the manuscript: John Hann; Steve Hann; Broome Wingate; C. H. Boyd; Michael P. Lane; Starr and Jami; Michael Heinikin, photographer; Debbie Blood; and Gary and Peggy Jackson.

1 Basic Materials and Techniques

Introduction

Hobbies and crafts have enjoyed an exciting resurgence of popularity over the last ten years. Today, more people than ever are exploring new and unusual creative and constructive hobbies. Do-it-yourself kits of various kinds, complete with material and instructions, are available in hobby, crafts, variety, and department stores as are ample supplies of open stock materials for all types of projects.

This wire art manual is intended to answer the needs of both beginners and experienced wire artists. The beginner will find a step-by-step course of instruction, including discussion and illustration of basic materials and methods on which to build. For those who have completed wire or string kits and wish to create their own projects, this manual also includes suggestions and techniques for more complex designs.

The authors, having designed the majority of the wire art kits now being manufactured in this country, have tried to provide in this manual all the basic information necessary to master, and enjoy, the craft of wire art.

The basic instructions in Chapter 1 apply to all projects in the book and should be read carefully before any projects are attempted.

Tools and Supplies

Necessary Tools

Only a few tools absolutely are necessary for the wire artist. These tools, shown in Figure 1-1, are a pair of needle- or long-nose pliers, a hammer, a rule, and a pencil.

Fig. 1-1 Necessary tools for wire art

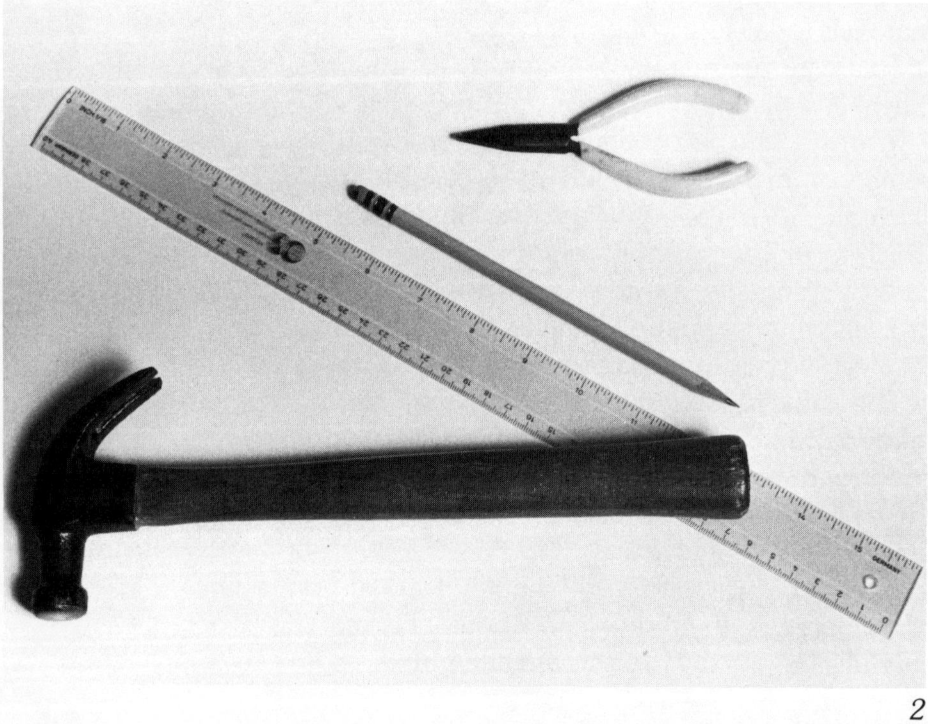

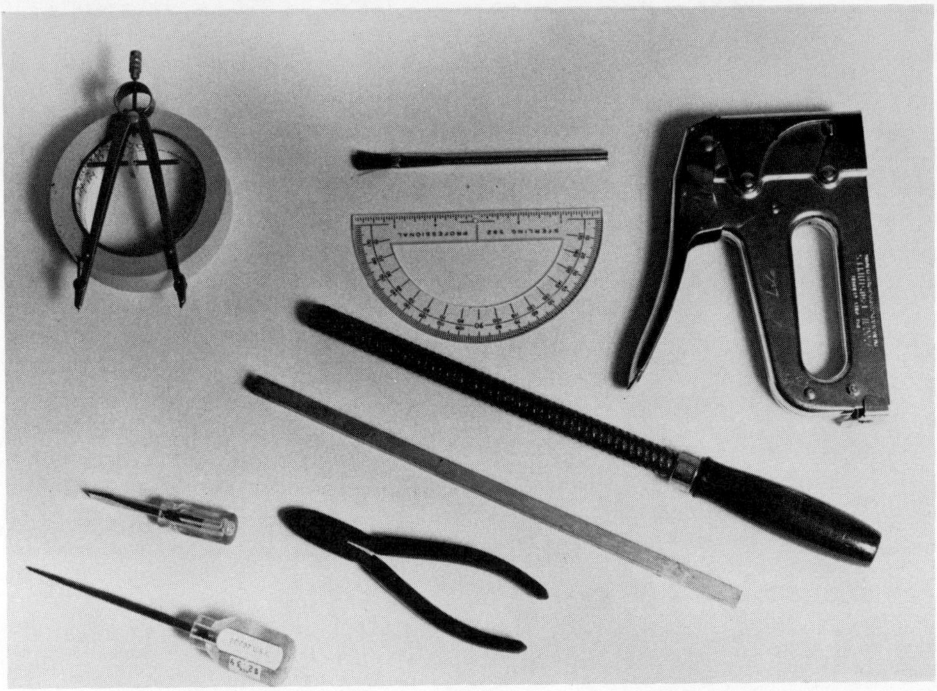

Fig. 1-2 Optional tools

Optional Tools

Additional tools that may be helpful to the wire artist, are a stapler, a protractor, a compass, tape, a nail bar, wire cutters, a rasp, and a paint brush. Most of these tools, shown in Figure 1-2, are standard, and special uses will be explained when necessary.

Backboards

A few of the most common backboards, shown in Figure 1-3, are plywood, lumber, and corkboard. Particle board also works well. Most lumberyards stock these and will cut to your specifications.

Fig. 1-3 Backboards

Board Coverings

Popular board coverings include velvet, vinyl, leather, and felt. Staining or painting the backboard are also possibilities. Fabric shops carry all of the coverings shown in Figure 1-4, and many other coverings you might wish to experiment with.

Fig. 1-4 Board coverings

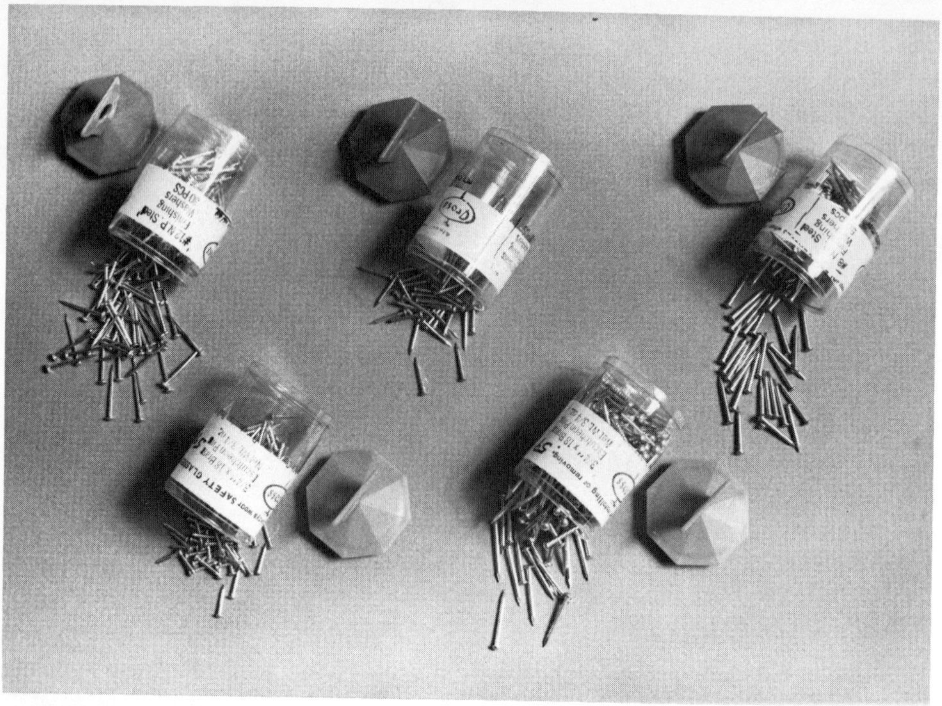

Fig. 1-5 Various kinds of nails

Nails

Nails, brads, escutcheon pins, and finishing nails, shown in Figure 1-5, are recommended, although any nail can be used. These may be found at any hardware store. We prefer ⅞-inch, 15-gauge escutcheon pins with about ½ inch of pin exposed above the board.

Wire

We use 26 or 28-gauge, coated copper wire, shown in Figure 1-6, but anything close to this, including metallic lamé, will do. Craft shops are the best places to locate these materials.

Fig. 1-6 Various kinds of wire

Paper

Any pad of paper or drawing paper can be used for drawing the pattern. If neither of these is available, cut up a grocery bag, but use a paper that will tear readily without dislodging the nails from the backboard. If you use heavy paper, cut it away rather than tearing it off.

Fig. 1-7 Paper for making patterns

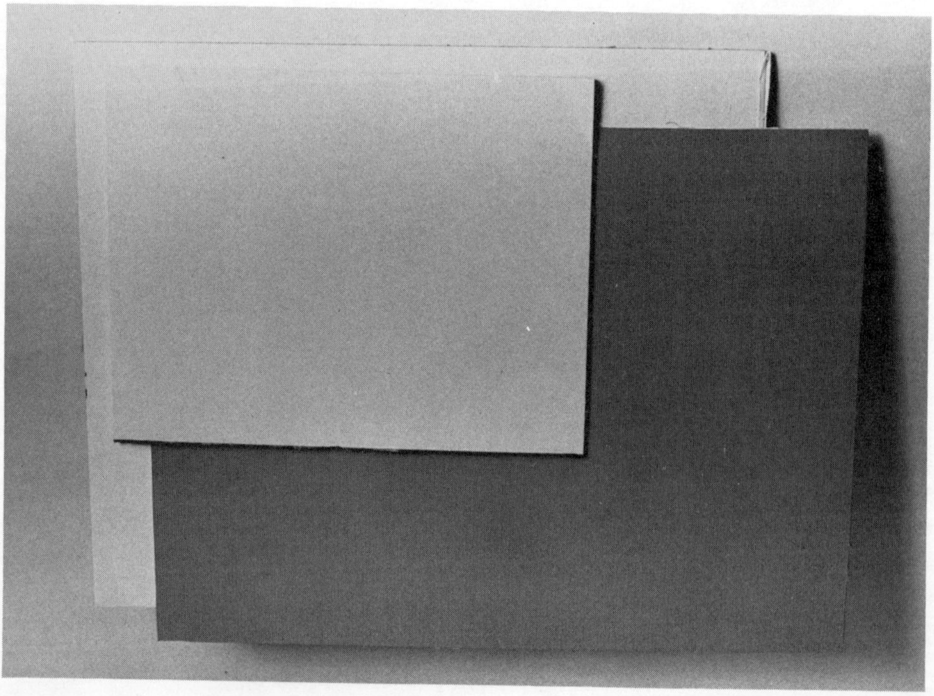

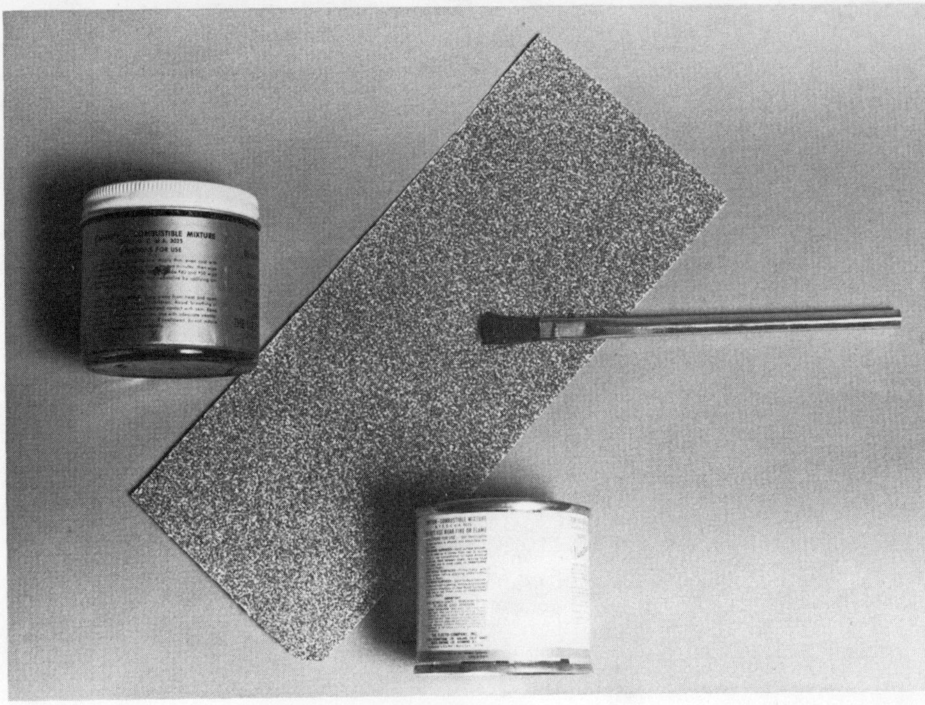

Fig. 1-8 Hull-making and woodworking accessories

Hull-Making and Woodworking Accessories

For some projects, wood (soft pine and redwood are easiest to work with), sandpaper, stain, and a paintbrush are necessary. A saw may be needed for larger projects.

Covering Backboards with Fabric

Centering Board on Fabric

Once you have selected your board and fabric, the first step is mounting the fabric on the board. Place the board in the center of the wrong side of the fabric. Be sure the fabric is at least two inches larger than the board on all sides. This border is necessary for tacking the fabric securely.

Fig. 1-9 Centering a backboard on fabric

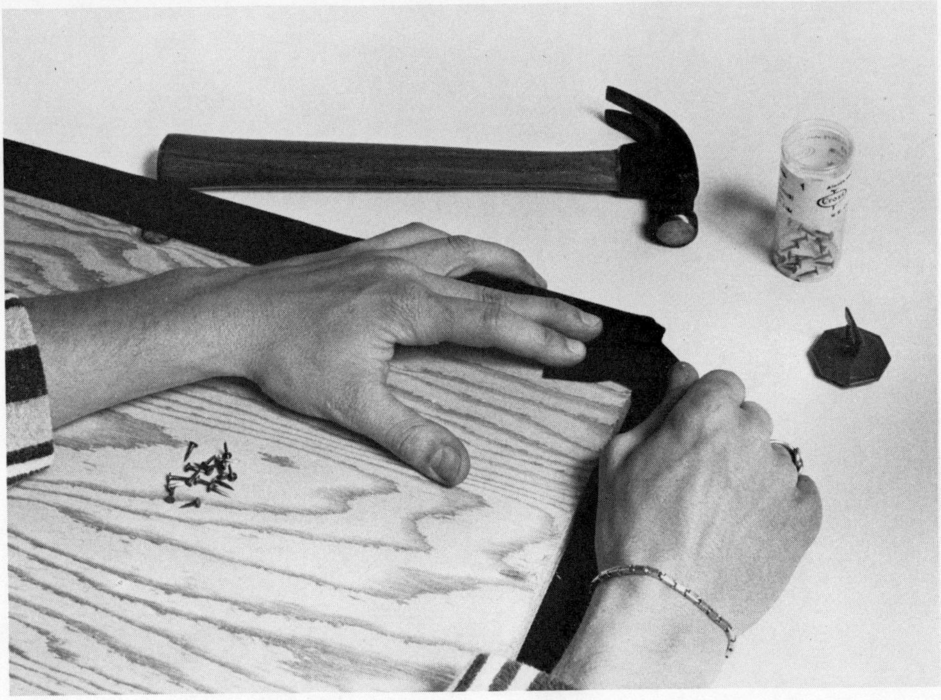

Fig. 1-10 Stretching fabric at the corner

Tacking Fabric to Board

Using small nails or tacks and a hammer if needed, tack down one long side of the fabric margin to the wrong side of the board. Turn the board around, pull the cloth taut, and tack down the second long side.

Next, gather the fabric at one corner and tack down where the gather is thickest. Continue around the board, stretching the fabric as you go and tacking it down one end at a time.

After tacking, check carefully for wrinkles. If you find any, stretch the fabric to the back and secure with a tack.

Fig. 1-11 Tacking fabric to the board

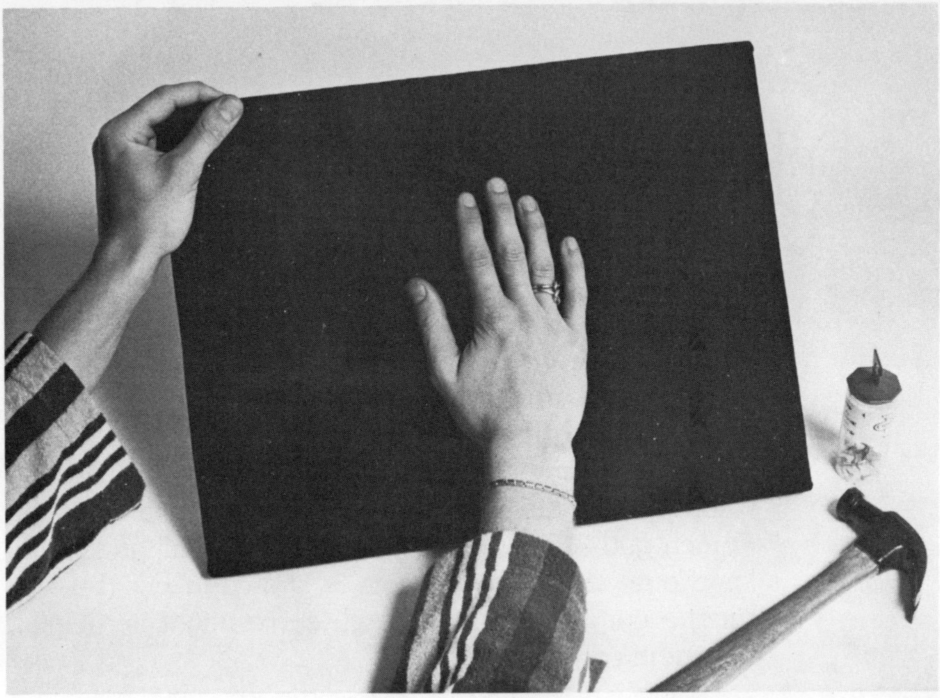

Fig. 1-12 Checking for wrinkles

Enlarging Patterns

To enlarge a pattern for nailing, draw a grid either directly on the design or on tracing paper placed on top of the design. For example, space the intersecting lines of the grid ¼ inch apart, as shown in Fig. 1-13.

Next, on another piece of paper, draw a ½-inch grid with approximately the same number of squares as the ¼-inch grid. Copy the design from the small grid to the large one, square by square, as shown in Fig. 1-14. A ruler, a compass, and a French curve might be helpful, depending on the design.

To reduce a pattern, reverse the process, drawing a ½-inch grid over the design and transferring it to a ¼-inch grid.

Fig. 1-13 Design on ¼-inch grid

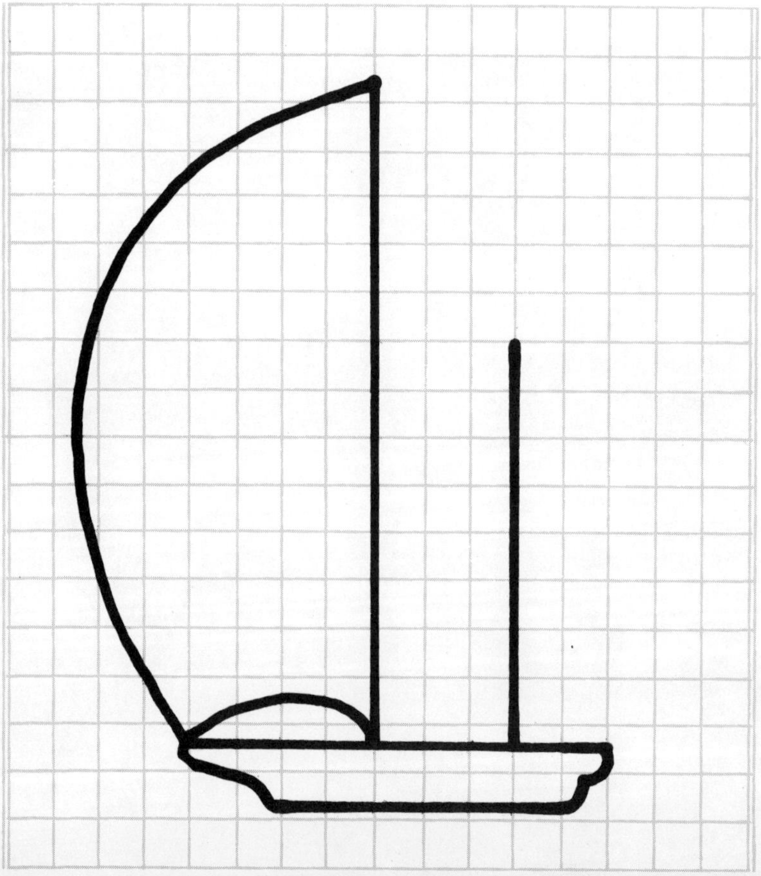

Fig. 1-14 Design on ½-inch grid

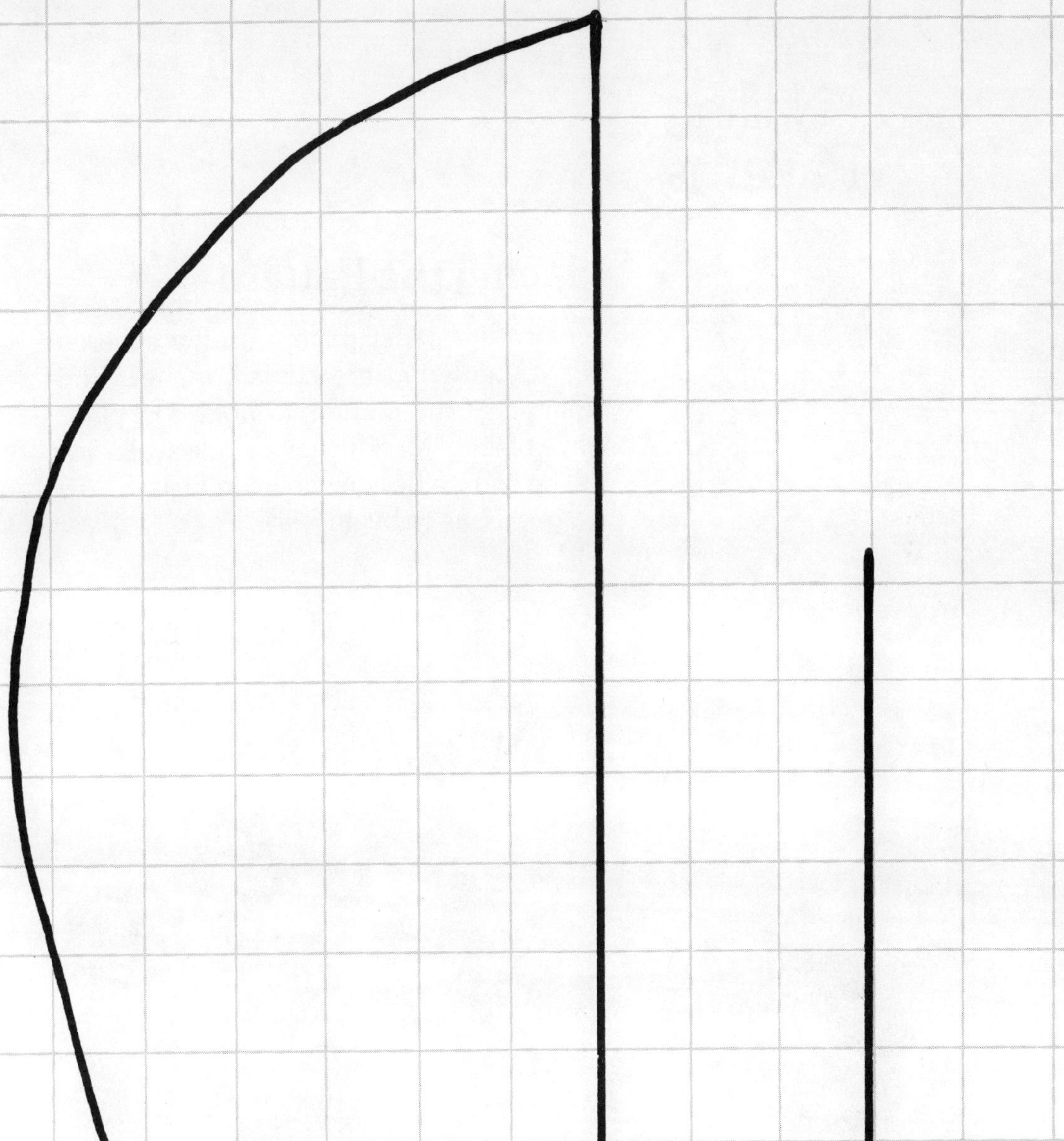

Nailing Patterns

Placing the Pattern

Place the paper pattern on the covered board, centering the subject matter, and taping it at the corners to hold it in place while nailing. Masking tape works well.

The square design shown in Figure 1-15 is a good one to begin with.

Fig. 1-15 Placing the pattern on the backboard

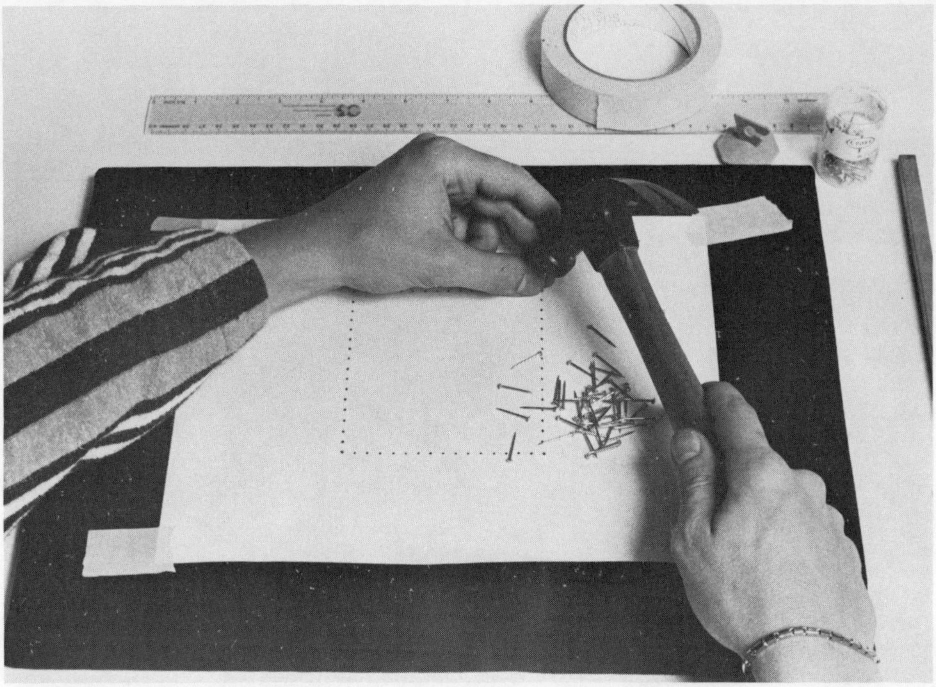

Fig. 1-16 Driving the nails into the backboard

Driving the Nails

Being careful not to hit your fingers, begin driving the nails into the board at even intervals, perhaps ¼-inch or ⅜-inch spacing. Try to keep all nailheads at the same height—⅜-inch to ½-inch height is recommended.

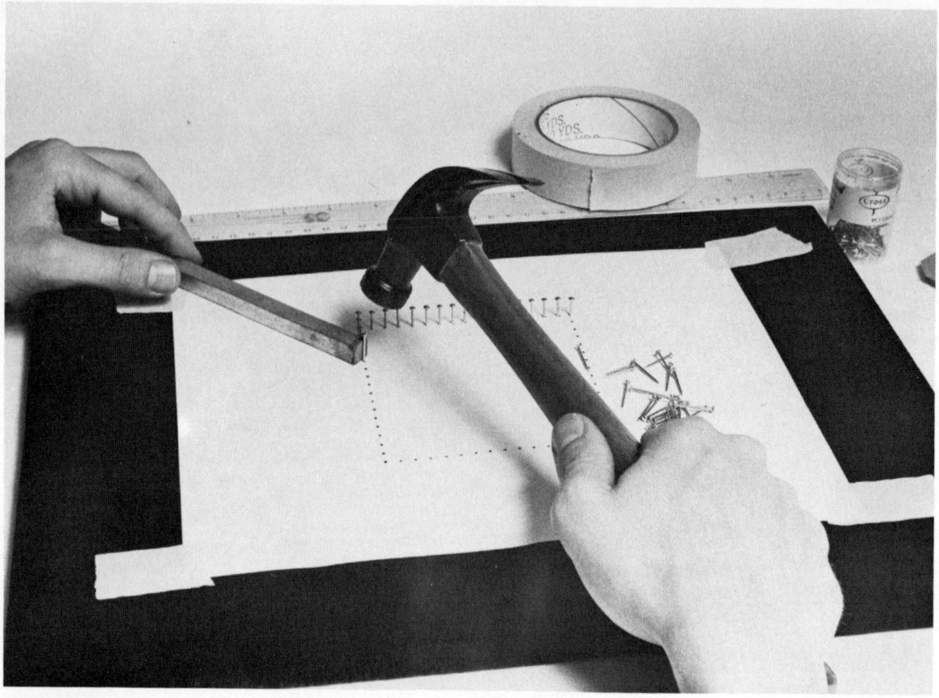

Fig. 1-17 Using the nail bar

Using the Nail Bar

The nail bar is very helpful in judging nail heights, as shown in Figure 1-17. These metal bars, ⅜-inch square and about 6 inches long, can usually be found in hardware stores. When you are nailing your own design, the nail bar can be used to help with spacing.

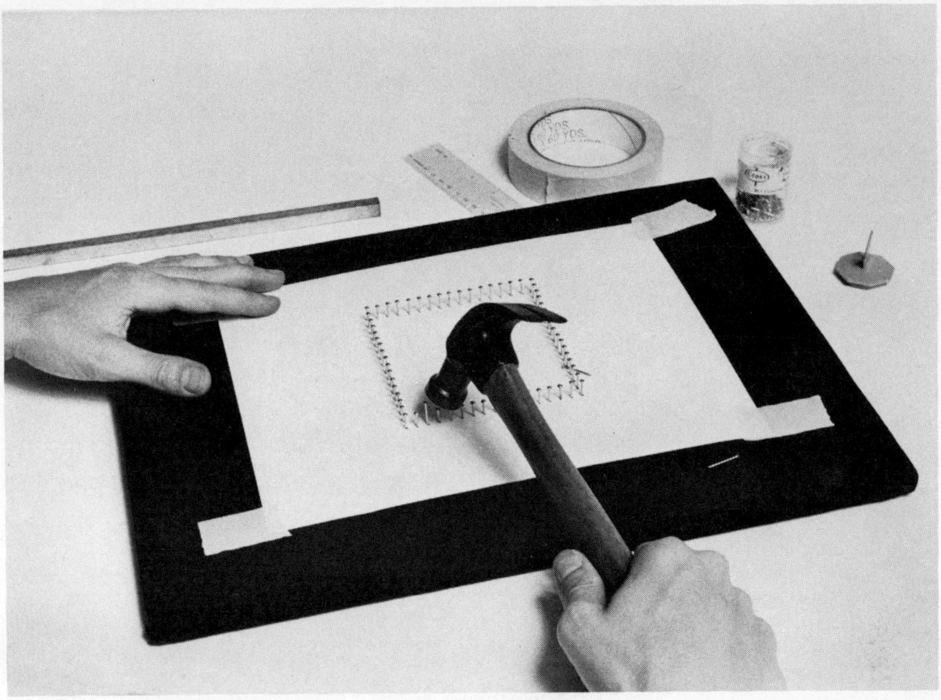

Fig. 1-18 Finishing nailing

Checking Nail Height

When the nailing is finished, recheck nail heights to be sure they are even and straight. The nail bar will come in handy here also.

Straightening Nails

Look at the nailed design from all angles to be sure the nails are as straight as possible. Use long- or needle-nose pliers to straighten any crooked nails.

Fig. 1-19 Straightening the nails

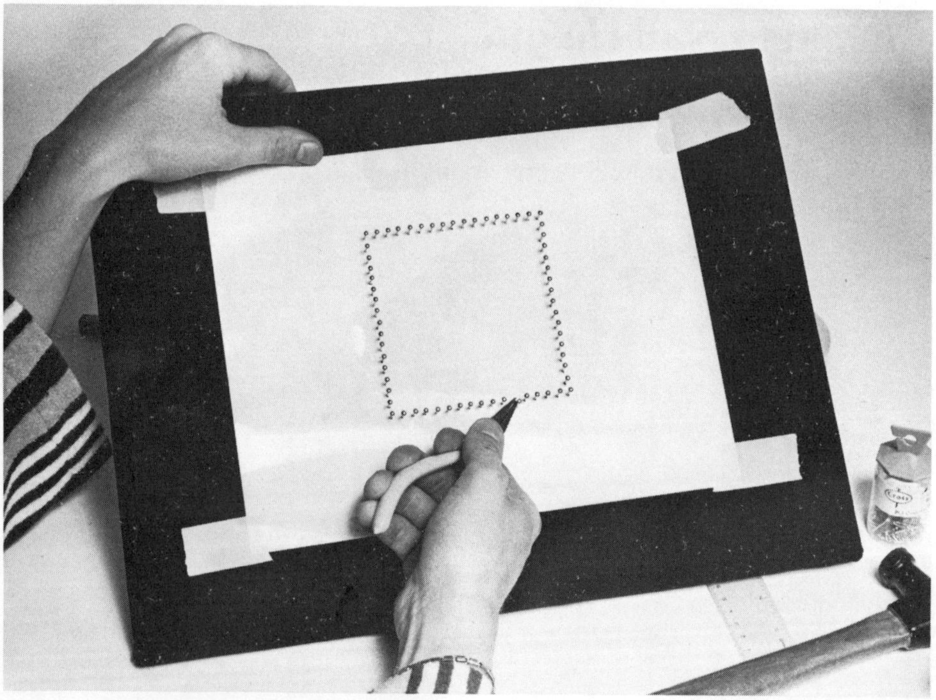

Removing the Pattern

When the nailing is finished, carefully tear the paper pattern away from the nails. If heavy paper was used, cut the pattern away gently so that the nails remain in position.

Fig. 1-20 Removing the pattern

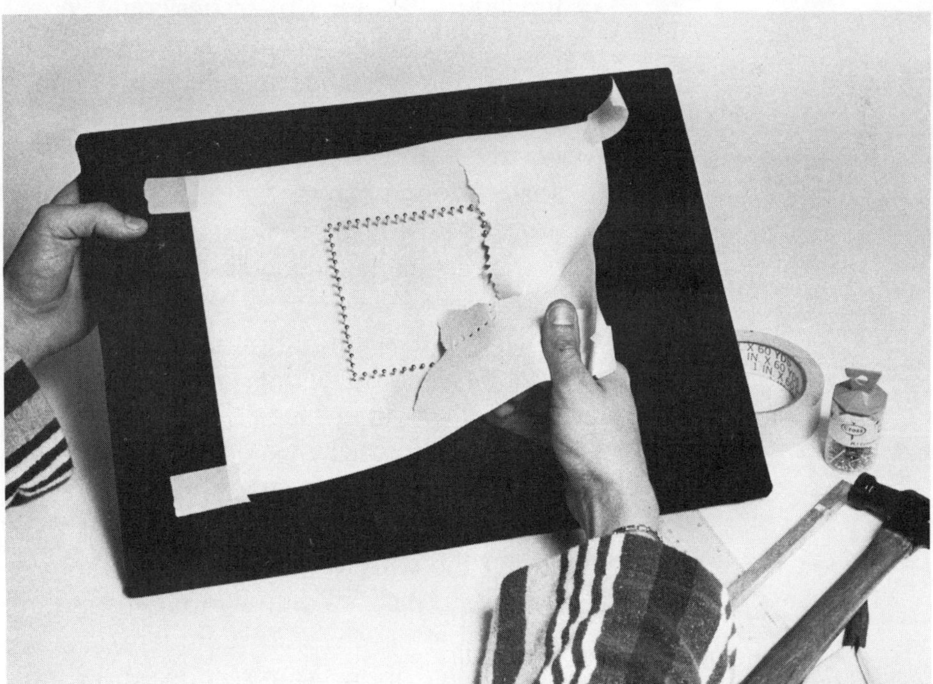

Basic Instructions for Wiring

Almost all the projects in this book will be presented in the following manner: (1) a photograph of the finished design; (2) a nailing pattern showing how to arrange the nails; (3) a wiring pattern showing how to wire the base layer of the design; and (4) a wiring pattern for the surface layer.

All the wiring patterns in this book use the letters "a" and "b" to designate certain nails. Nail "a" is the starting point and nail "b" is the next nail to which the wire is brought in the wiring sequence. Next to each "a" and "b" nail will be an arrow—a solid arrow next to "a" and an outline arrow next to "b". These arrows indicate the direction in which the wiring will be carried out.

To begin, secure the wire to nail "a" by wrapping it four times around the nail. When the solid arrow tells you that you will be wiring toward the left, wrap the wire clockwise; if the arrow points to the right, wrap the wire counterclockwise. After securing the wire to nail "a", bring the wire directly to nail "b" and wrap it around the nail, either clockwise or counterclockwise, depending upon the direction of the outline arrow. Pull the wire straight and taut, then bring it back to the nail nearest "a" in the direction of the solid arrow. Again, wrap the nail and pull it taut, then bring it back to the nail nearest "b" in the direction of the outline arrow. Continue around the pattern until you reach nail "a" again. Wrap the wire four times around nail "a" again and cut off close to the nail.

Most of the designs in this book use two layers of wiring. When working the base layer, push the wire tightly down against the backboard. When working the surface layer, push the wire tightly up against the nailhead.

Before attempting your first project, follow the step-by-step procedure outlined below and illustrated by the accompanying photographs. All these basic instructions must be understood and kept in mind when any of the projects in this book are attempted.

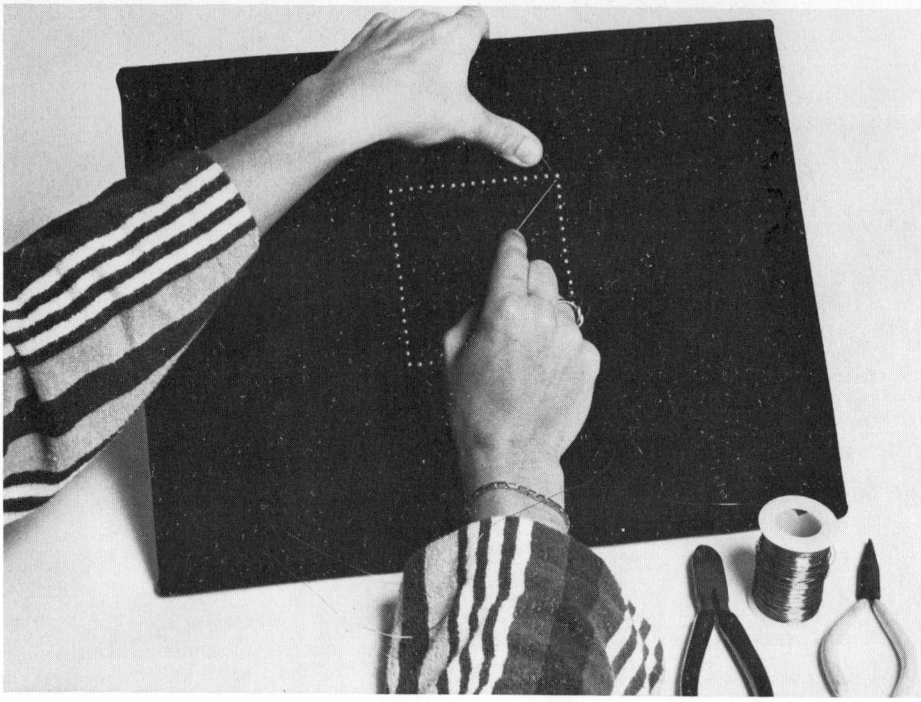

Fig. 1-21 Placing the first wire

Placing the First Wire

After wrapping at nail "a", proceed to nail "b". Be sure all wire of this first, or base layer, is pushed down to the fabric. This will add depth to the finished piece.

Wiring of the Base Layer

Following the arrows on the pattern, continue wiring the base layer. Be sure to keep a slight amount of tension on the wire and keep the wire pushed down throughout the wiring of the base layer.

Fig. 1-22 Wiring the base layer

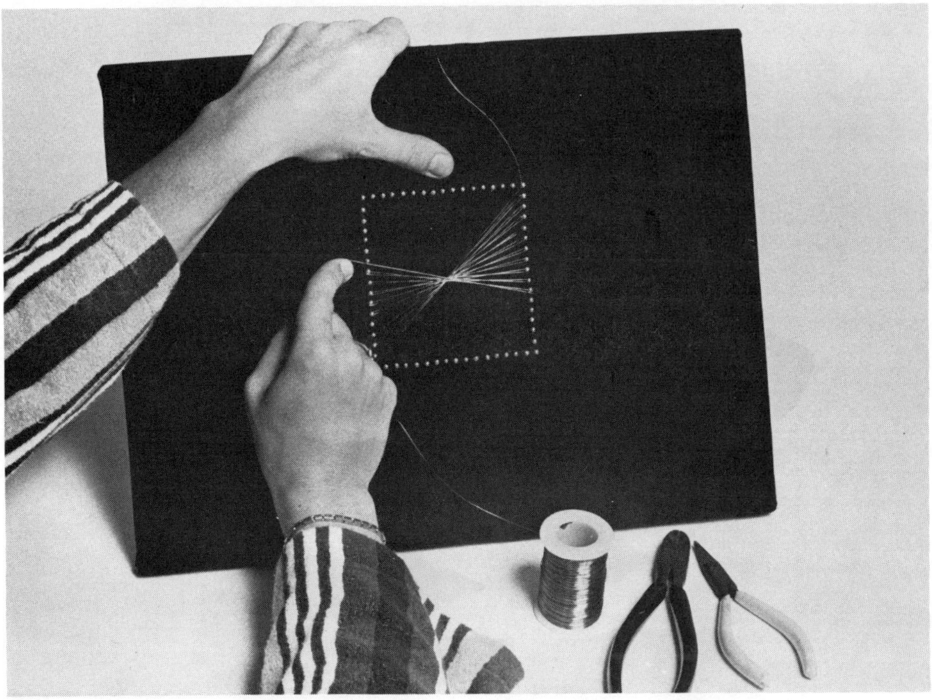

Finishing the Base Layer

After completing the base layer, wrap wire at nail "a" and cut close to the nail with the wire cutters or break with your pliers if wire cutters are not available.

Fig. 1-23 Finishing the base layer

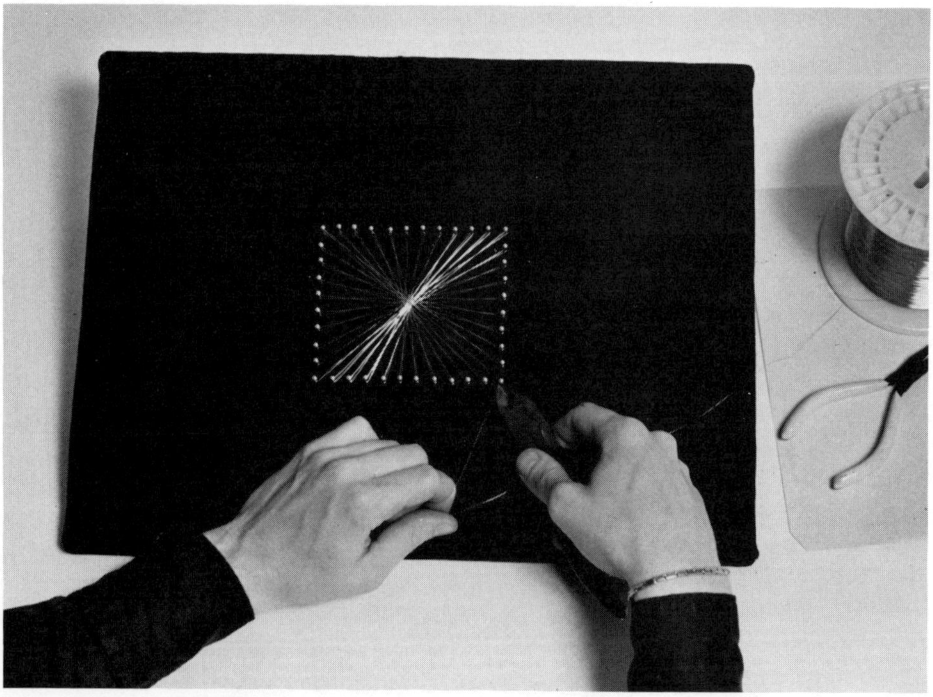

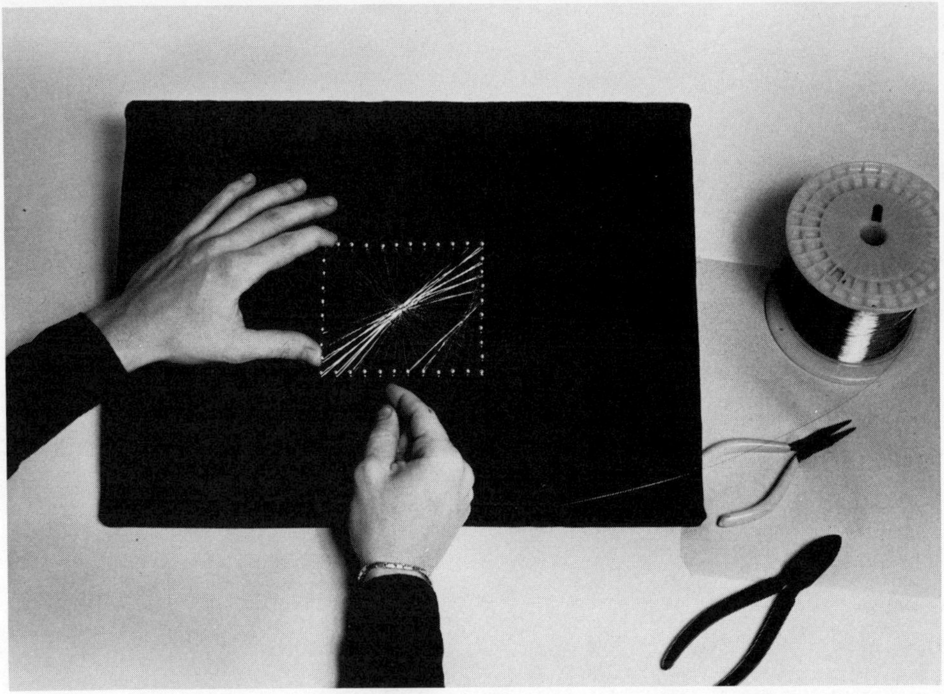

Fig. 1-24 Beginning the surface layer

Beginning the Surface Layer

Starting at nail "a" as indicated on the surface layer pattern, wrap and proceed to nail "b", keeping the wire at the *top* of the nails on this layer. Be sure to keep tension on the wire as you wrap.

Wiring the Surface Layer

Keeping the wire at the top of the nails, proceed in the direction of the arrows, continuing to maintain tension on the wire to prevent sagging.

Fig. 1-25 Wiring the surface layer

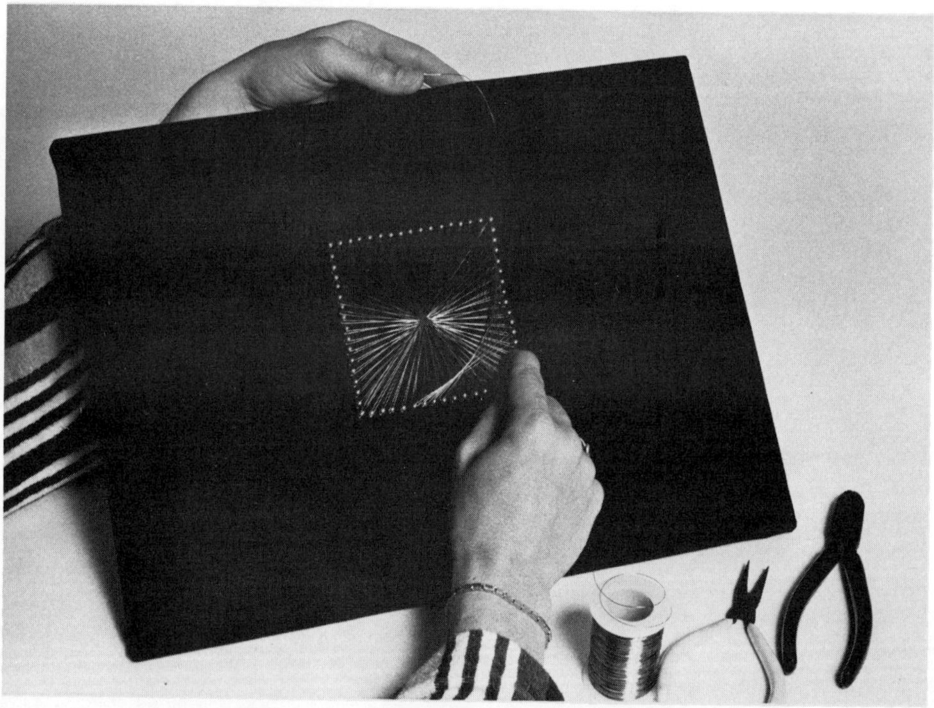

Finished!

Once again, wrap and cut at nail "a".

Fig. 1-26 Finishing the surface layer

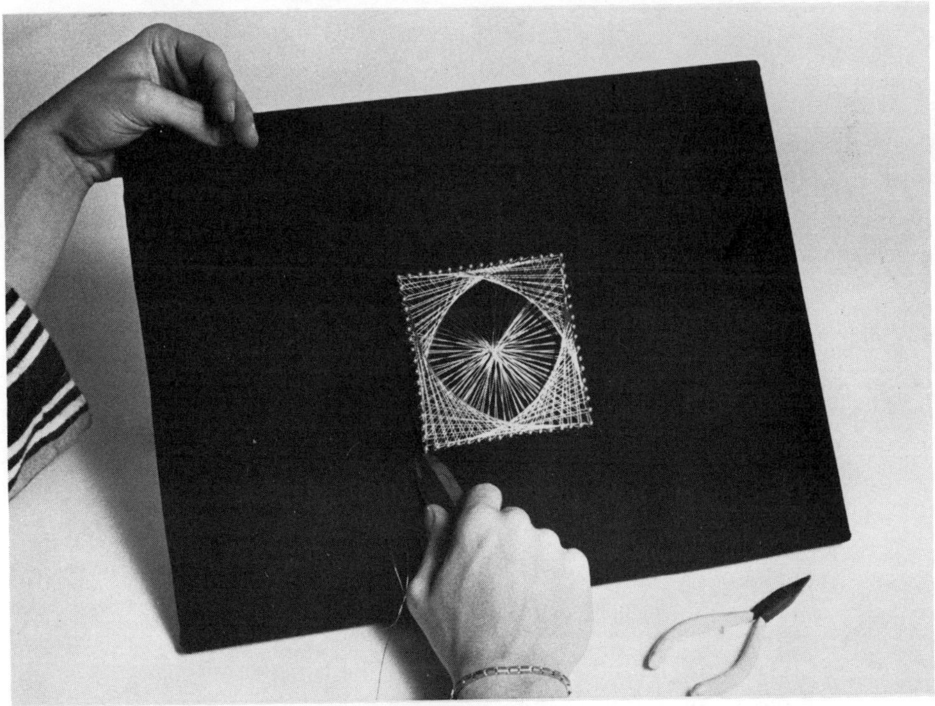

Fig. 1-27 Painting a finished design

Painting

You may wish to paint your finished design to obtain a special effect: the color contrast helps to bring out the depth of the design. Use a metallic gold or silver lacquer paint. Gold leaf paint works very well and its rich color complements the copper. Place a piece of cardboard between the base and surface layers while dabbing the paint on. Two layers of paint may be necessary to cover the wire completely.

2 Basic Geometric Designs

Geometric forms are the basic shapes found in all of nature, such as squares, circles, and triangles. Of course, there are variations of all these.

The basic "a" to "b" system described in Chapter 1 is used in all the projects in Chapter 2. Again, the "a" direction is indicated by the solid arrow and the "b" direction is indicated by the outline arrow.

These basic projects are important, as all the following projects in this manual build on techniques introduced in this chapter.

Square

Base Layer

Fig. 2-1 shows how the finished design will look if all the directions are followed correctly. The nailing pattern for this design is shown in Fig. 2-2.

To work this design, begin at nail "a" as shown in Fig. 2-3 and proceed to "b"; continue in the direction shown by the arrows. Stop at nail "a". The wire will form a crisscross pattern in the middle.

Surface Layer

To form a rim around this pattern, begin at surface pattern nail "a" as shown in Fig. 2-4 and proceed to "b". The only difference between the base layer and the surface layer is the number of nails skipped or used.

Fig. 2-1 Square

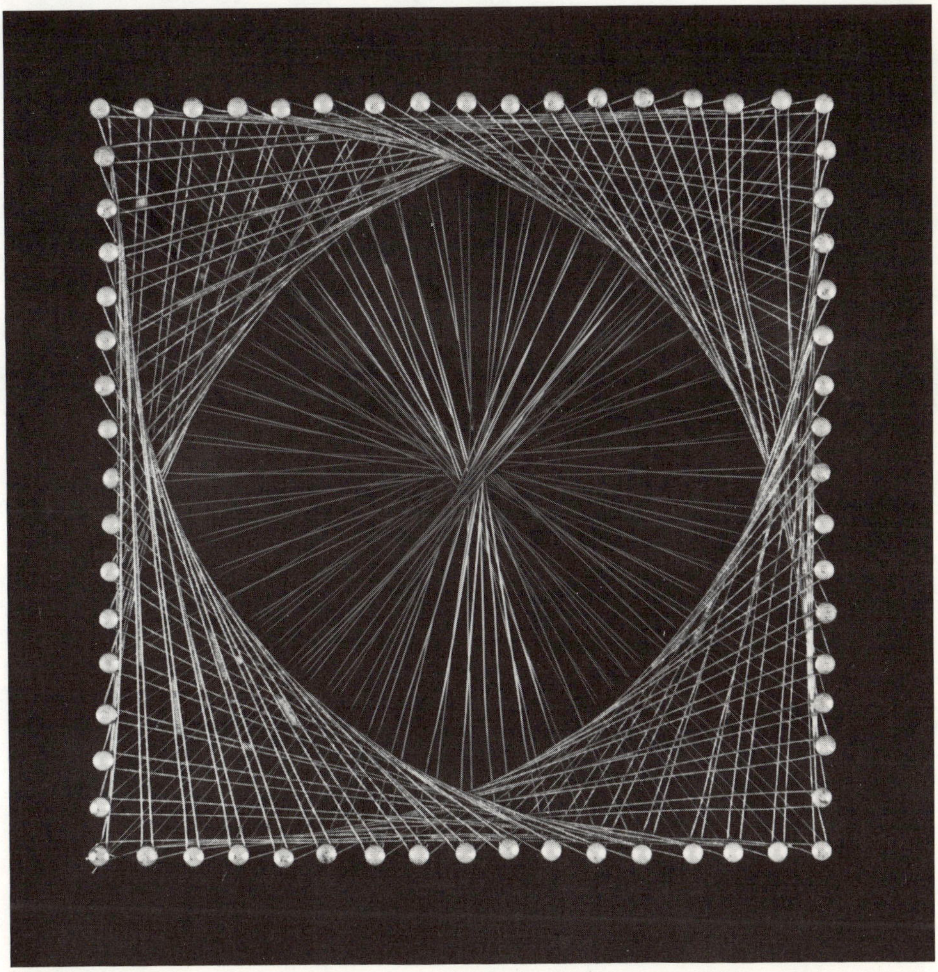

Fig. 2-2 Nailing pattern for square

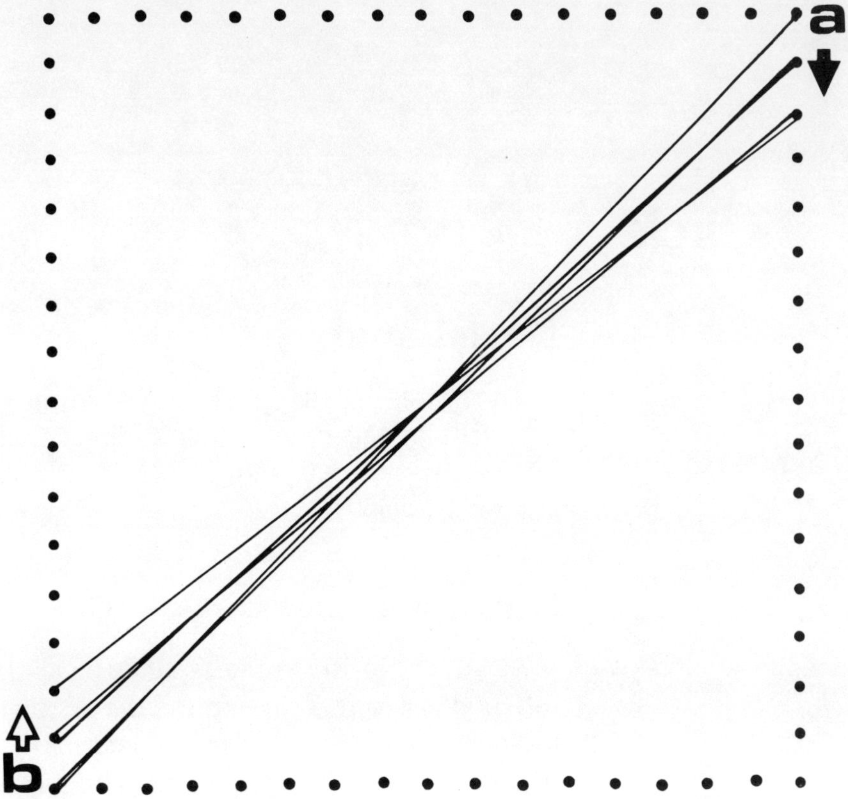

Fig. 2-3 Base layer of square

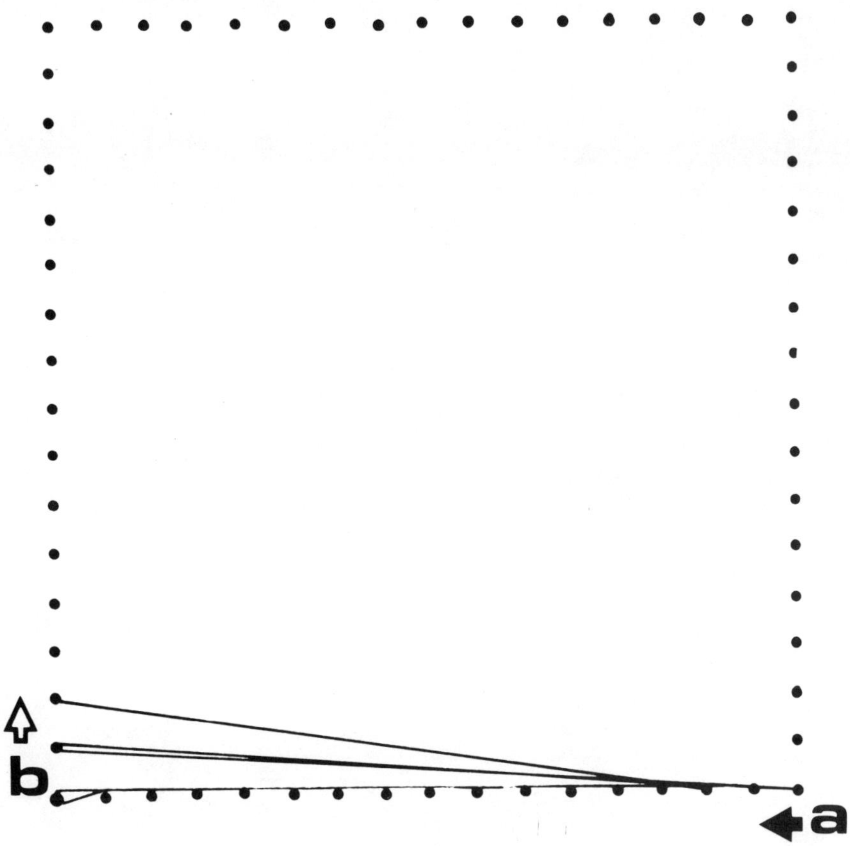

Fig. 2-4 Surface layer of square

Circle

Base Layer

The wire in this pattern will form a crisscross in the center; follow directional arrows as shown in Fig. 2-7. End at nail "a" once again.

Surface Layer

As shown in the surface pattern in Fig. 2-8, you will form a rim around the edge of the nails. The size of the rim is determined by the amount of nails skipped. The more nails skipped, the larger the rim. Smaller rims add more definition to the finished design.

Fig. 2-5 Circle

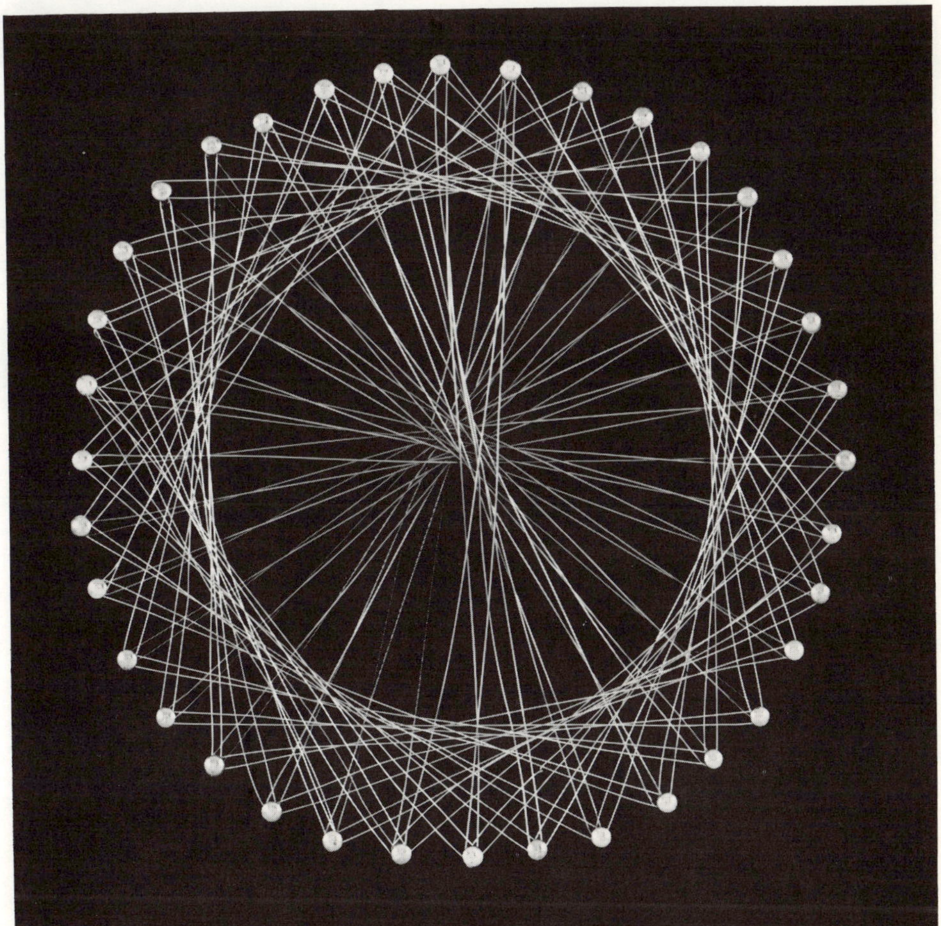

Fig. 2-6 Nailing pattern for circle

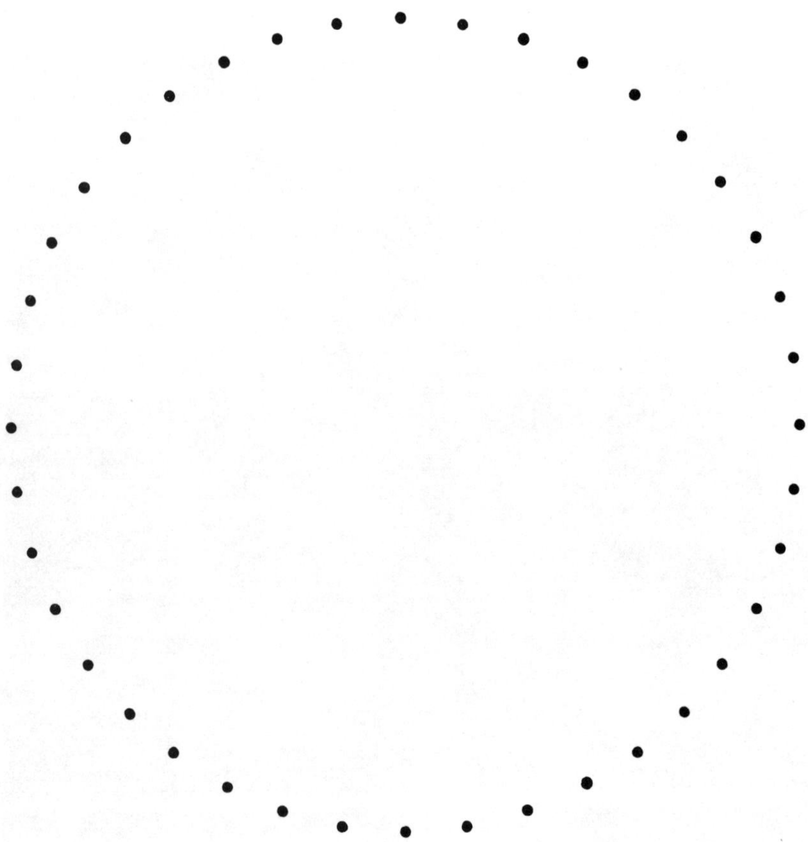

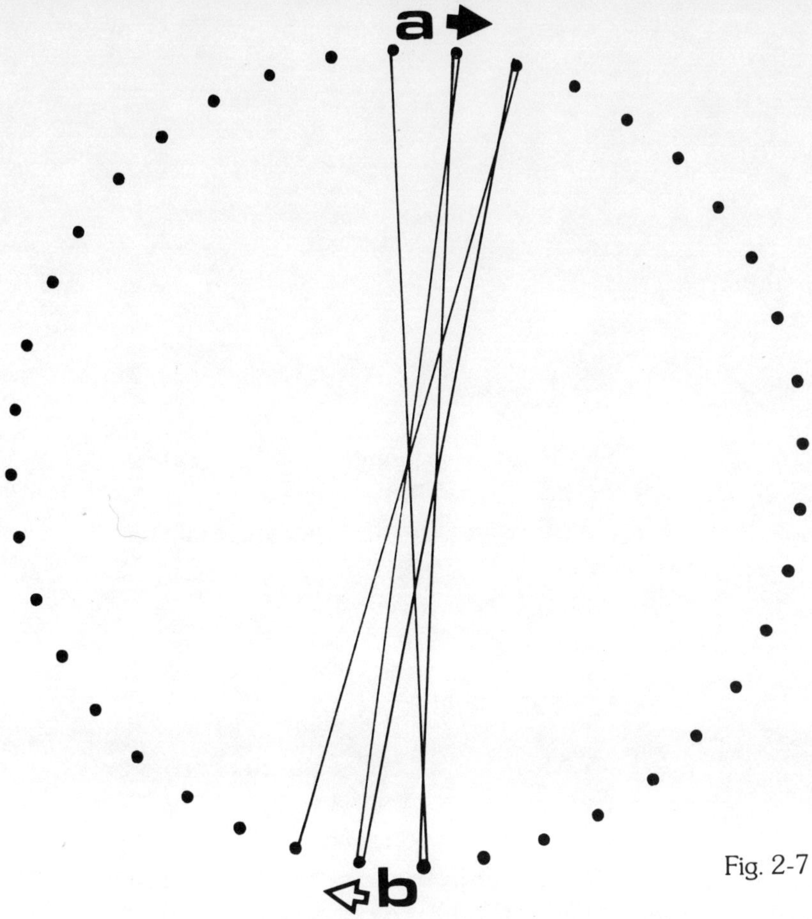

Fig. 2-7 Base layer of circle

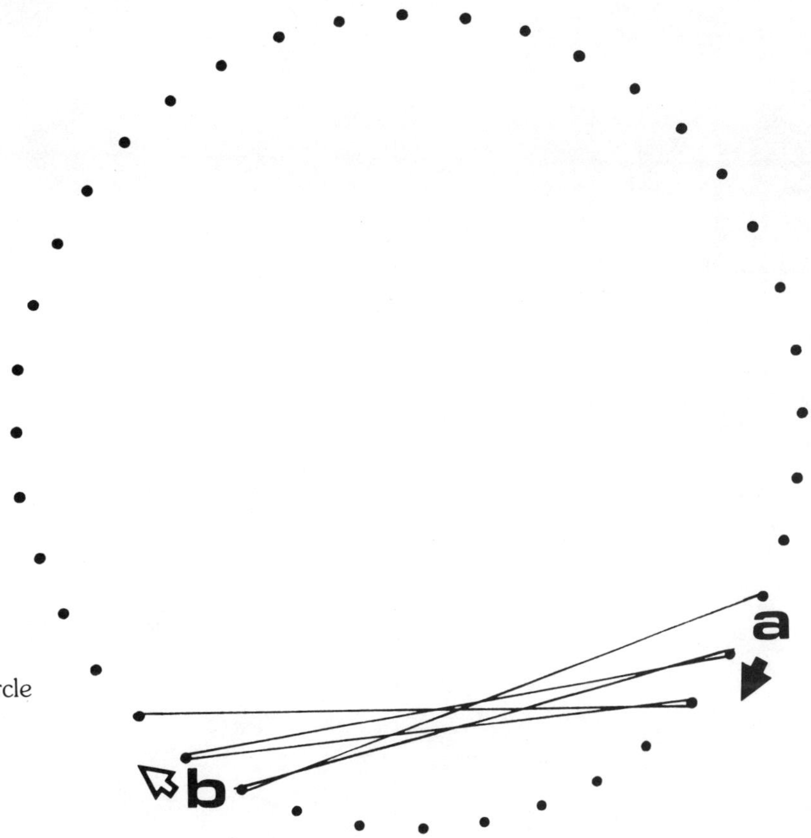

Fig. 2-8 Surface layer of circle

Rectangle

Base Layer

The rectangle is much like the square. On the base layer, shown in Fig. 2-11, the wire will cross in the middle and you will have the same crisscross pattern as in all base layers of this style.

Surface Layer

The size of any arch, in the corners, is determined by the amount of nails skipped. By skipping fewer nails, a smaller arch is achieved; skipping more nails creates a larger arch. Fig. 2-12 shows the wiring pattern for the surface layer of the rectangle.

Fig. 2-9 Rectangle

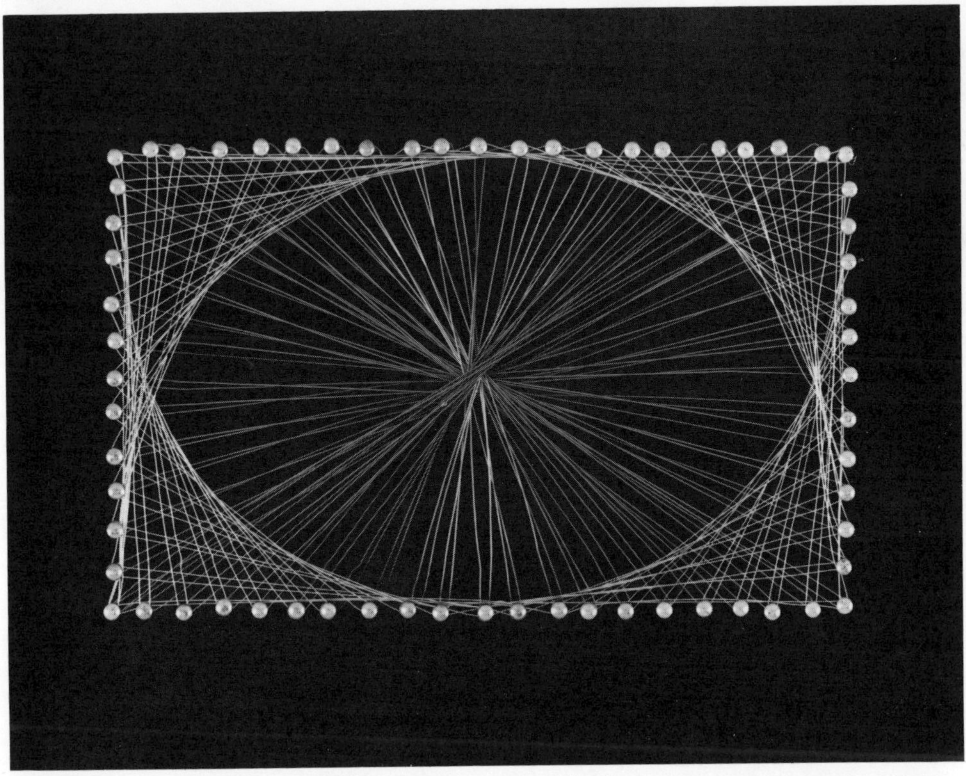

Fig. 2-10 Nailing pattern for rectangle

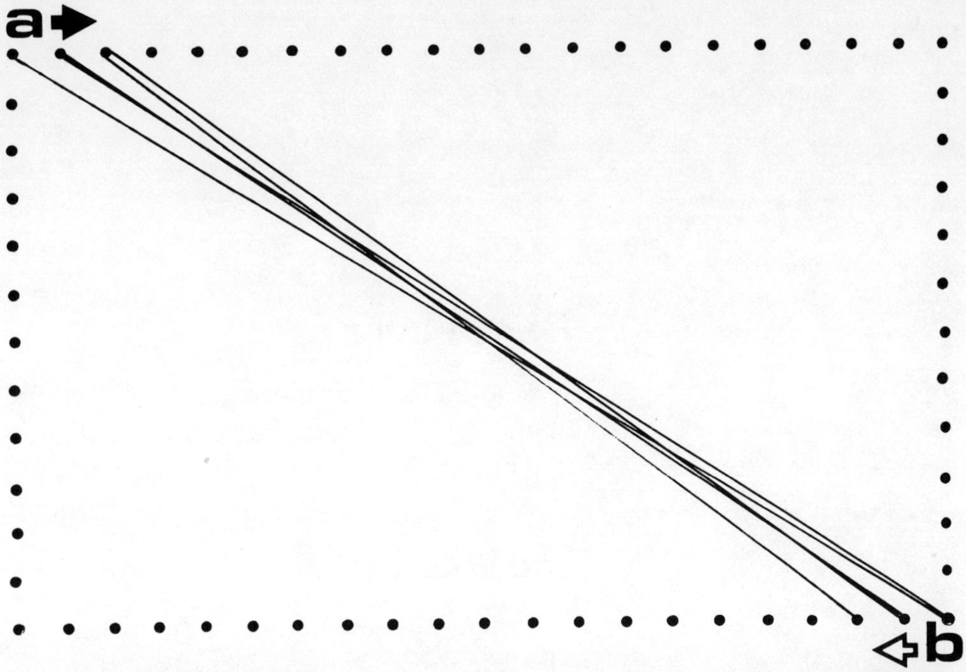

Fig. 2-11 Base layer of rectangle

Fig. 2-12 Surface layer of rectangle

Curve

Base Layer

Stop the wire at the nail marked with a diamond. This is necessary on any design that has an open instead of a closed design.

Surface Layer

Stop at the nail marked with a diamond. The curve is useful in abstracts and many other designs, as the surface layer gives even more depth to the design.

Fig. 2-13 Curve

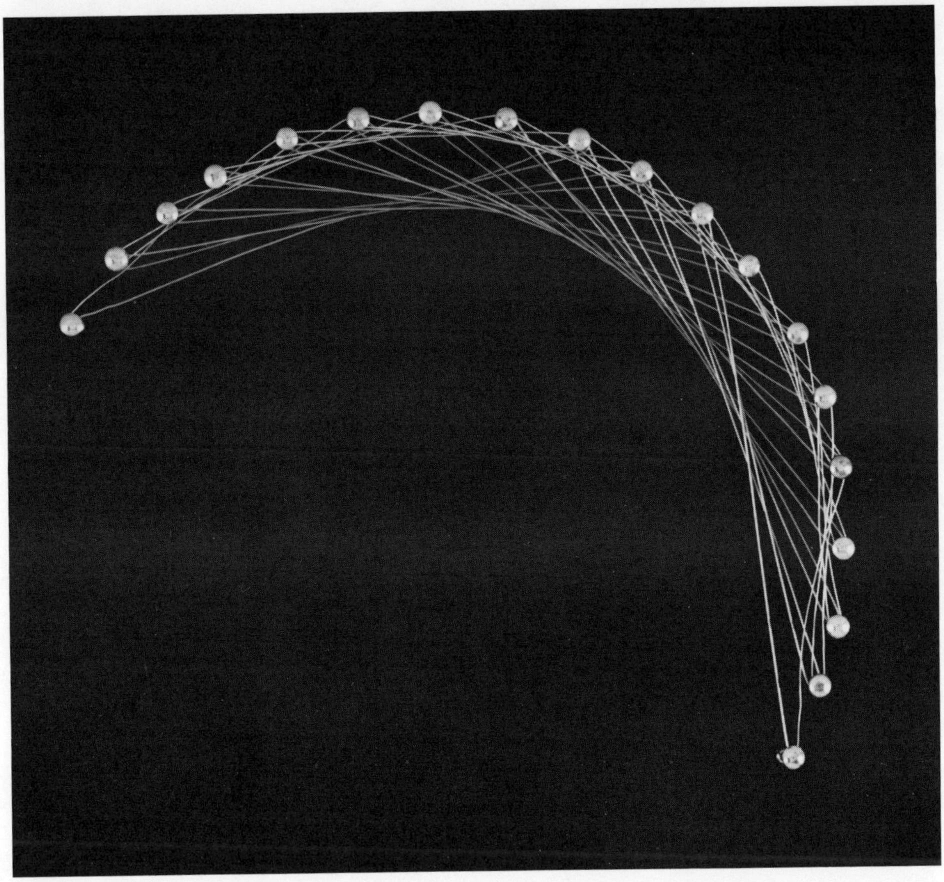

Fig. 2-14 Nailing pattern for curve

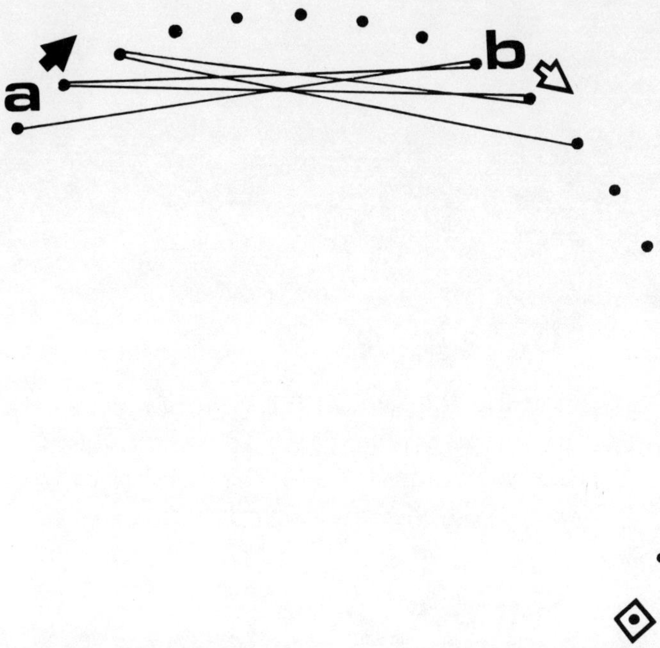

Fig. 2-15 Base layer of curve

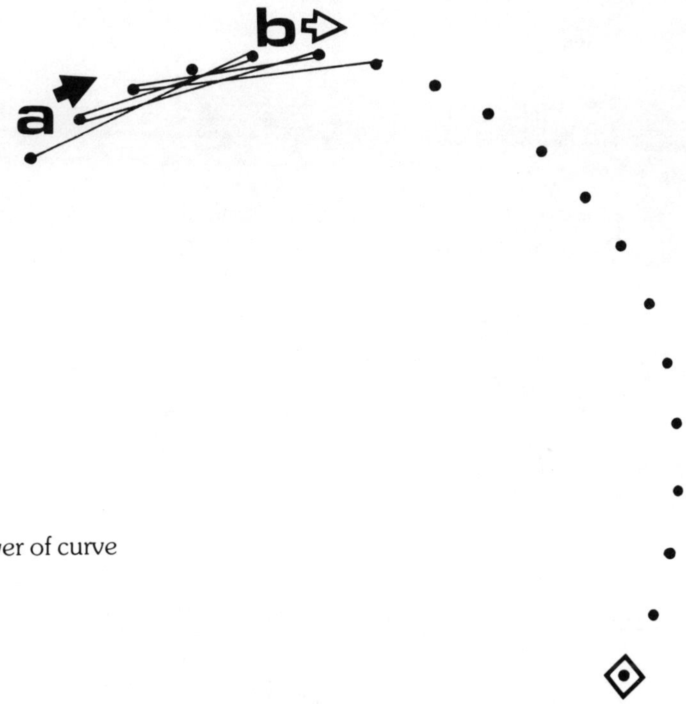

Fig. 2-16 Surface layer of curve

Angle

Base Layer

Stop the wire at the nail marked with a diamond on Fig. 2-19. The size of this wire arch is determined by the number of nails skipped between "a" and "b".

Surface Layer

Stop wiring at the nail marked with the diamond on the surface pattern shown in Fig. 2-20. Angles are helpful in almost any abstract design, and they are very useful in ship designs in forming the slant of the mast.

Fig. 2-17 Angle

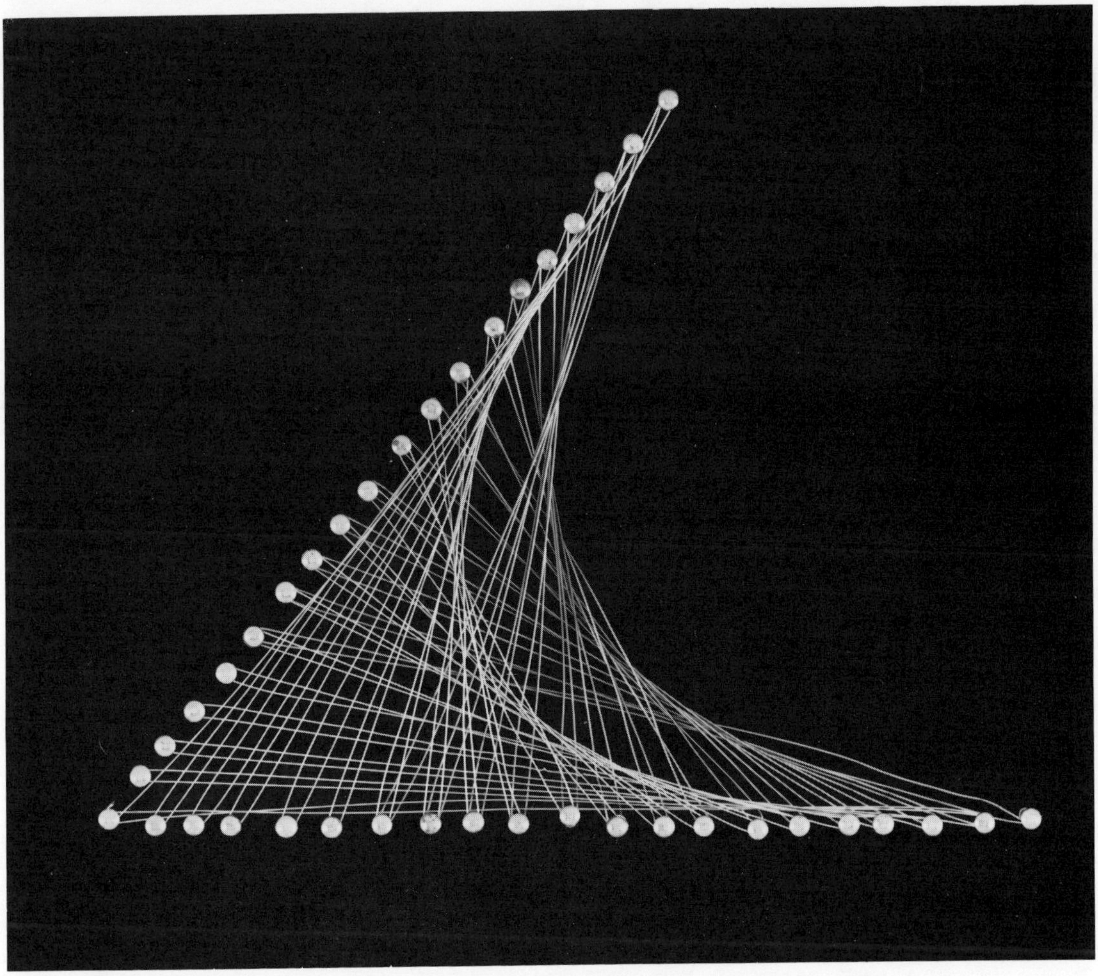

Fig. 2-18 Nailing pattern for angle

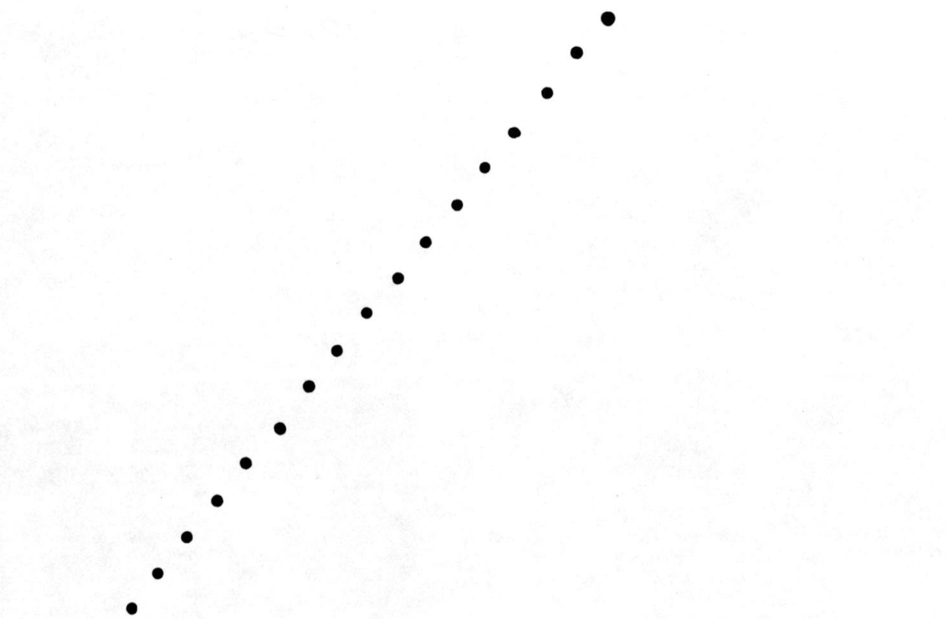

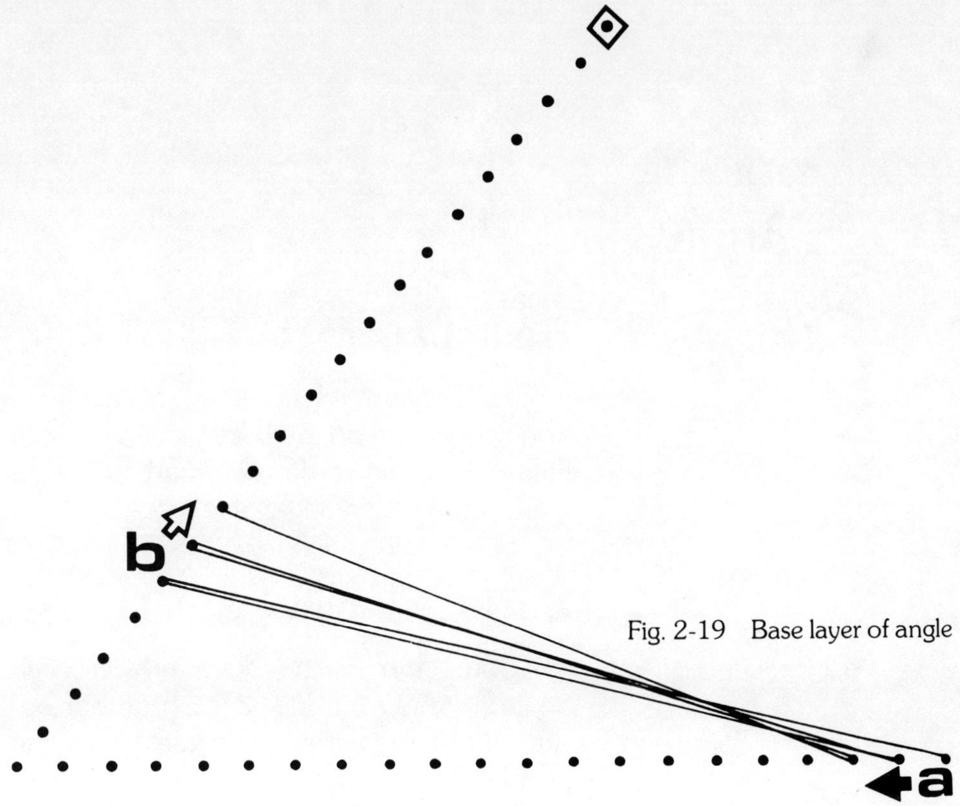

Fig. 2-19 Base layer of angle

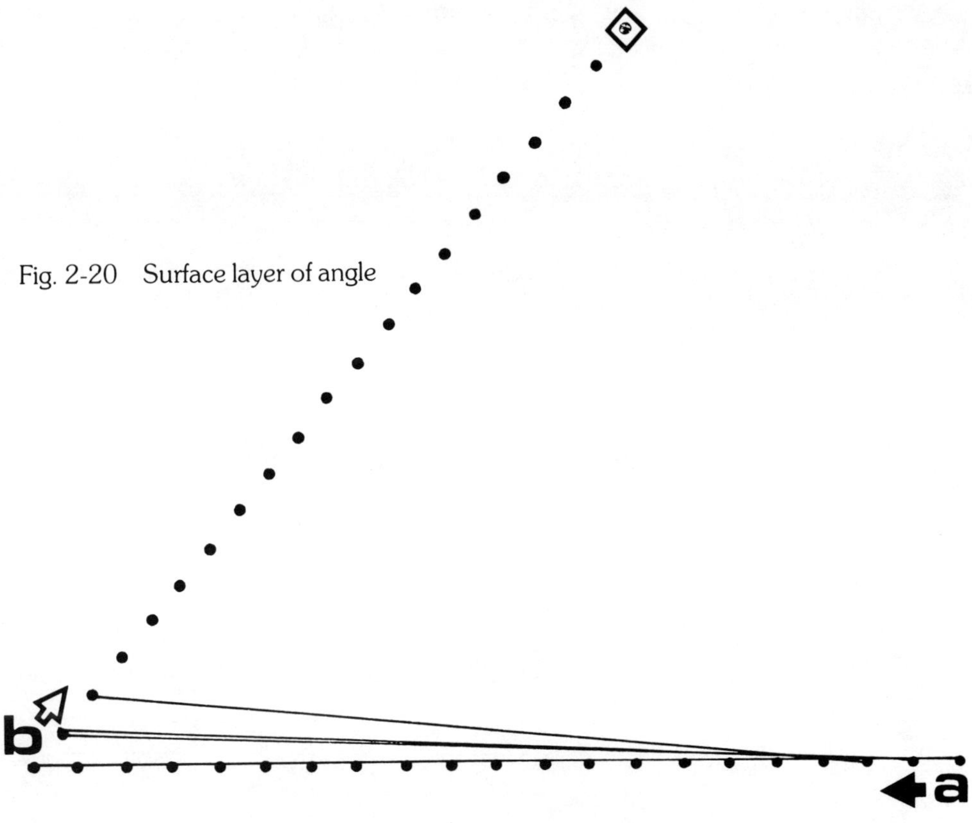

Fig. 2-20 Surface layer of angle

Opposite Angles

Base Layer

This design involves wiring in two directions, as shown on the base layer pattern in Fig. 2-23. Stop at the nail marked with a diamond on each angle of this design.

Surface Layer

Again, stop at the diamond on each angle as shown in Fig. 2-24 (number beside the solid arrow coincides with the proper diamond for that wiring sequence). These opposite angles form a pattern almost identical to that of a schooner mast.

Fig. 2-21 Opposite angles

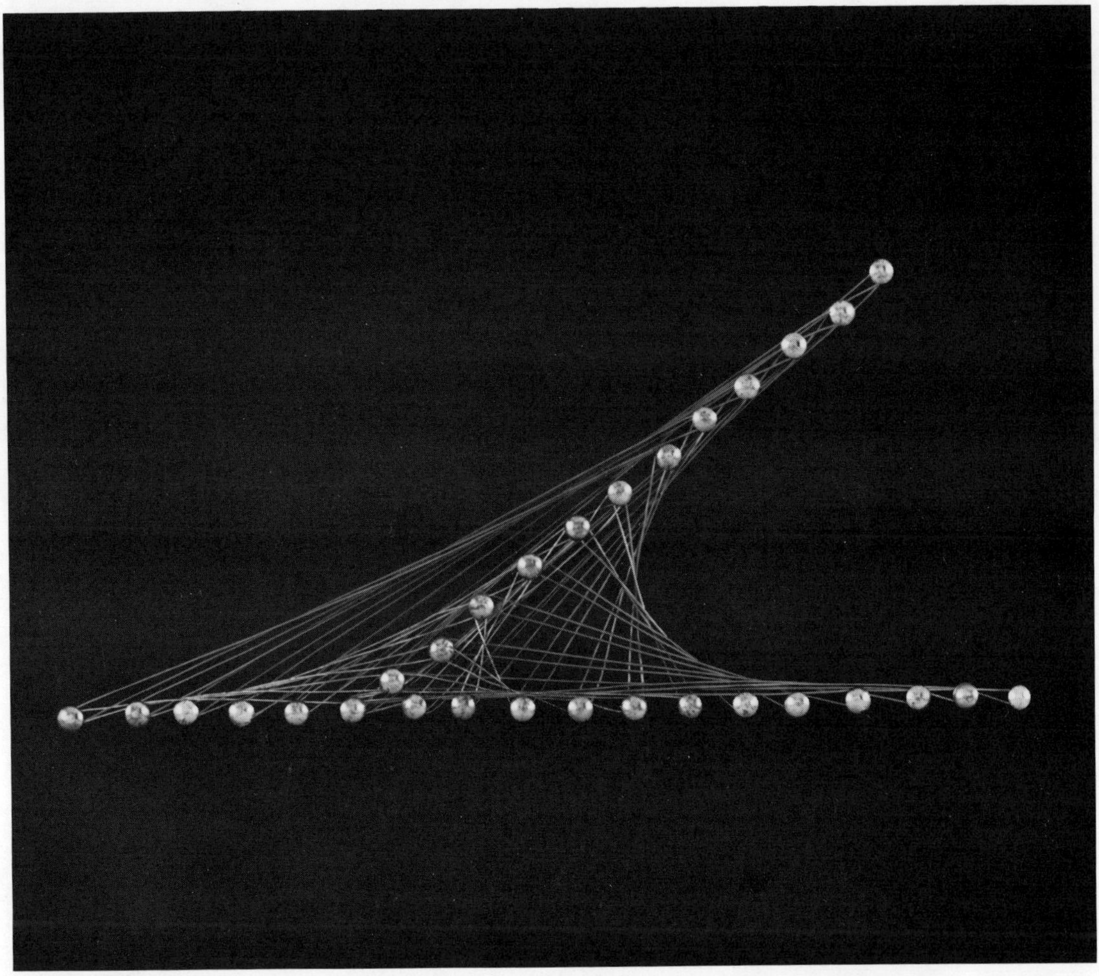

Fig. 2-22 Nailing pattern for opposite angles

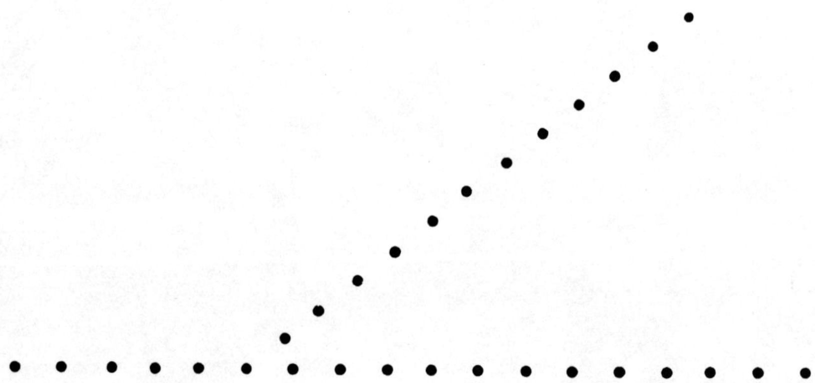

Fig. 2-23 Base layer of opposite angles

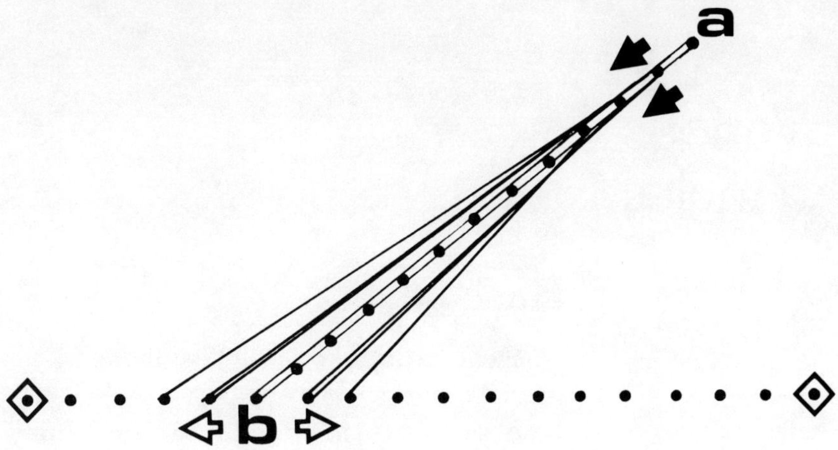

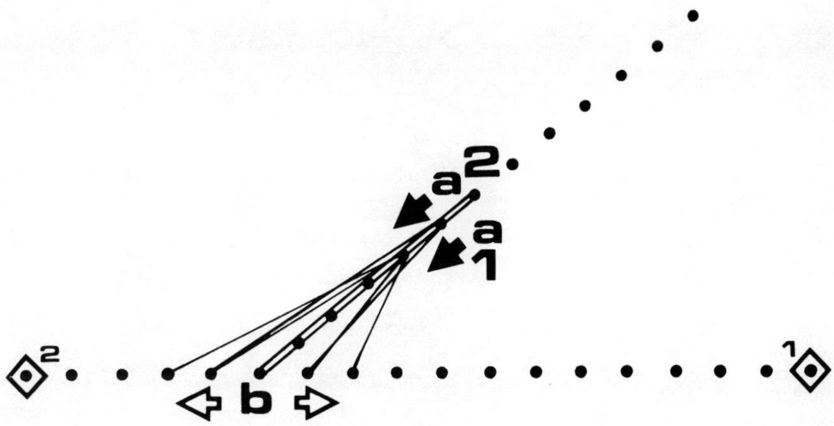

Fig. 2-24 Surface layer of opposite angles

Various Angles

Base Layer

Always stop wiring at the diamond on each of these patterns. The arches will have similar stopping points for uniformity of design.

Surface Layer

This design is an exercise involving almost every possible angle. Different approaches to this project such as different weights of wire, skipping nails, lighter base layer, or lighter surface layer will produce a variety of striking designs. To achieve a "lighter" layer, try skipping every other nail.

Fig. 2-25 Various angles

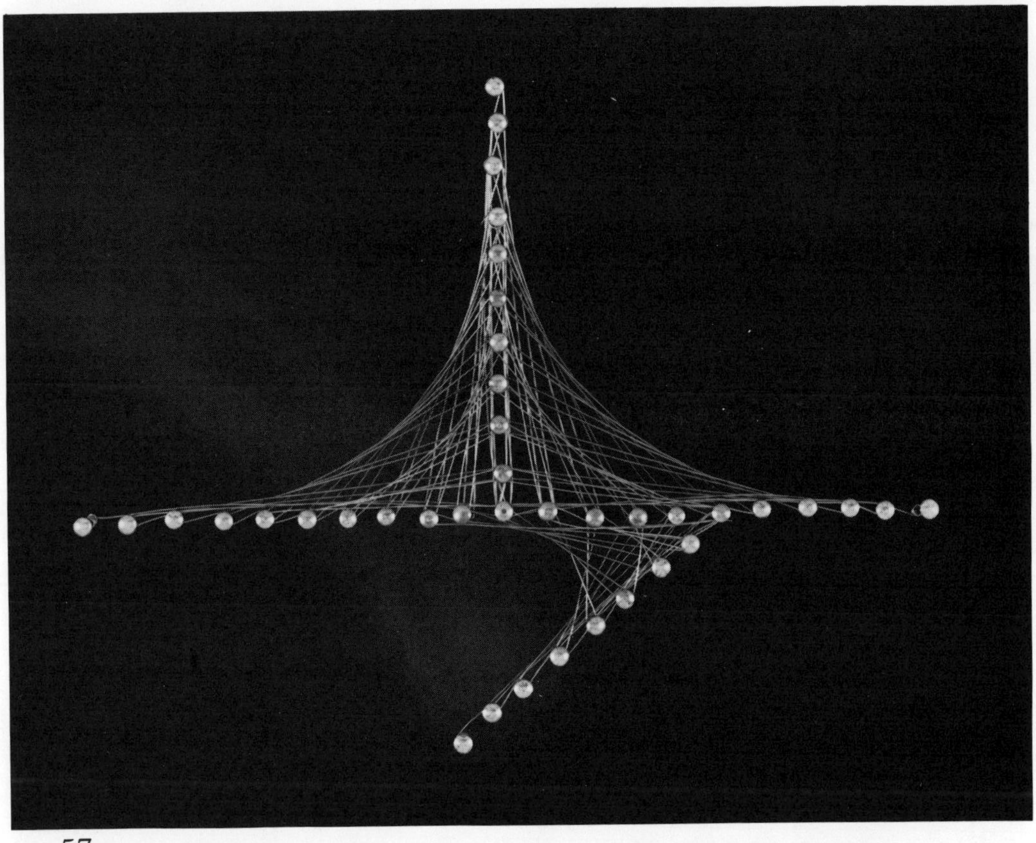

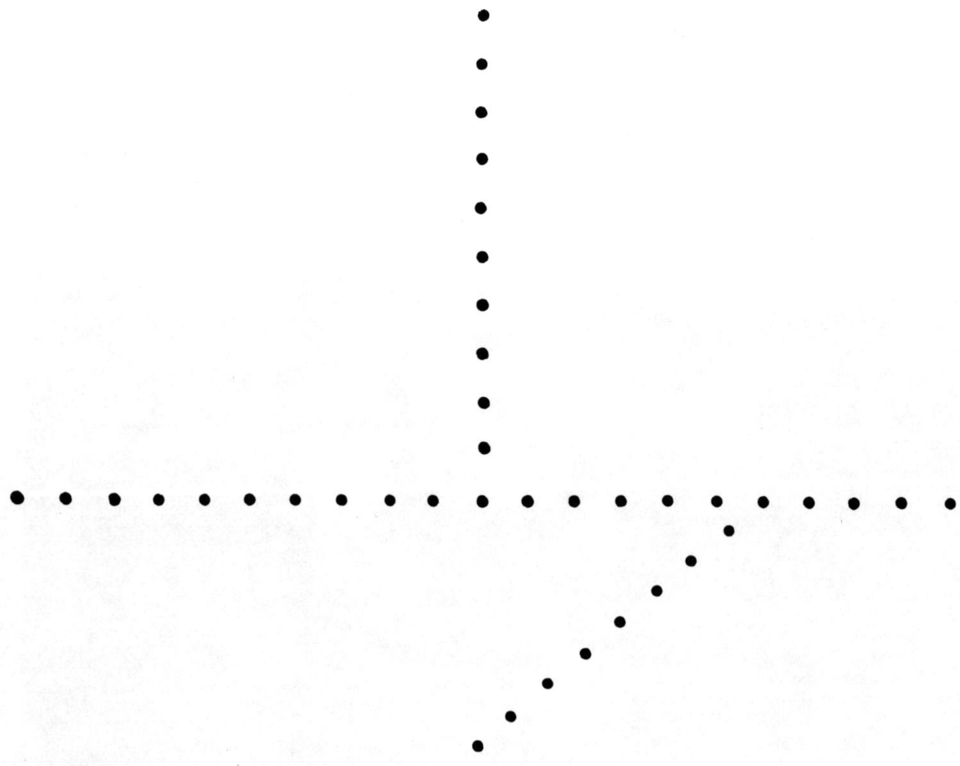

Fig. 2-26 Nailing pattern for various angles

Fig. 2-27 Base layer of various angles

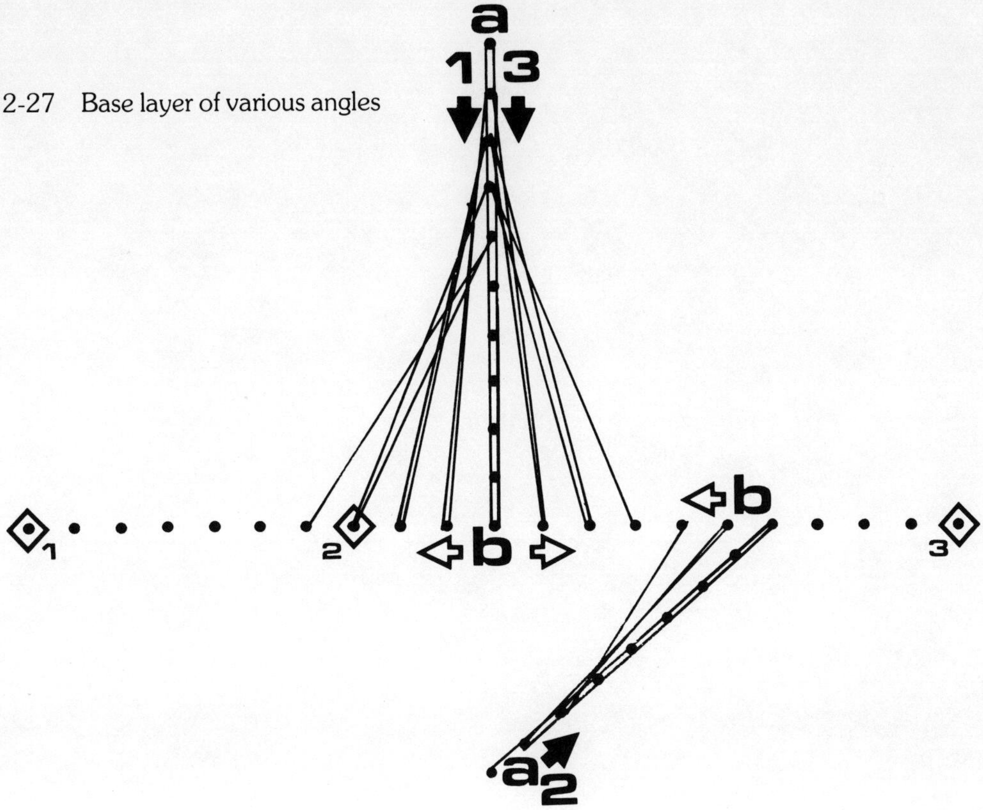

Fig. 2-28 Surface layer of various angles

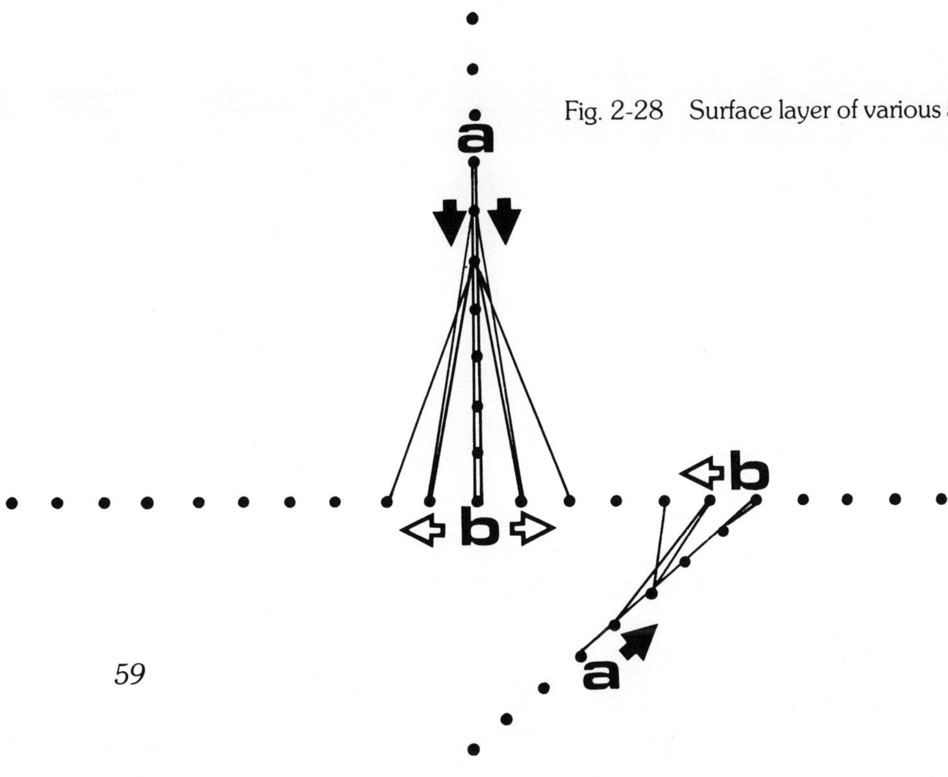

3
Combining Basic Geometric Designs

The combining of the basic designs presented in Chapter 2 can produce almost any pattern desired. Although the projects in this chapter may seem simple, they cover nearly every aspect of the art form. Cars, boats, animals, and people are all simply combinations of basic geometric designs arranged in specific ways.

Double Square

Base Layer

Both squares are done exactly the same as the one presented at the beginning of Chapter 2. This combination is used in many abstract designs.

Surface Layer

Try spacing the wire for the surface arches in several different ways. To enlarge or decrease the size of the surface rim of wire, increase or decrease the number of nails skipped. The more nails skipped, the larger the rim of wire. This will show you how much difference a slight change can make.

Fig. 3-1 Double square

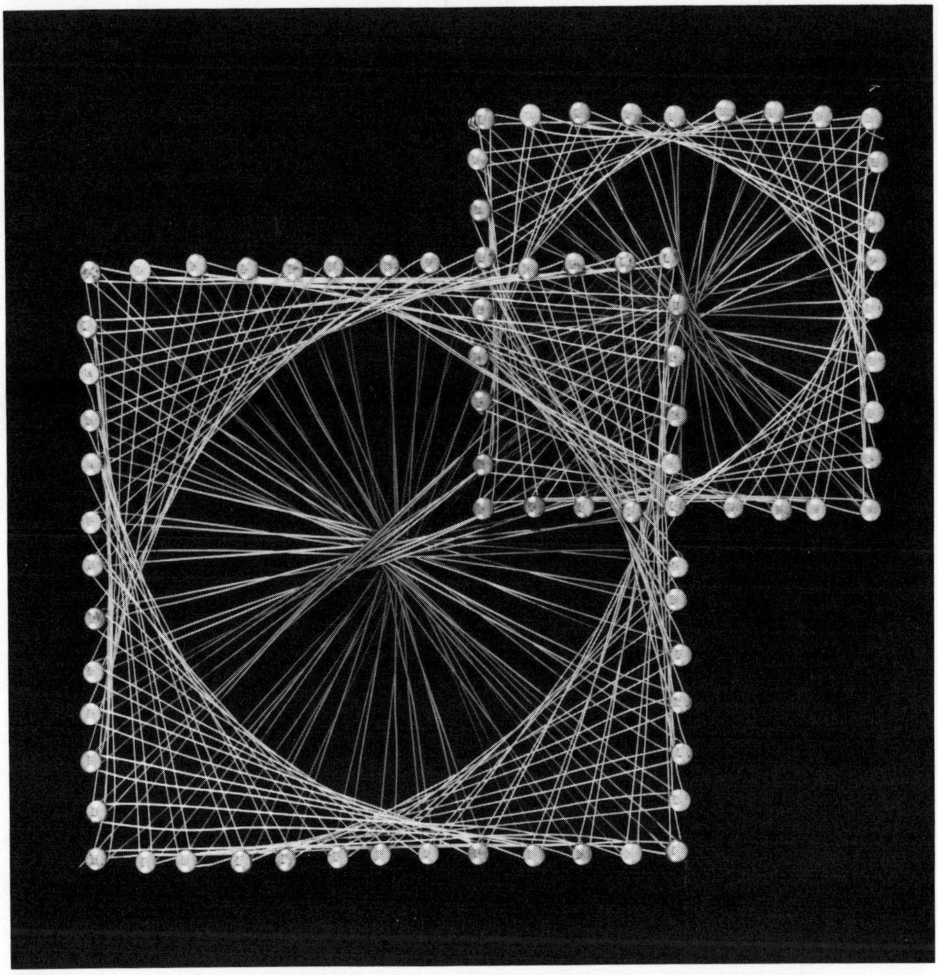

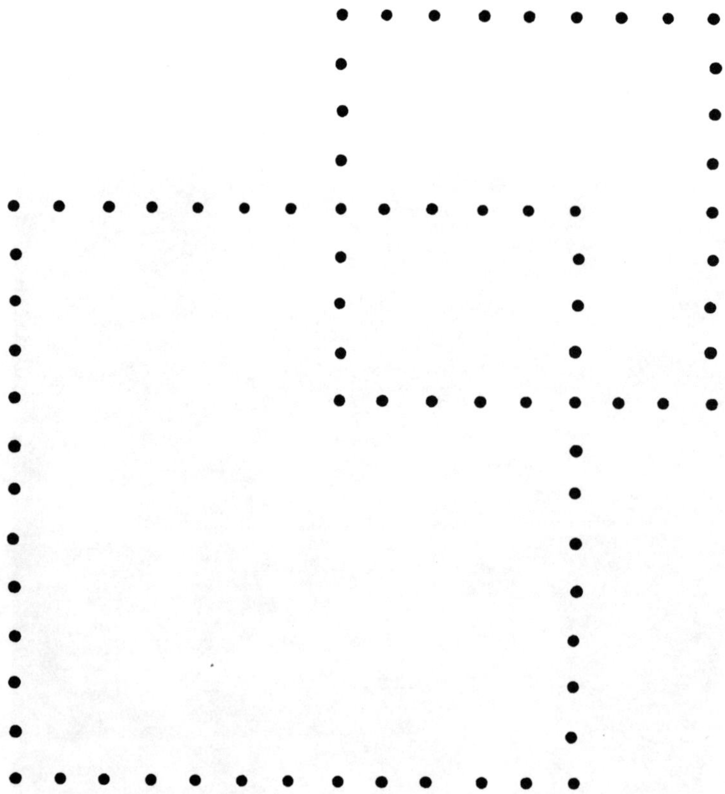

Fig. 3-2 Nailing pattern for double square

Fig. 3-3 Base layer of double square

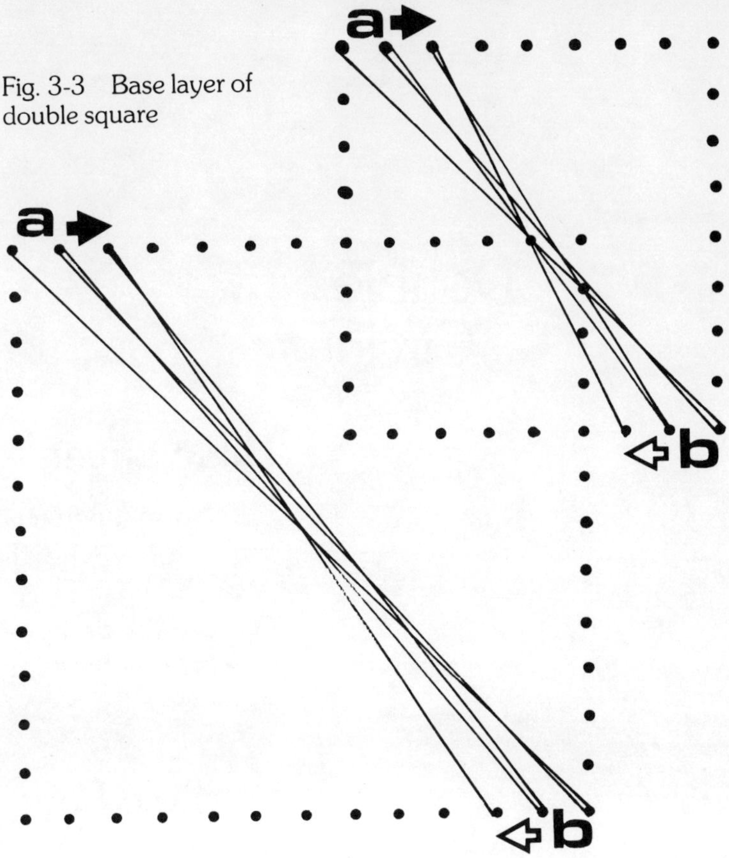

Fig. 3-4 Surface layer of double square

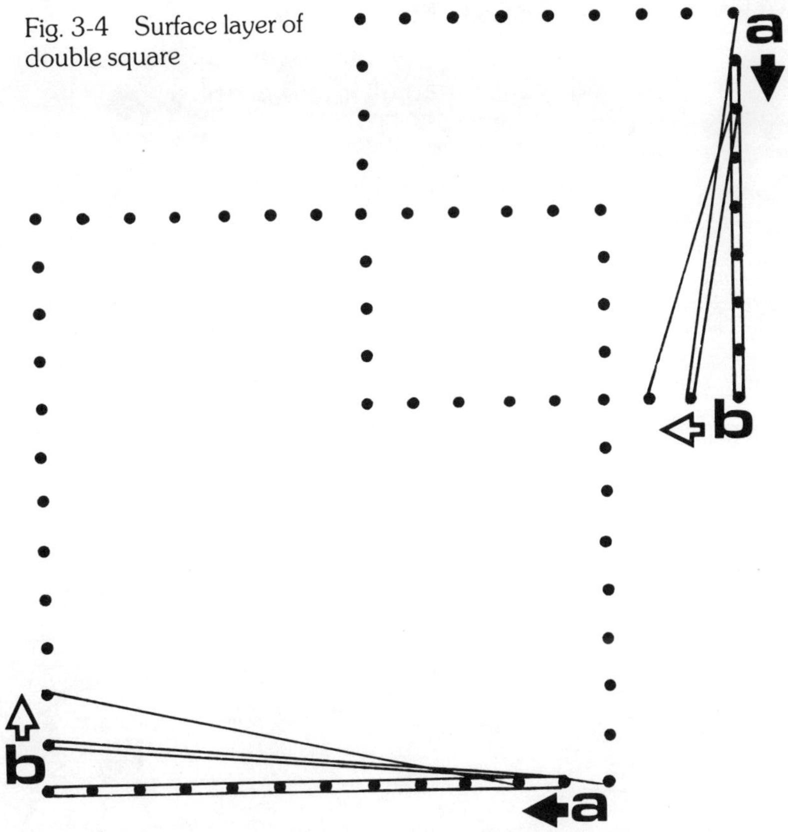

Double Circle

Base Layer

To form a perfect cross in the center of a circle, follow the directions for the base layer shown in Fig. 3-7. An attractive variation on this design involves using the surface layer pattern for both the base and the surface.

Surface Layer

The spacing of the nails can change the look of these circles dramatically. Using a small rim of wire gives the design more definition. Most vehicles have wheels, of course, but circles also can be used in designs for animals and people.

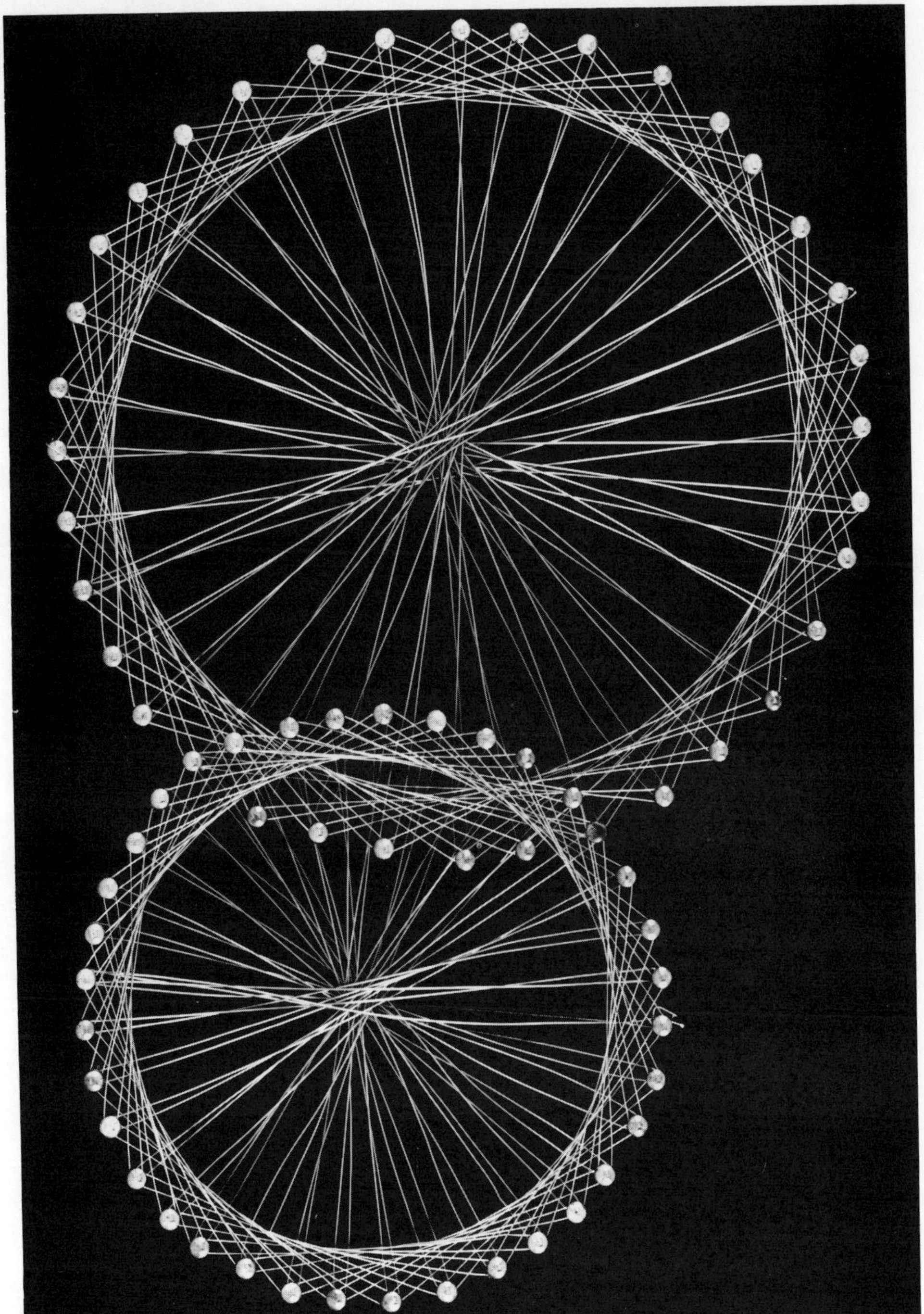

Fig. 3-5 Double circle

Fig. 3-6 Nailing pattern for double circle

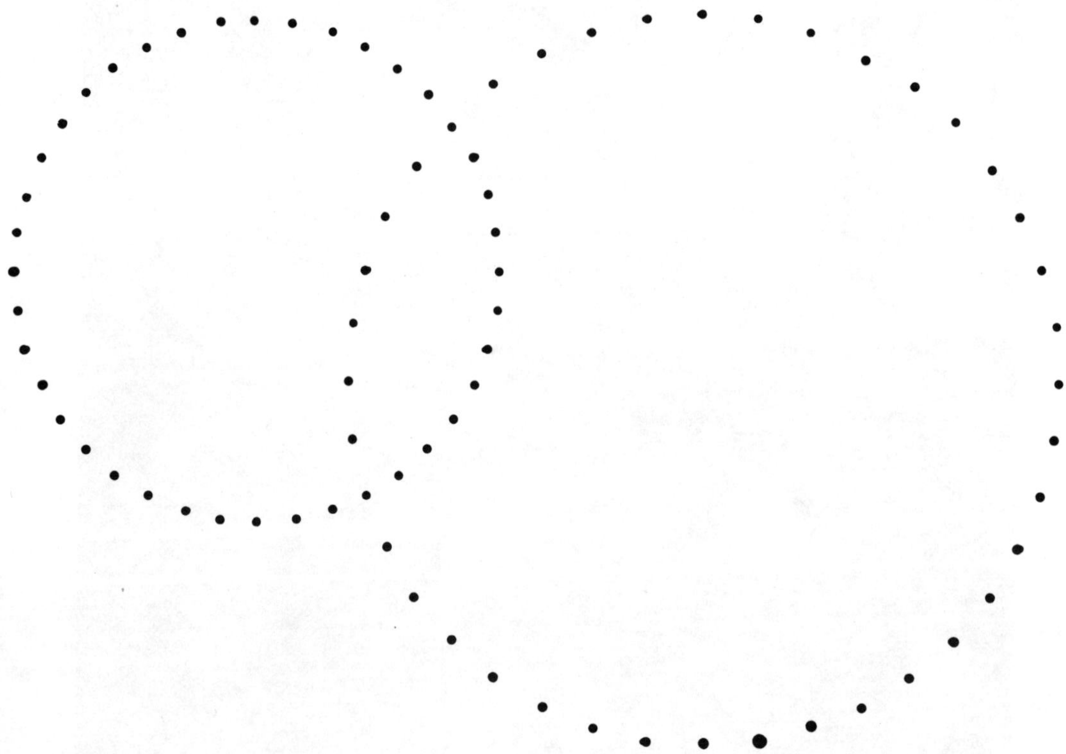

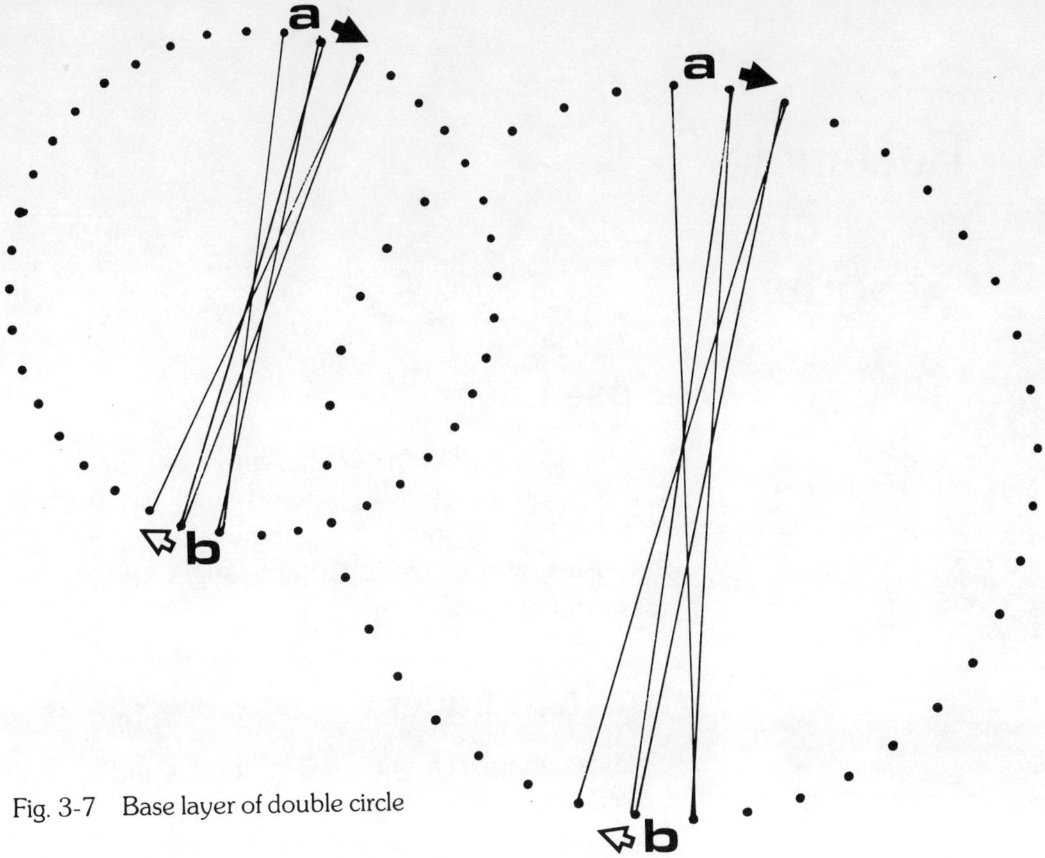

Fig. 3-7 Base layer of double circle

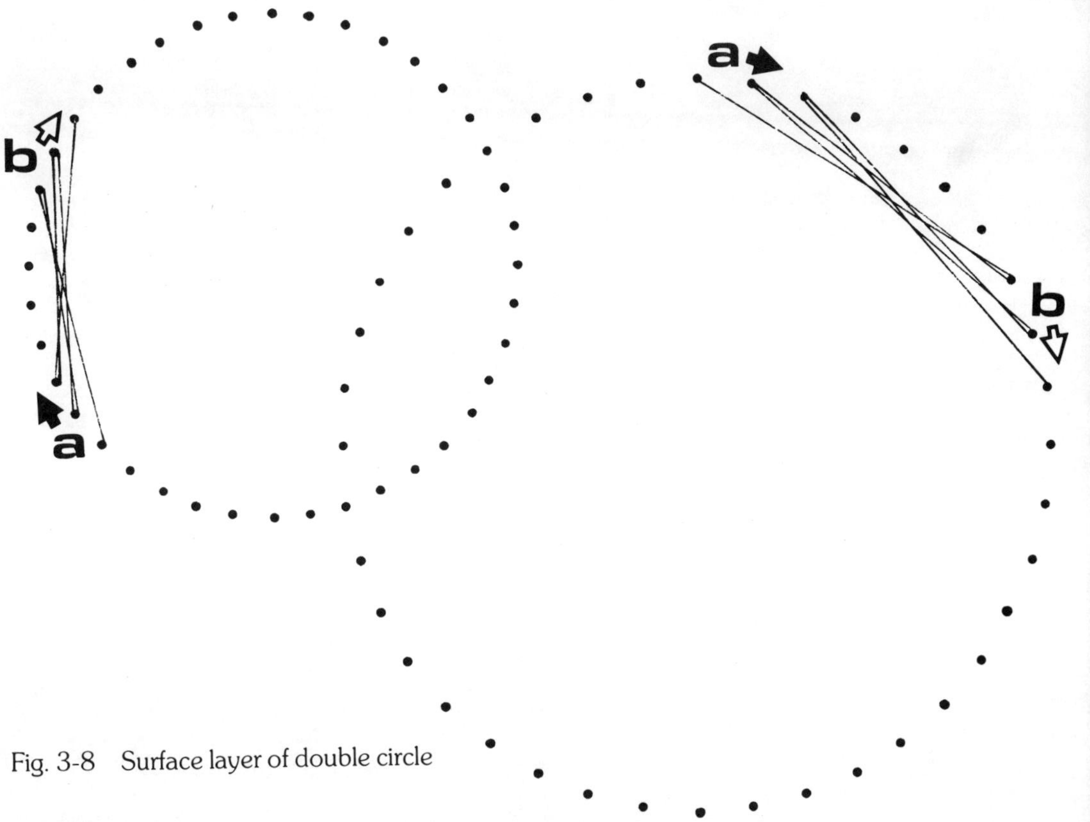

Fig. 3-8 Surface layer of double circle

Rectangle and Square

Base Layer

This project is almost the same as the double square design shown in Fig. 3-1, but it can be worked in a variety of ways. Try using two or more surface layers and no base layer.

Surface Layer

These shapes can be used in houses and bridges very effectively. They also apply to any cubist design you may wish to try.

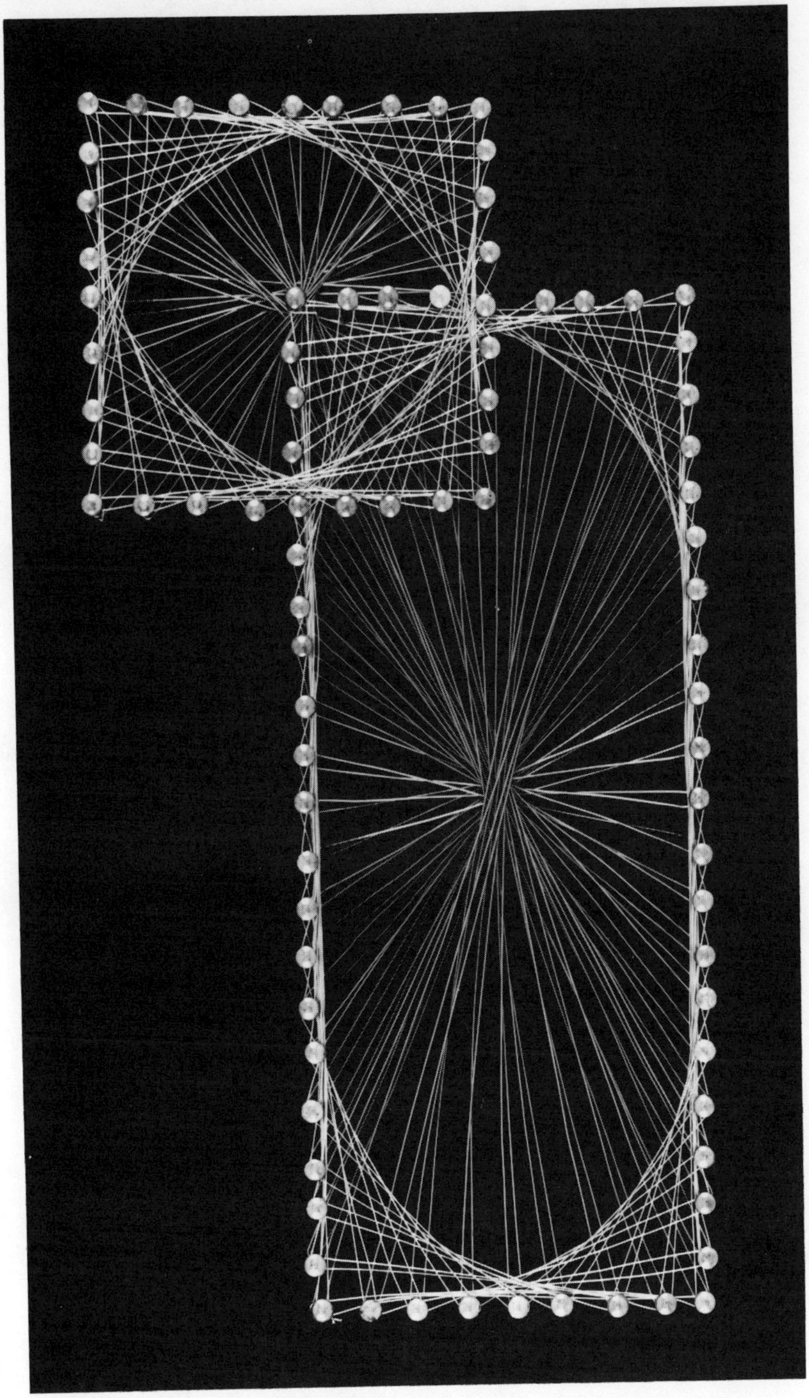

Fig. 3-9 Rectangle and square

Fig. 3-10 Nailing pattern for rectangle and square

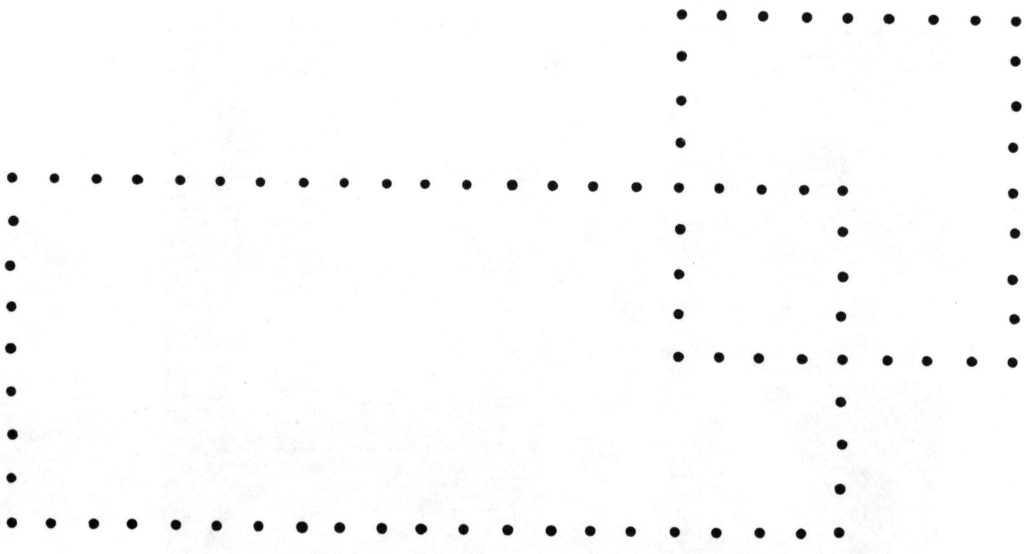

Fig. 3-11 Base layer of rectangle and square

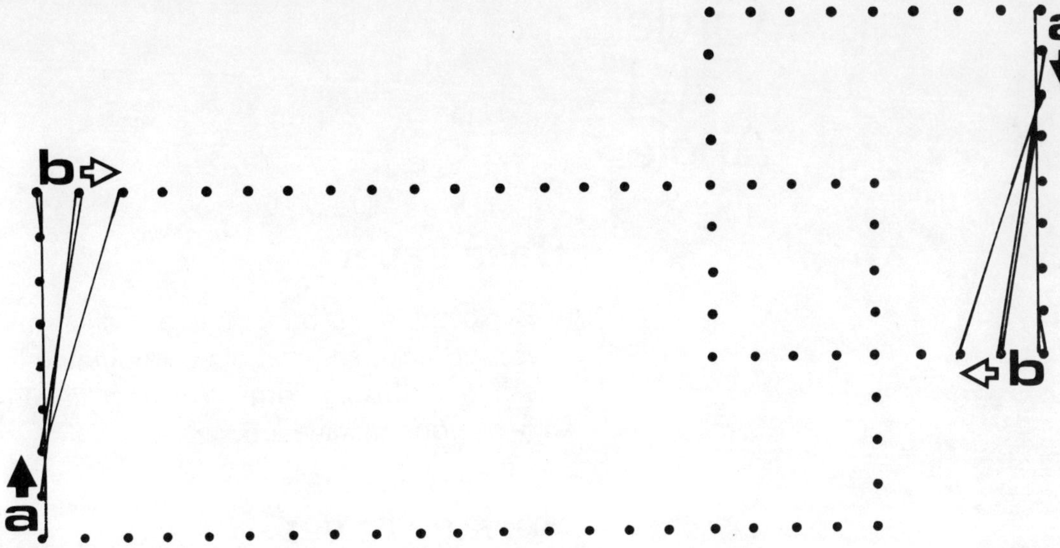

Fig. 3-12 Surface layer of rectangle and square

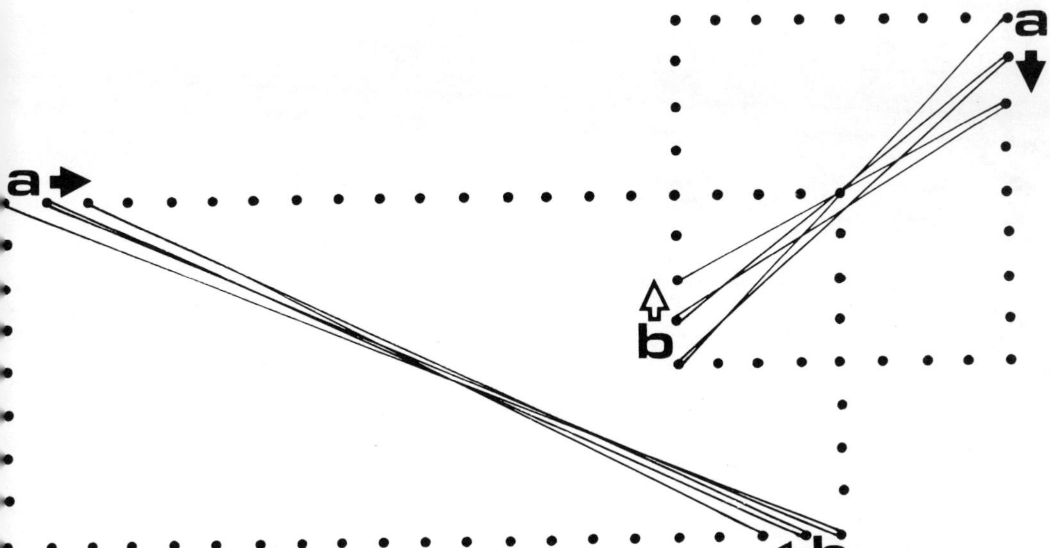

Circle and Angle

Base Layer

By combining basic designs such as these, you can see that almost anything is possible in this art form. You are limited only by your imagination.

Surface Layer

These surface rims and arches can be altered by skipping more or fewer nails, as noted in earlier chapters.

Fig. 3-13 Circle and angle

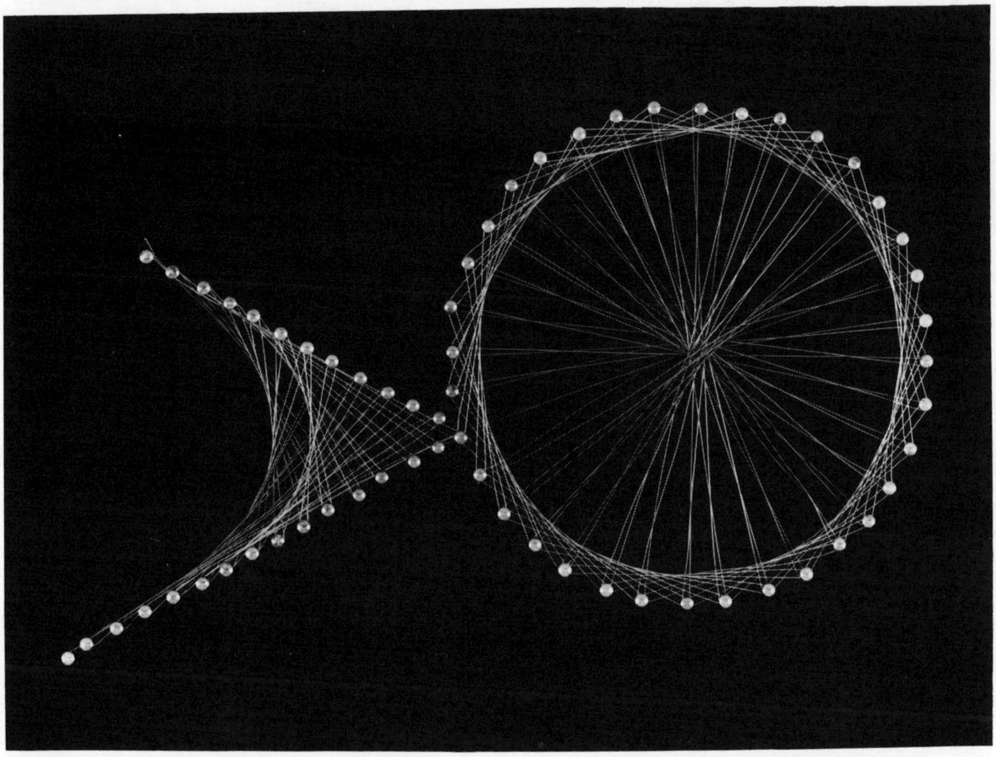

Fig. 3-14 Nailing pattern for circle and angle

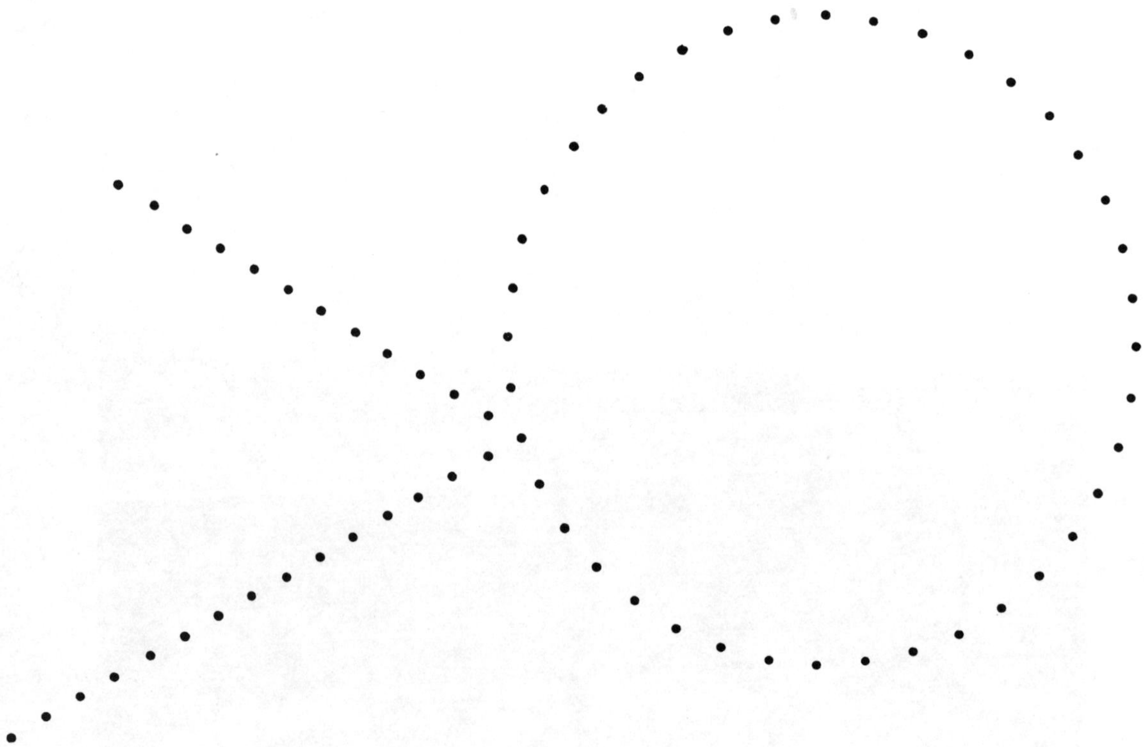

Fig. 3-15 Base layer of circle and angle

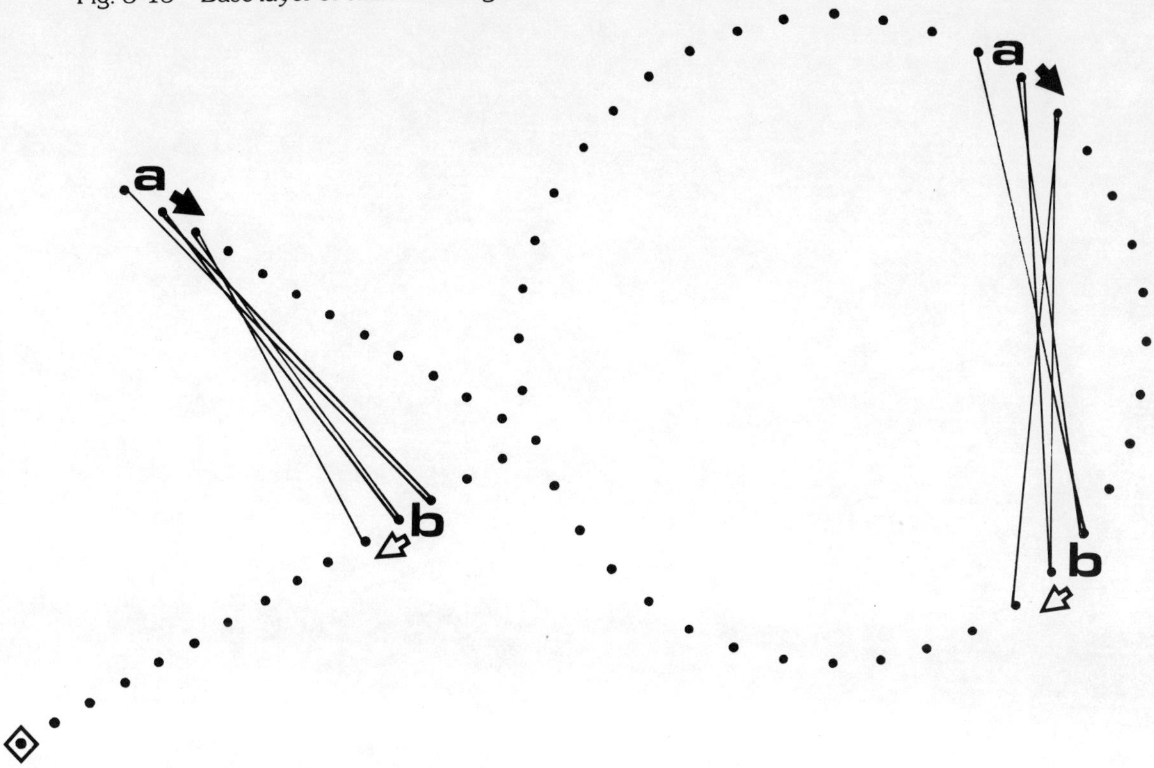

Fig. 3-16 Surface layer of circle and angle

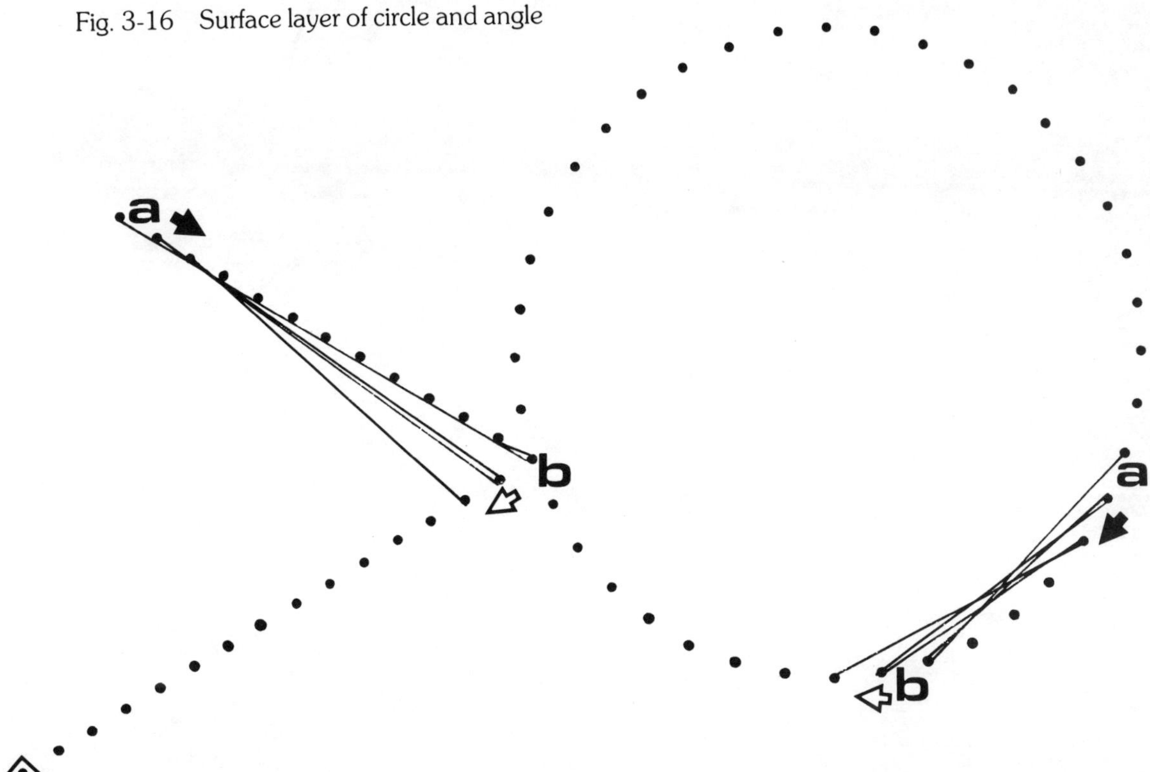

4
Using Three Layers

Sometimes three layers of wire may enable you to achieve more depth in your sculptures.

Diamond

First Layer

The crisscross base is very effective on diamonds, as it is on almost any shape when used to fill an enclosed wired area.

Fig. 4-1 Diamond

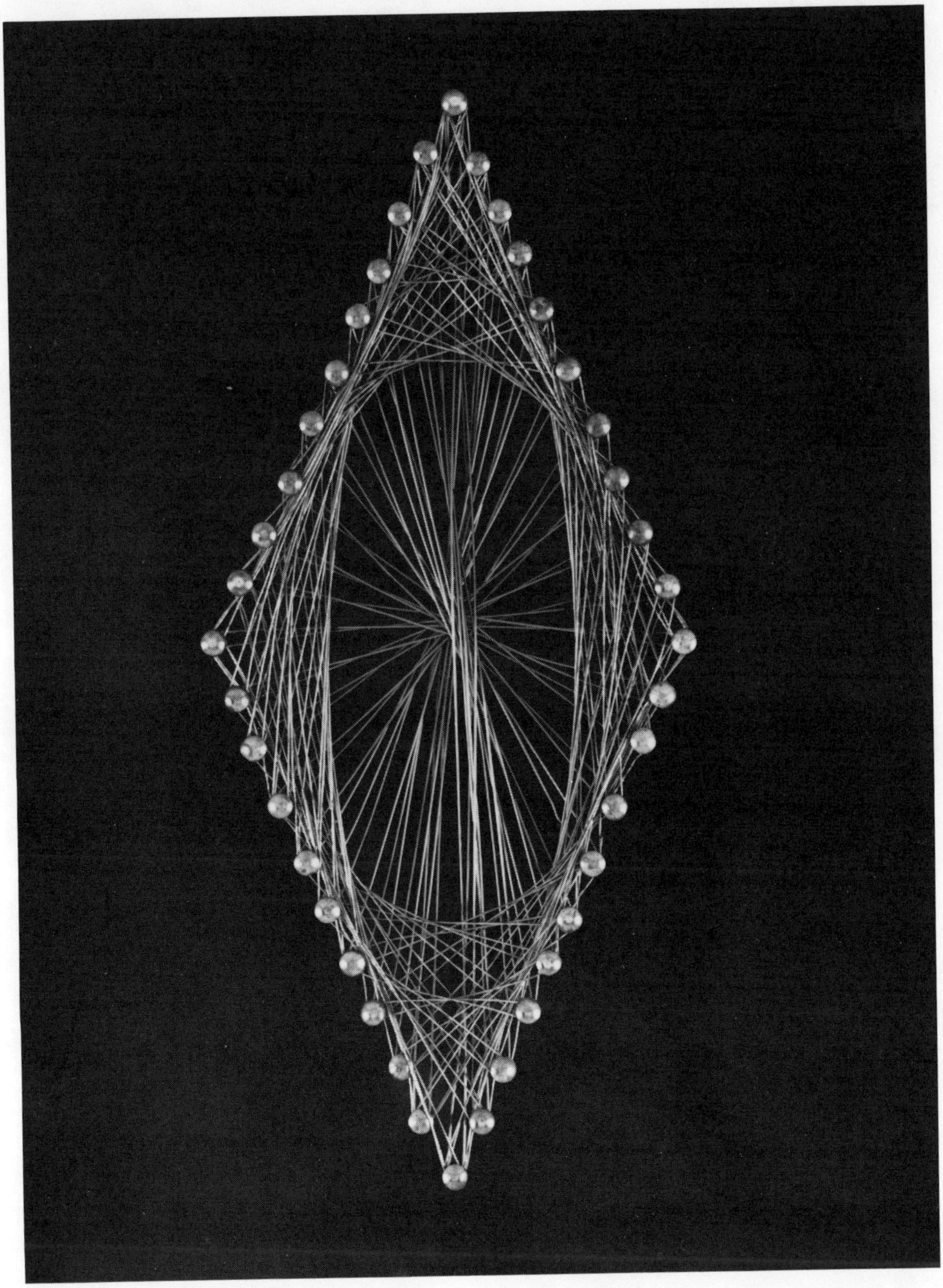

Second Layer

As this project will show, you are not limited to using two layers on any of these, or on your own designs. However, too much wire can make your design look too busy, while too little can make it look unfinished.

Fig. 4-2 Nailing pattern for diamond

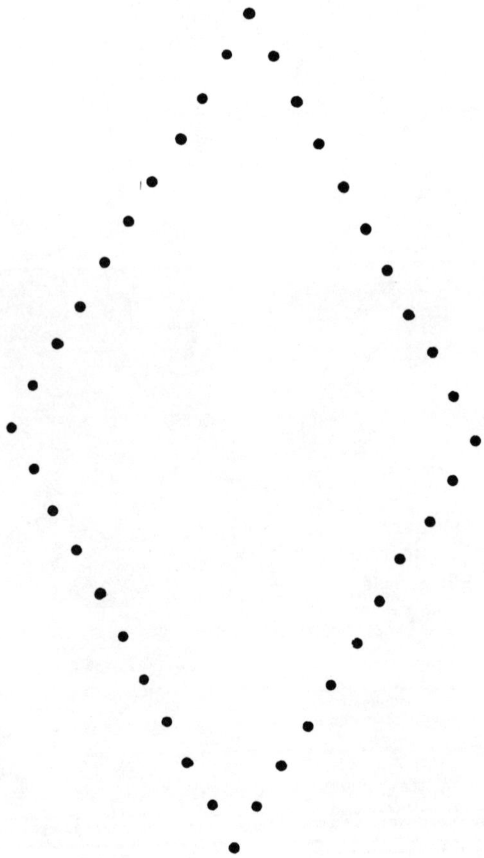

Fig. 4-3 First layer of diamond

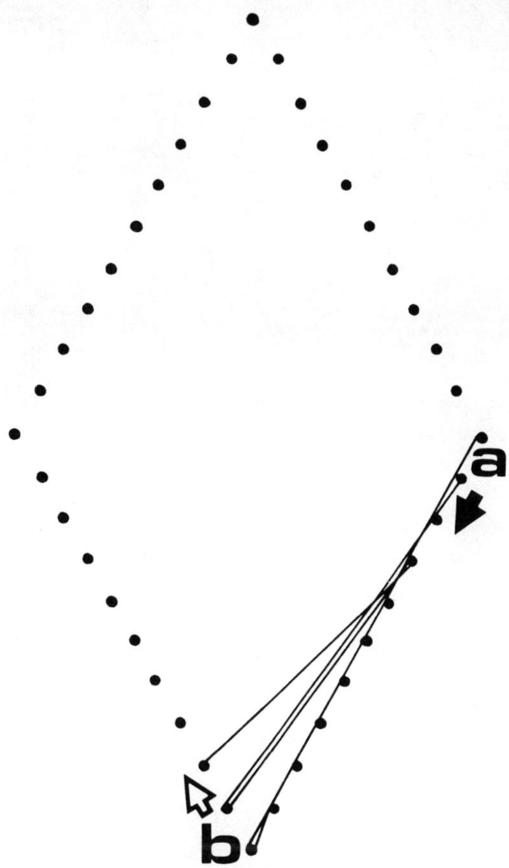

Fig. 4-4 Second layer of diamond

Third Layer

Some wire sculptures have as many as twelve layers and require a long and heavy nail. We suggest ¾ inch nails for a project involving three layers.

Fig. 4-5 Third layer of diamond

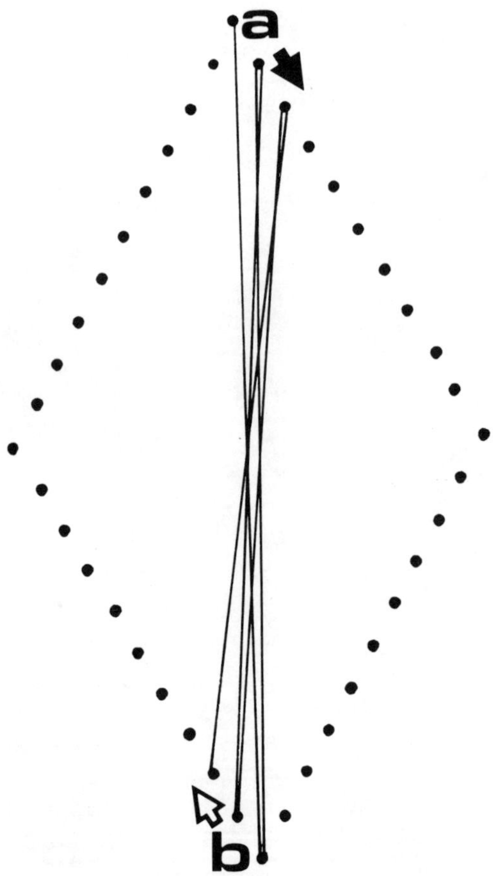

5

Abstract Designs

The designs shown in this chapter are basic. Try using your own ideas and experiment with variations on these designs. This will help give you an idea of the many possibilities of wire sculpture.

Snowflake

Base Layer

The wiring for only one section of the snowflake is shown because each segment is done in exactly the same fashion. The numbers in the pattern represent different segments, each one wired the same way.

Surface Layer

The number of nails skipped on these patterns should be the same for each section of the snowflake. Skip as many as you like, but keep each section the same as the others.

Fig. 5-1 Snowflake

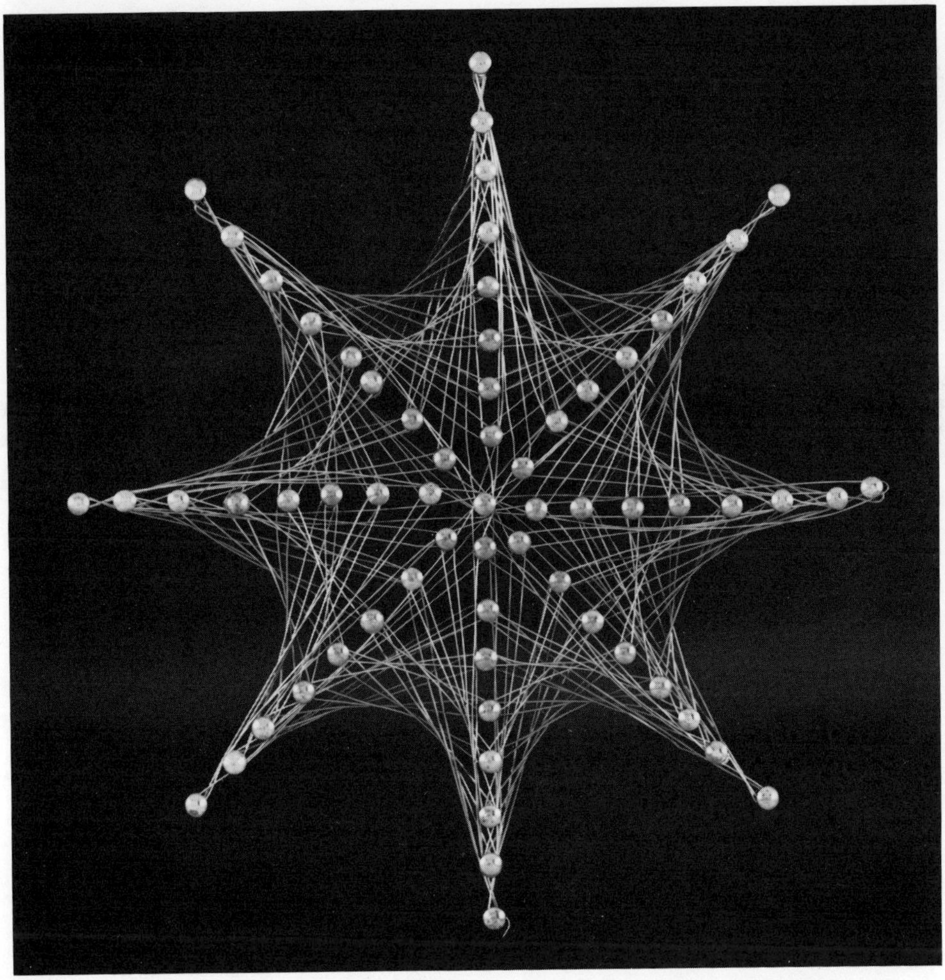

Fig. 5-2 Nailing pattern for snowflake

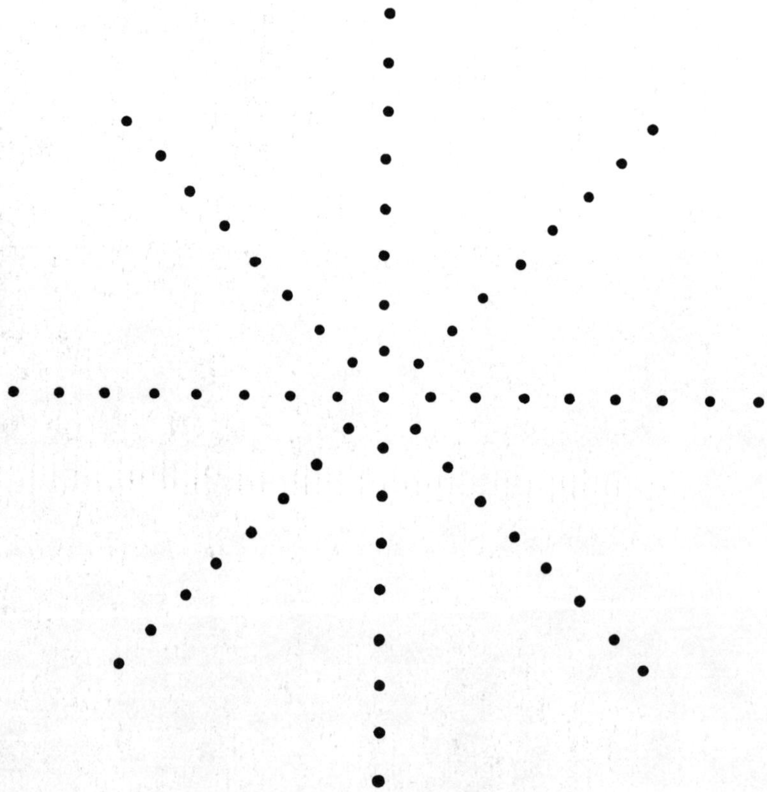

Fig. 5-3 Base layer of snowflake

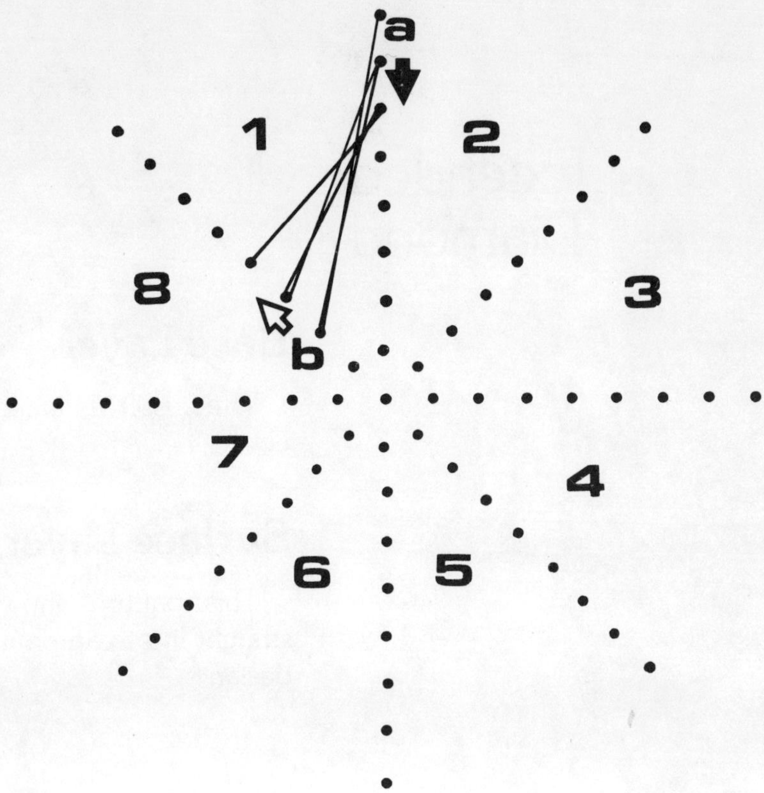

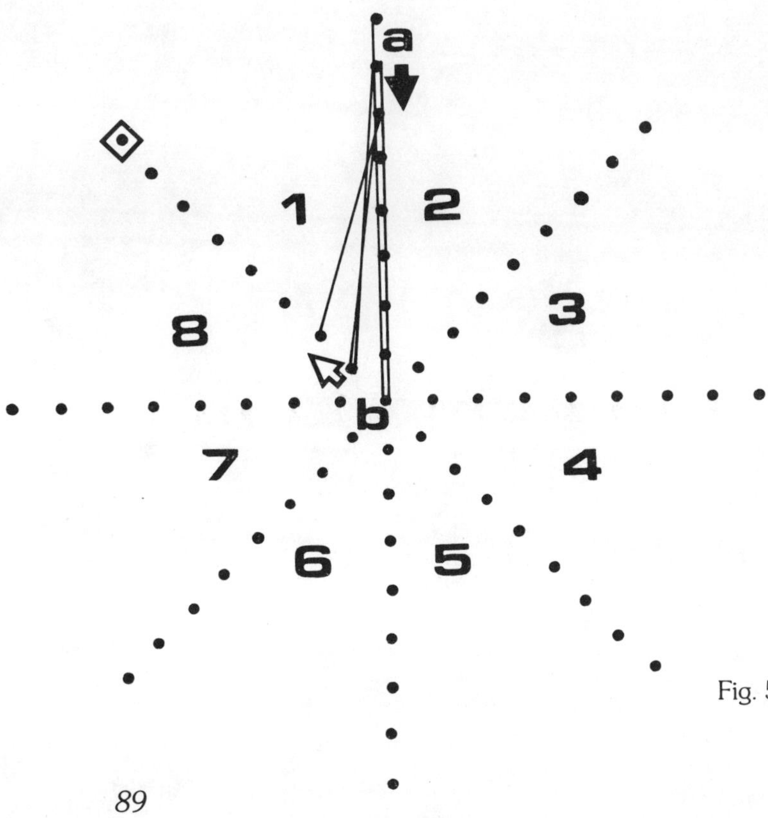

Fig. 5-4 Surface layer of snowflake

Extended Diamond

Base Layer

The crisscross base is used for this project.

Surface Layer

This pattern shows how the use of straight lines can change the look of your design.

Fig. 5-5 Extended diamond

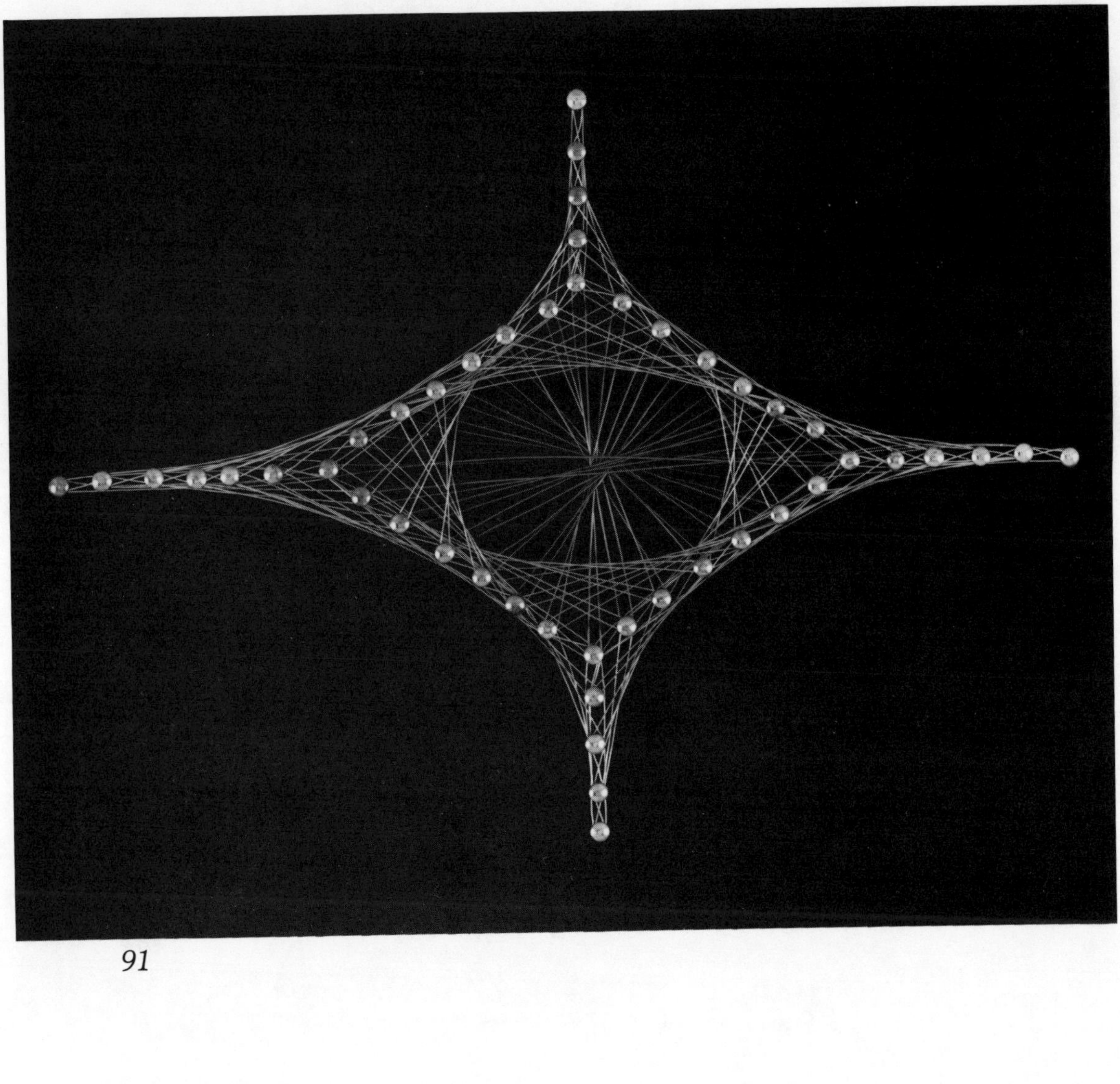

Fig. 5-6 Nailing pattern for extended diamond

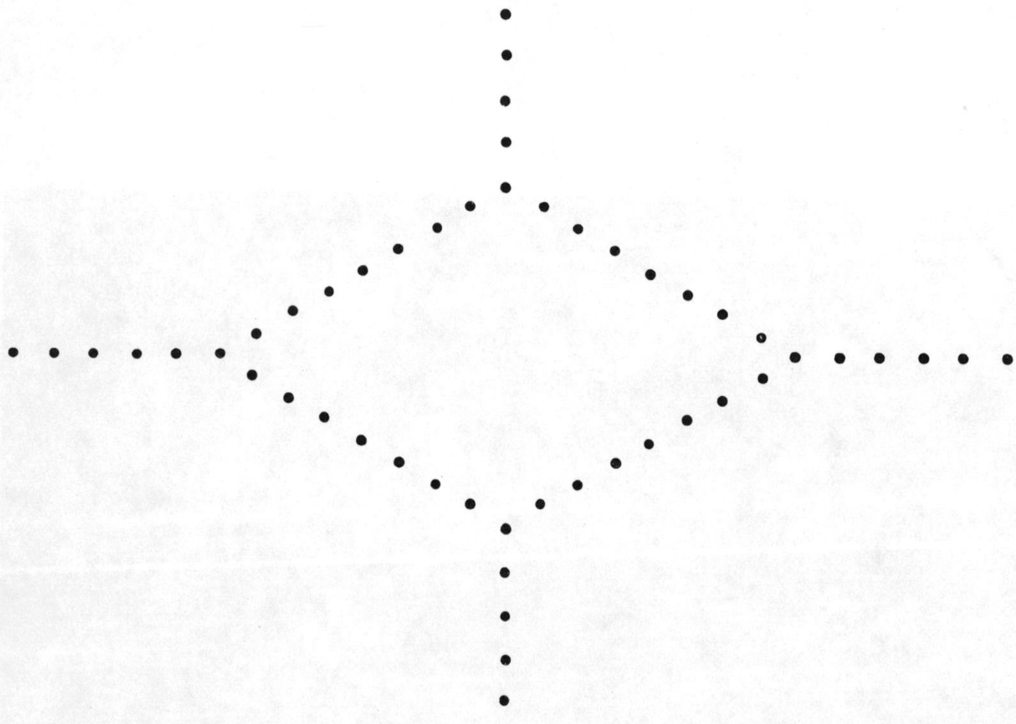

Fig. 5-7 Base layer of extended diamond

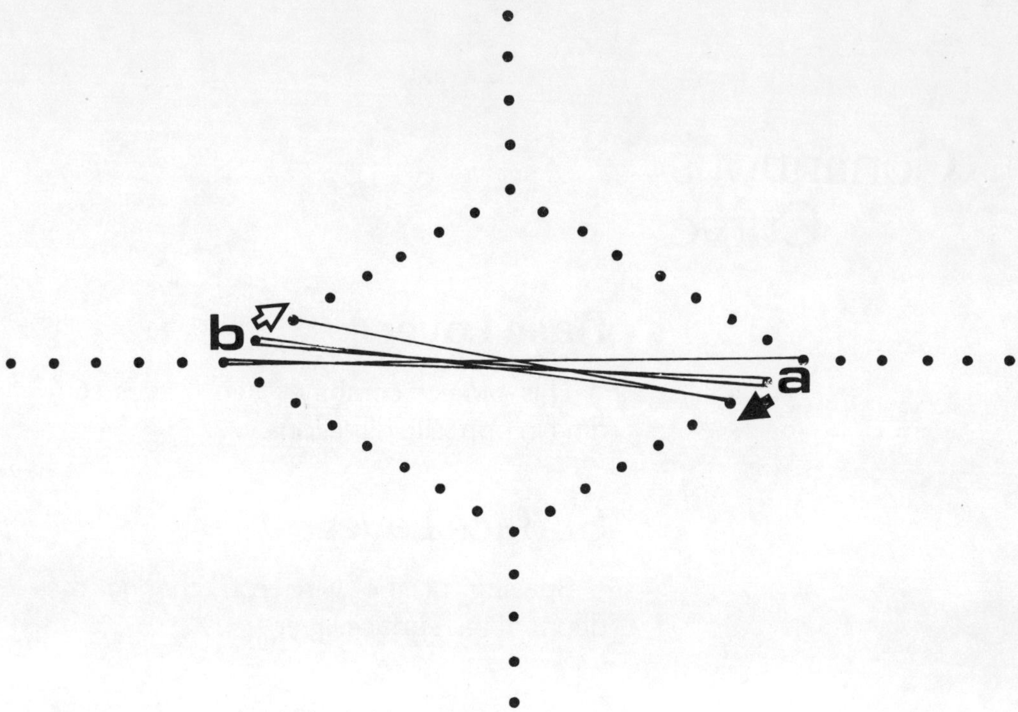

Fig. 5-8 Surface layer of extended diamond

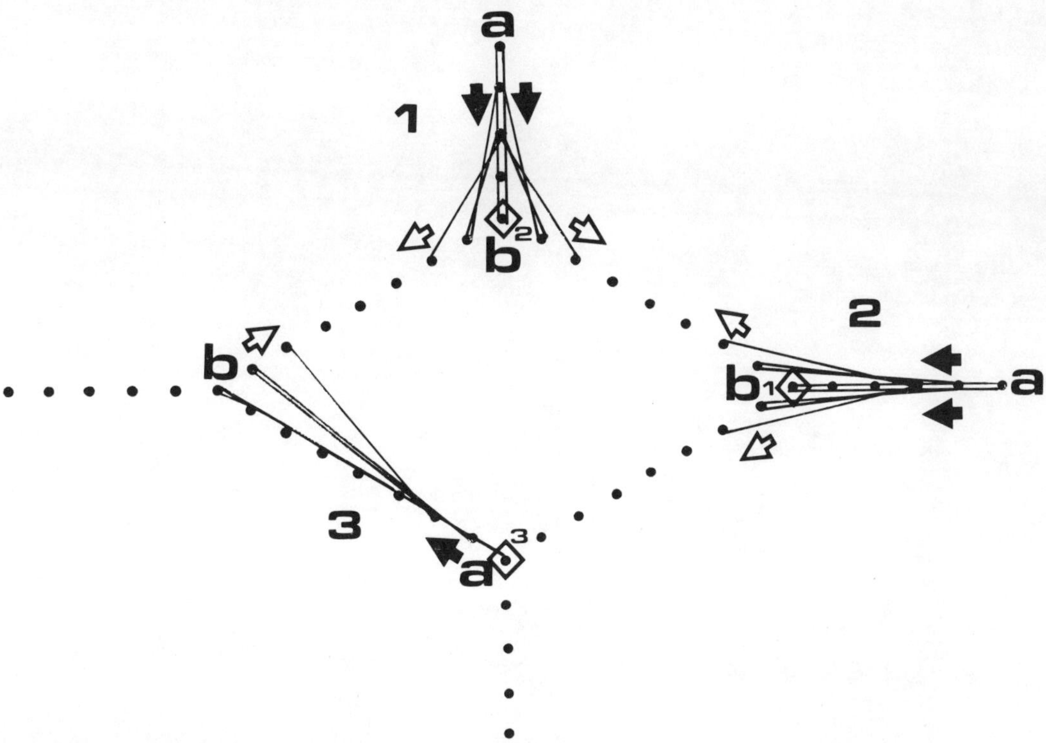

Continuous Curve

Base Layer

This project combines two curves running in opposite directions.

Surface Layer

Spacing of the wire can change the depth of this surface layer.

Fig. 5-9 Continuous curve

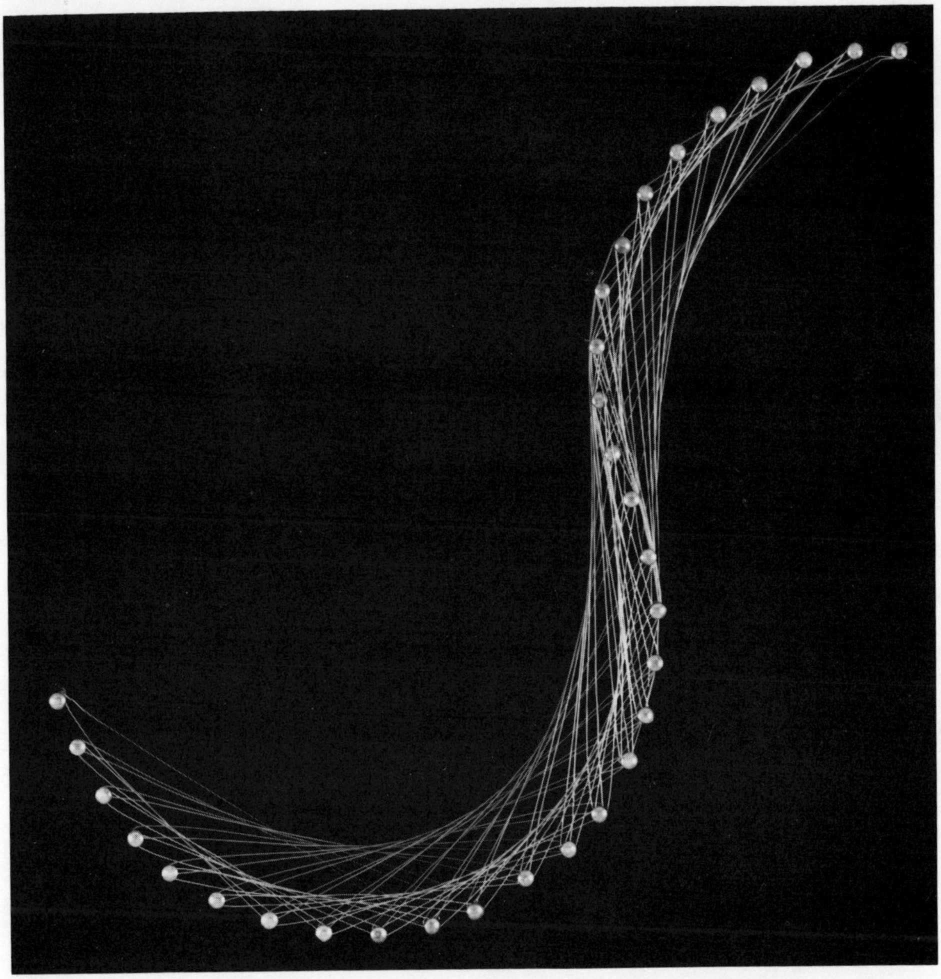

Fig. 5-10 Nailing pattern for continuous curve

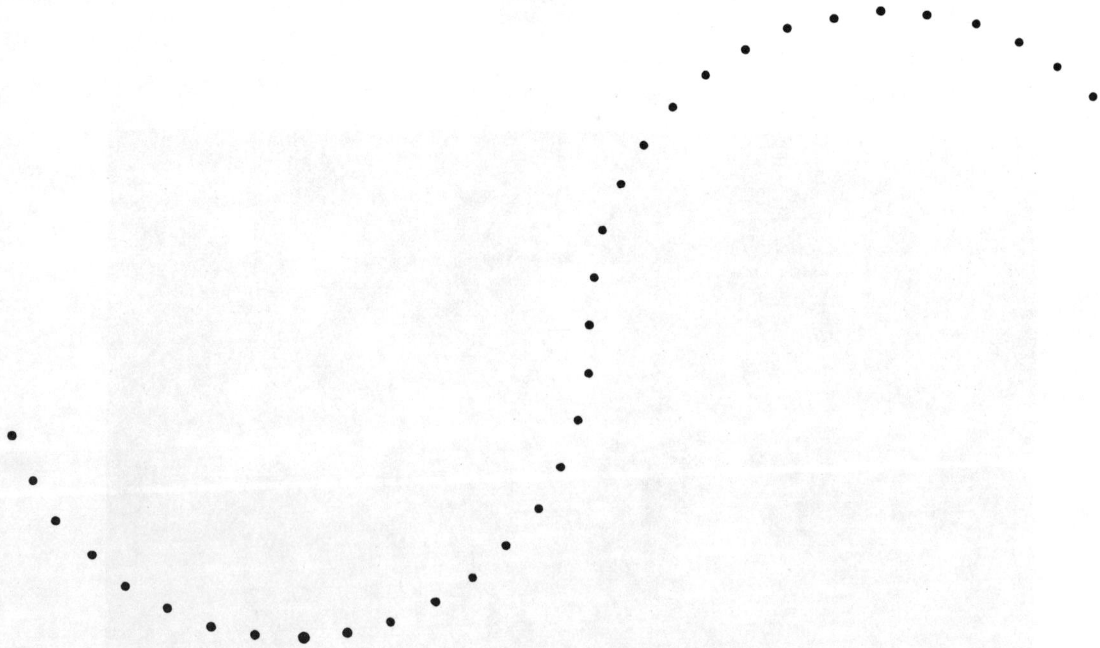

Fig. 5-11 Base layer of continuous curve

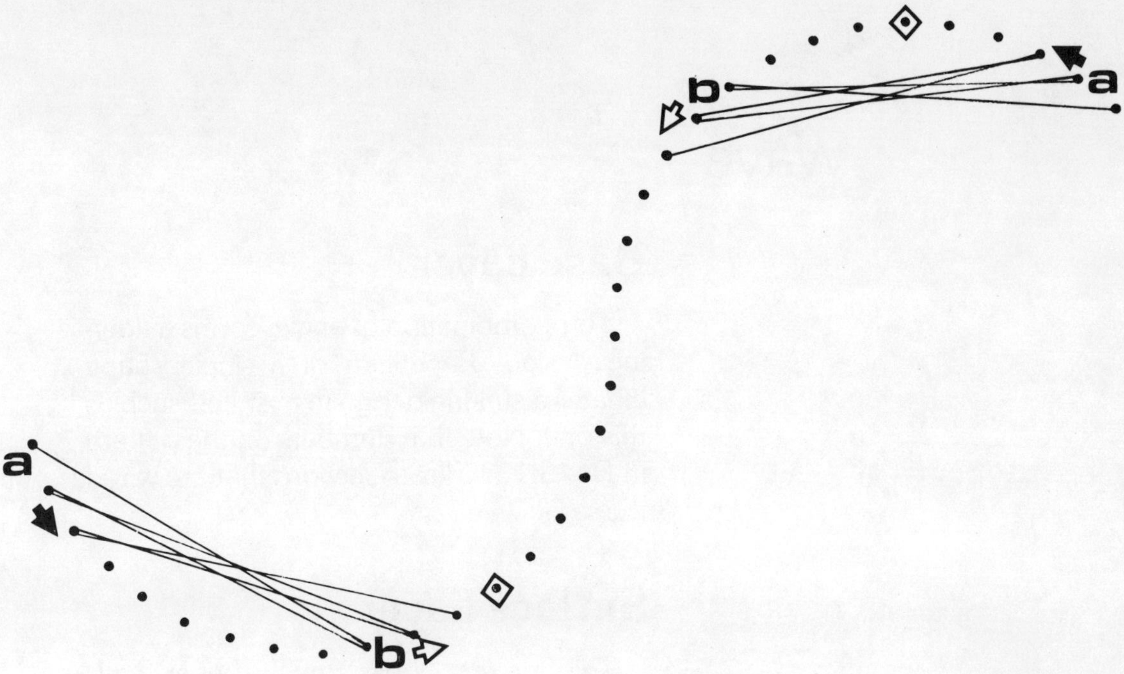

Fig. 5-12 Surface layer of continuous curve

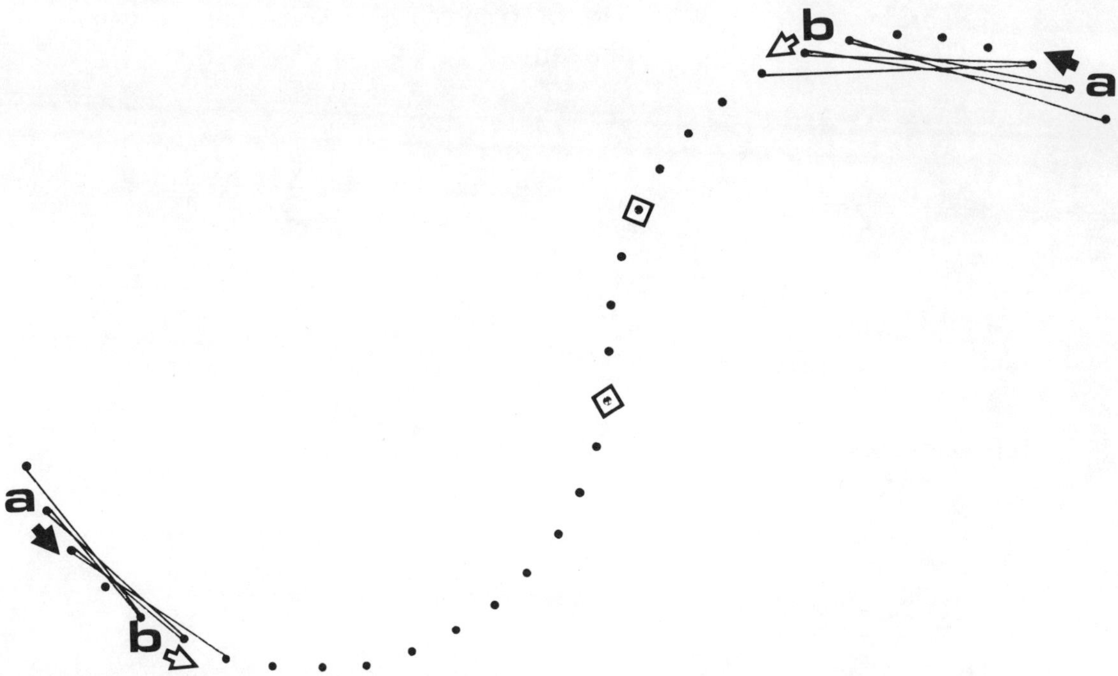

Wave

Base Layer

This combination of angles forms a flowing design. Repetition of a single shape creates a striking design in abstracts such as this one. Note that numbers on the pattern in Fig. 5-15 indicate sections that are wired the same way.

Surface Layer

This project looks much better with heavier gauge wire on the surface layers, but be sure the reduction in gauge from layer to layer is uniform. Wire tension is very important on this design. Numbers in Fig. 5-16 indicate sections that are wired the same.

Fig. 5-13 Wave

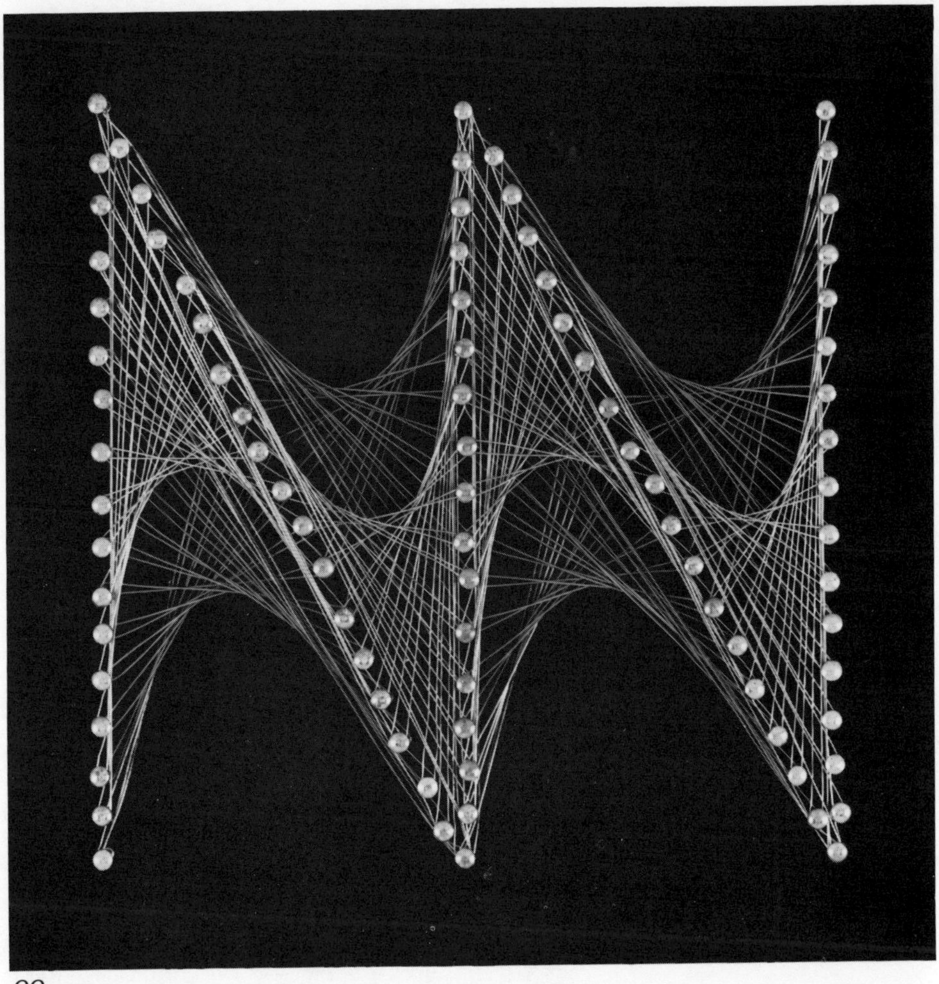

Fig. 5-14 Nailing pattern for wave

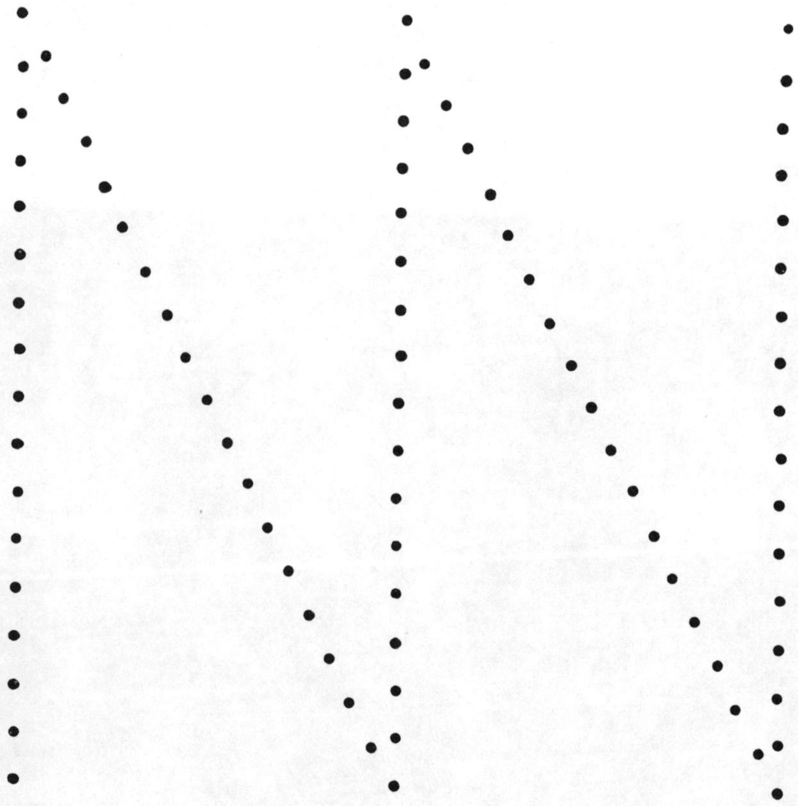

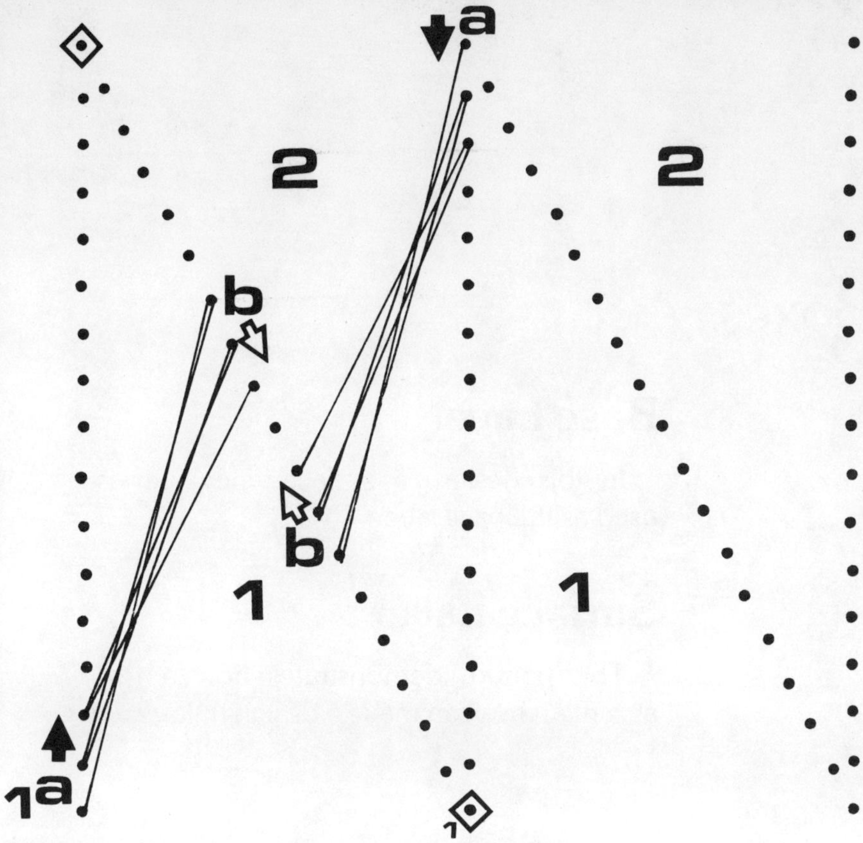

Fig. 5-15 Base layer of wave

Fig. 5-16 Surface layer of wave

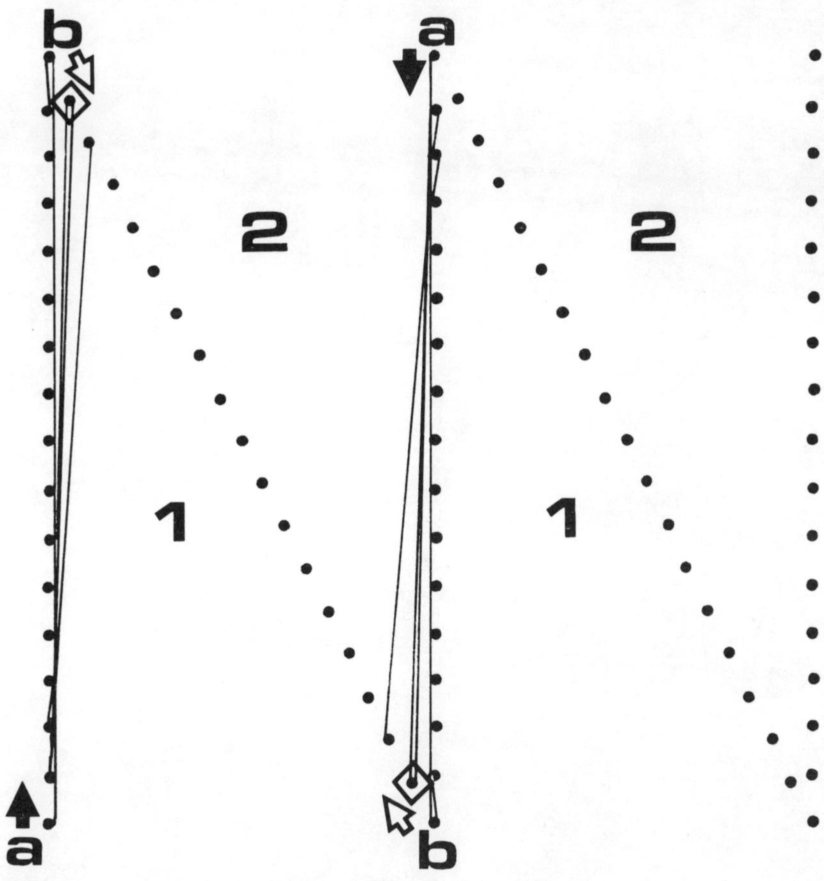

Boxes

Base Layer

In this design, a surface-type layer is used as the base layer.

Surface Layer

This pattern demonstrates how a few accent arches can make a design unique.

Fig. 5-17 Boxes

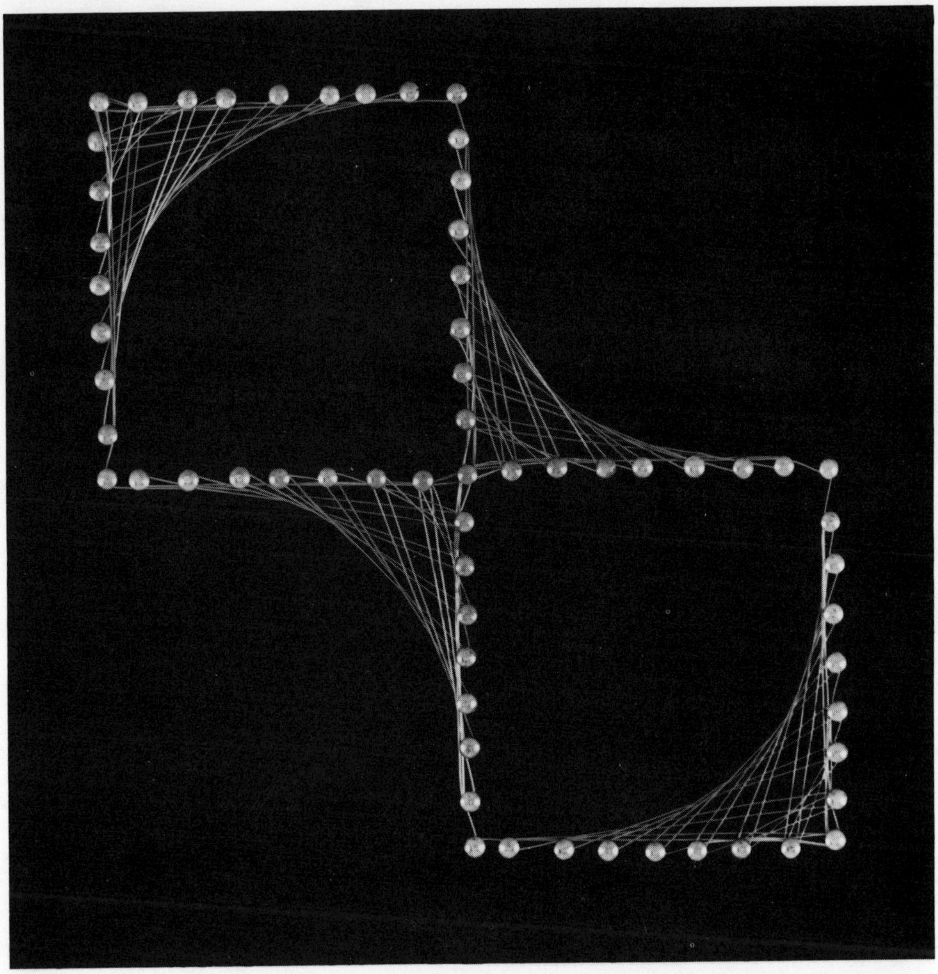

Fig. 5-18 Nailing pattern for boxes

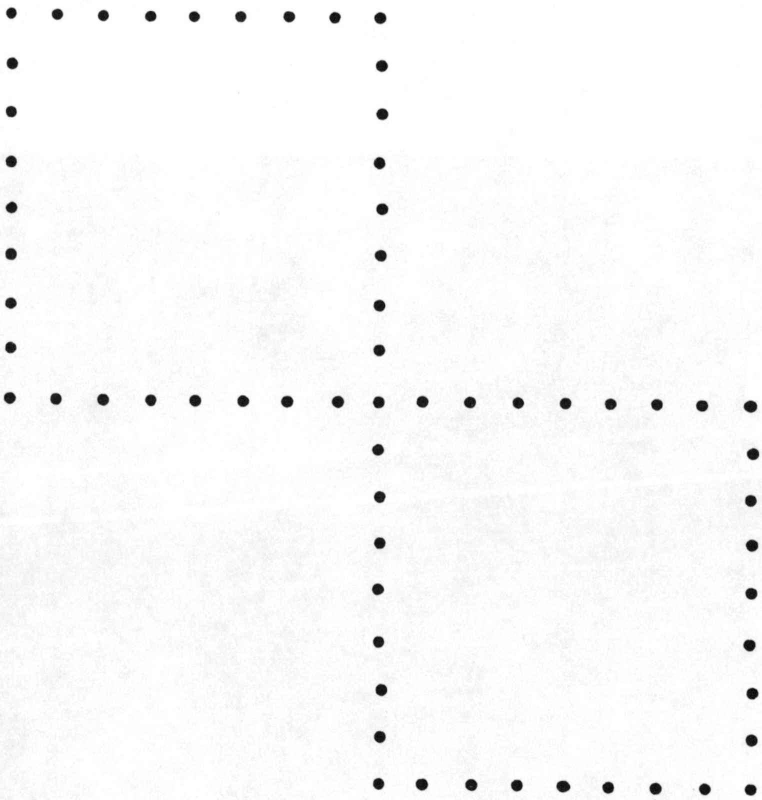

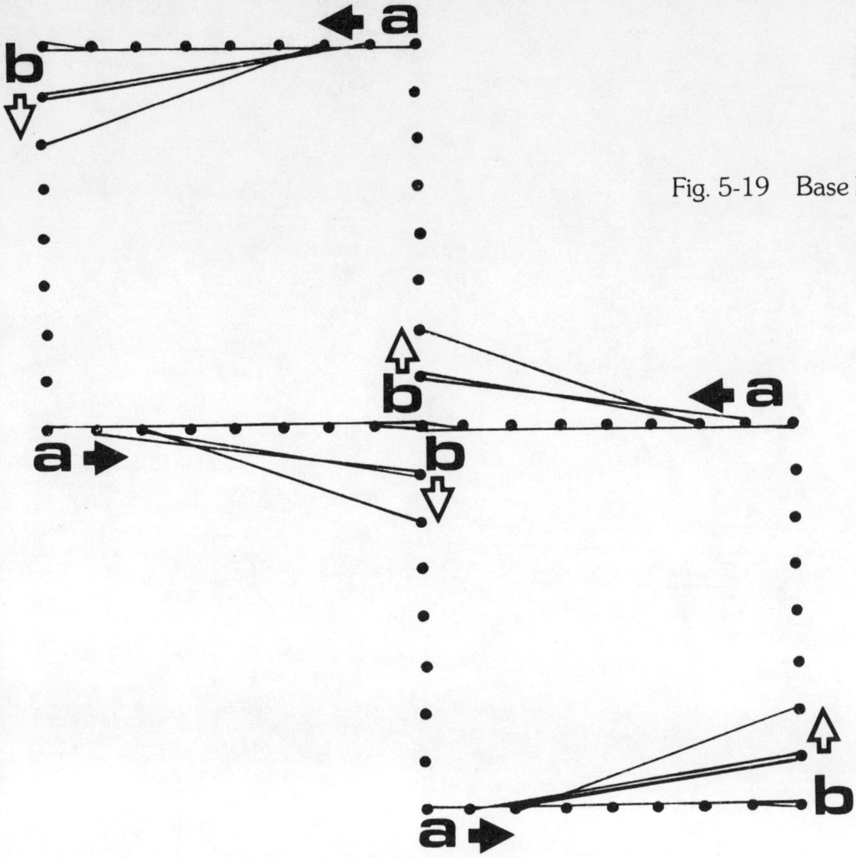

Fig. 5-19 Base layer of boxes

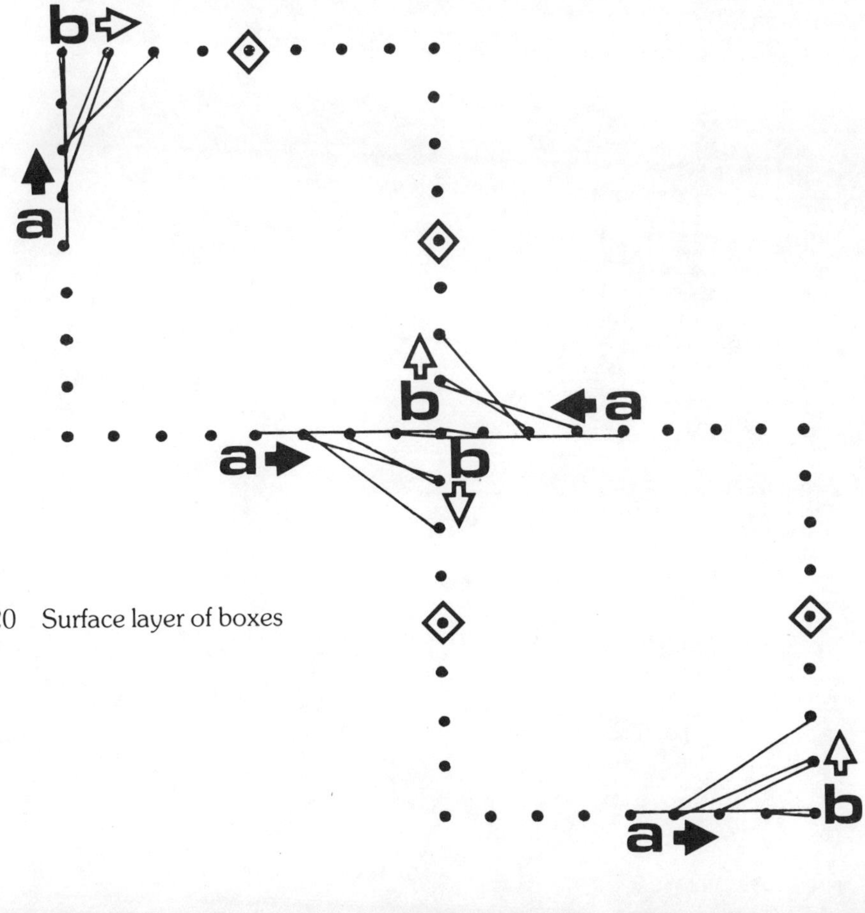

Fig. 5-20 Surface layer of boxes

6
Ships

Almost any kind of sailing vessel will lend itself to wire sculpture. If a wooden hull is to be added to the design, however, the task can become more complex. Once mastered, though, the finished appearance is well worth the extra effort.

All ship design projects include a pattern showing the rigging for the masts.

Hull Making

To make a hull, first draw the design on the wood you have chosen. Then saw or sand the wood to the shape outlined. Next, sand the surface until smooth and stain it with an appropriate wood stain. If you wish, finish with Varethane or varnish. To attach the hull, use finishing nails or ⅜″ brass nails.

Fig. 6-1 Hull making

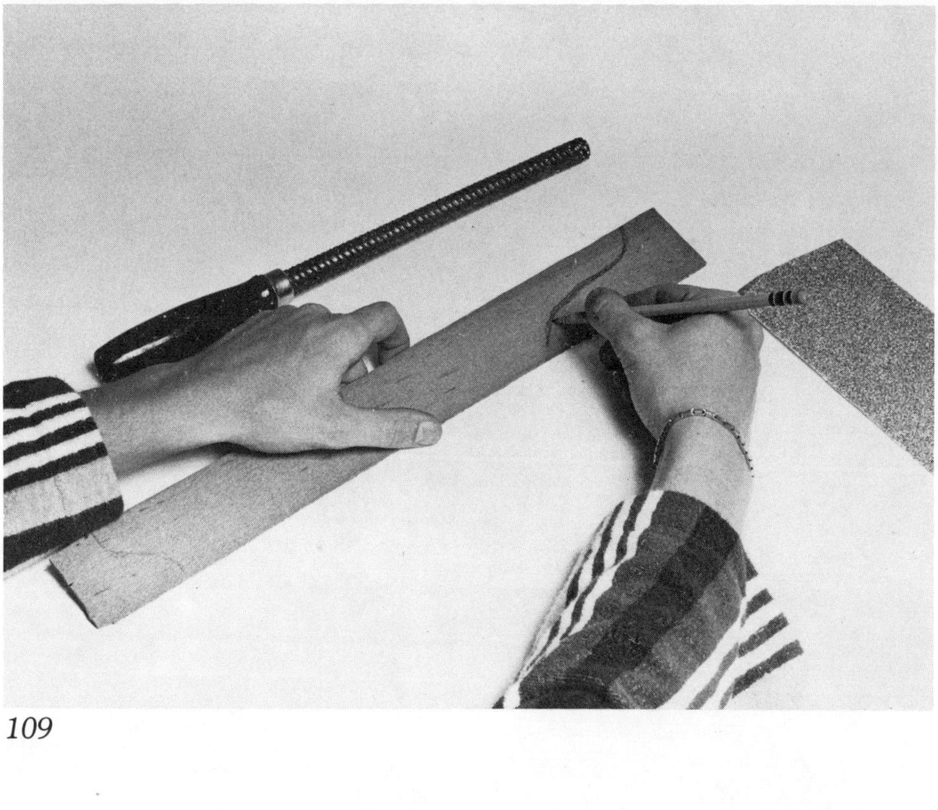

Two-Masted Schooner

Base Layer

The base layer will form the back part of the sails. Be sure that all wires are pushed against the fabric and that the wire is taut while wrapping.

Surface Layer

The surface layer may be painted with a gold or silver enamel paint to give the design more depth.

Rigging

Attach hull with nails and follow the line drawings for the rigging. Lamé wire is popular for this. If you are using finishing nails to attach the hull, countersink the nails and fill with wood putty for a finished look.

Fig. 6-2 Two-masted schooner

Fig. 6-3 Nailing pattern for two-masted schooner

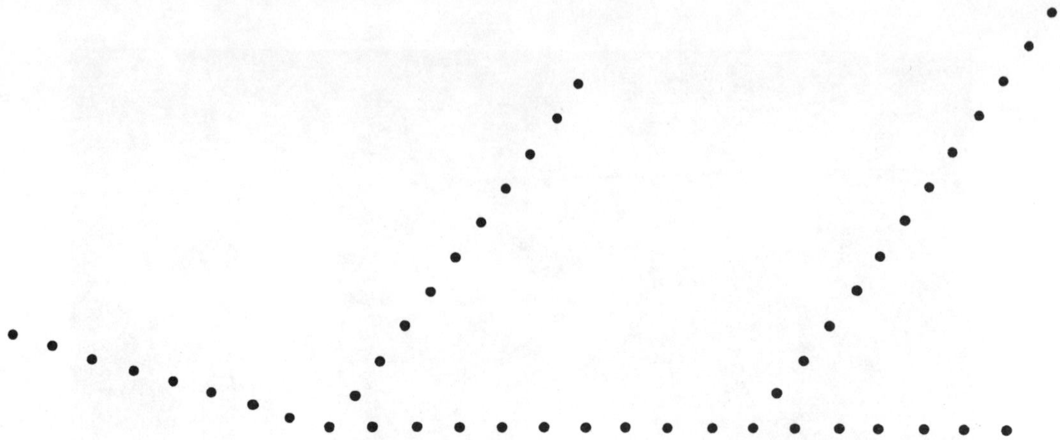

Fig. 6-4 Base layer of schooner

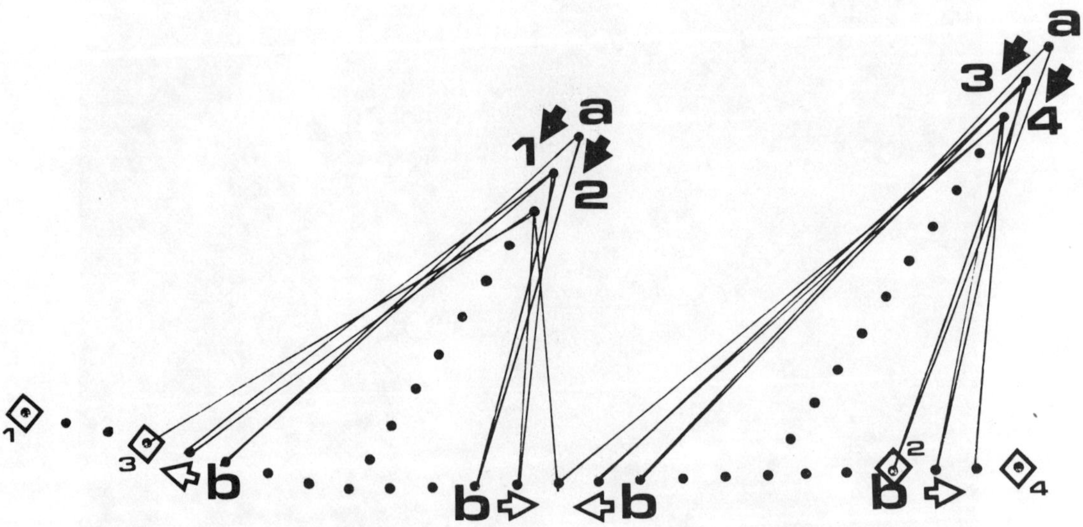

Fig. 6-5 Surface layer of schooner

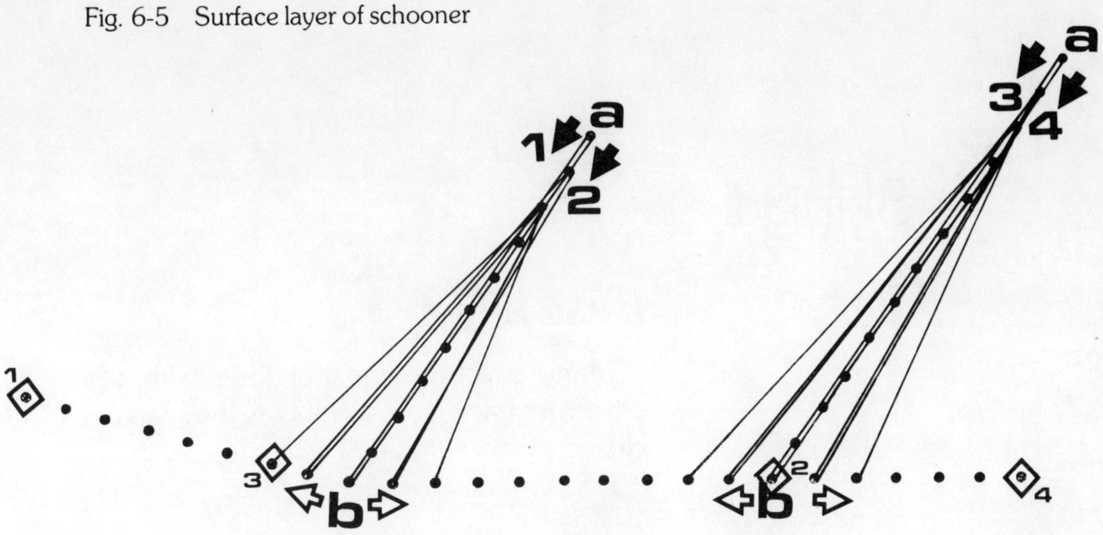

Fig. 6-6 Rigging for schooner

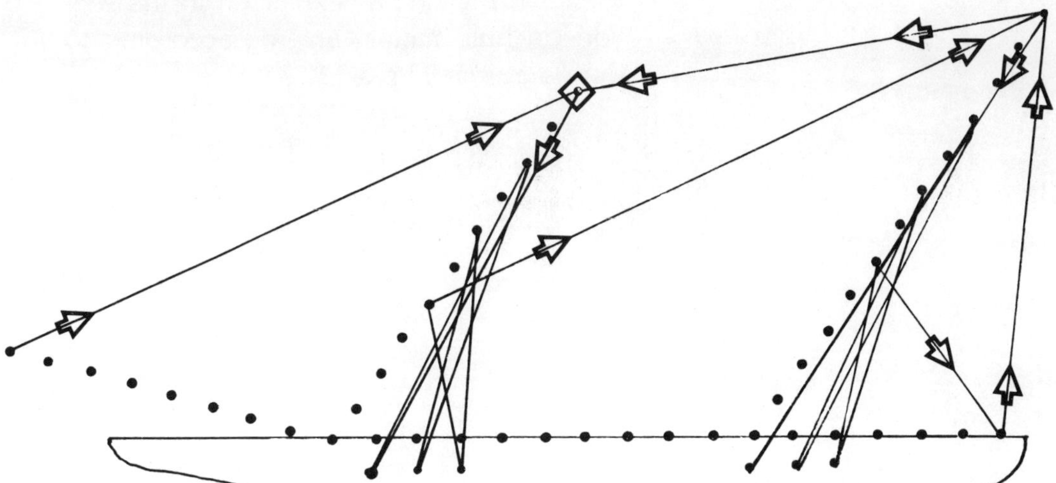

Skipjack

Base Layer

Many sailboats can be done with the crisscross base layer as long as they have a closed sail form to work within.

Surface Layer

By skipping fewer nails and adding more layers, simple designs become very intricate. Try dressing this ship up by surrounding each pattern with lamé or using more than one surface layer, or by experimenting with your own ideas.

Rigging

Attach the hull as explained in the section on hull making and rig according to the diagram in Fig. 6-11.

Fig. 6-7 Skipjack

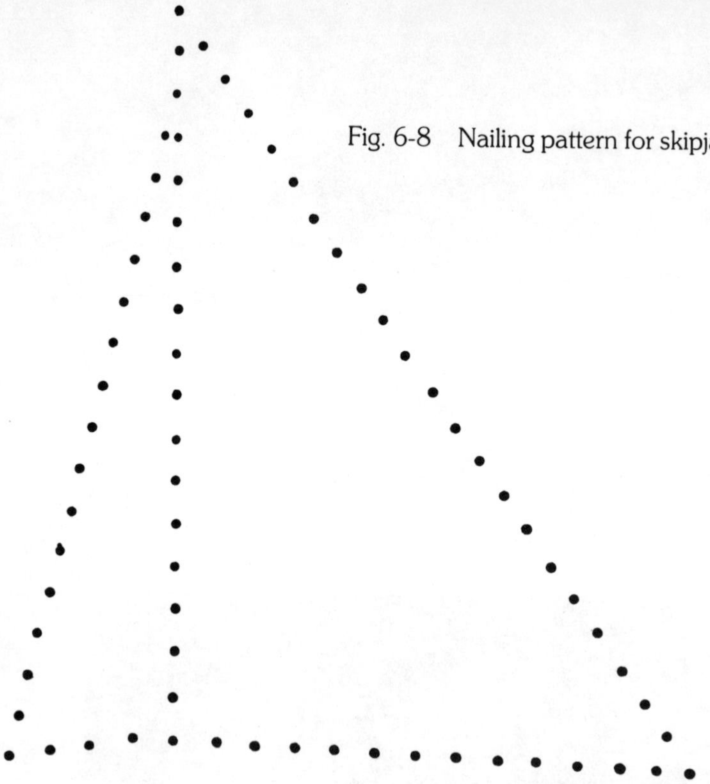

Fig. 6-8 Nailing pattern for skipjack

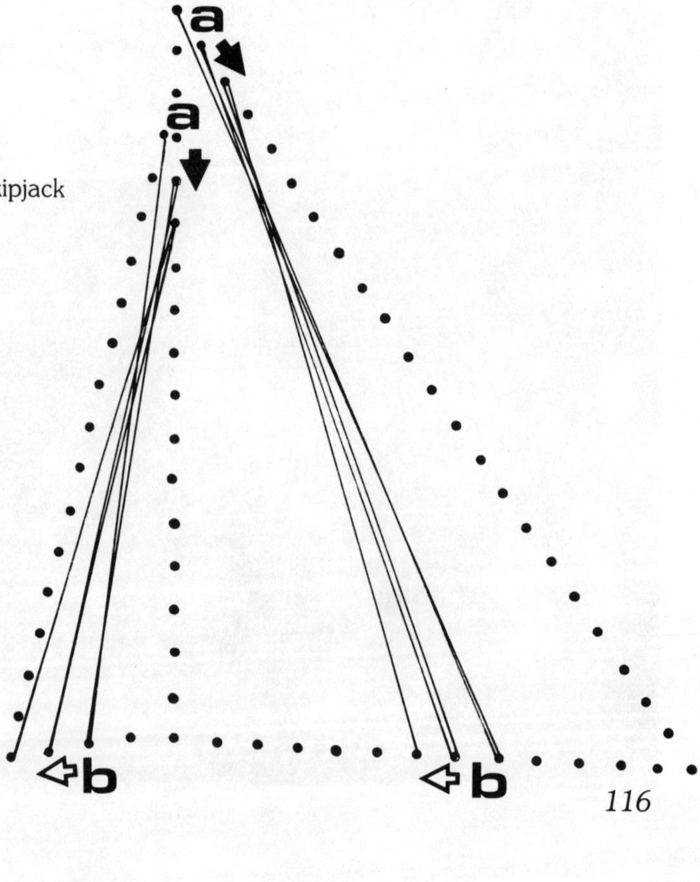

Fig. 6-9 Base layer of skipjack

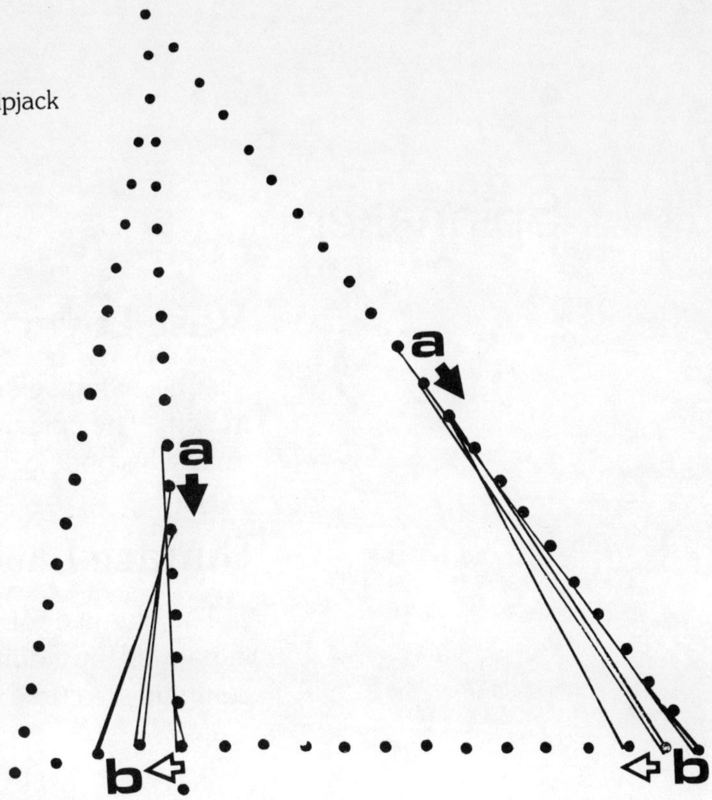

Fig. 6-10 Surface layer of skipjack

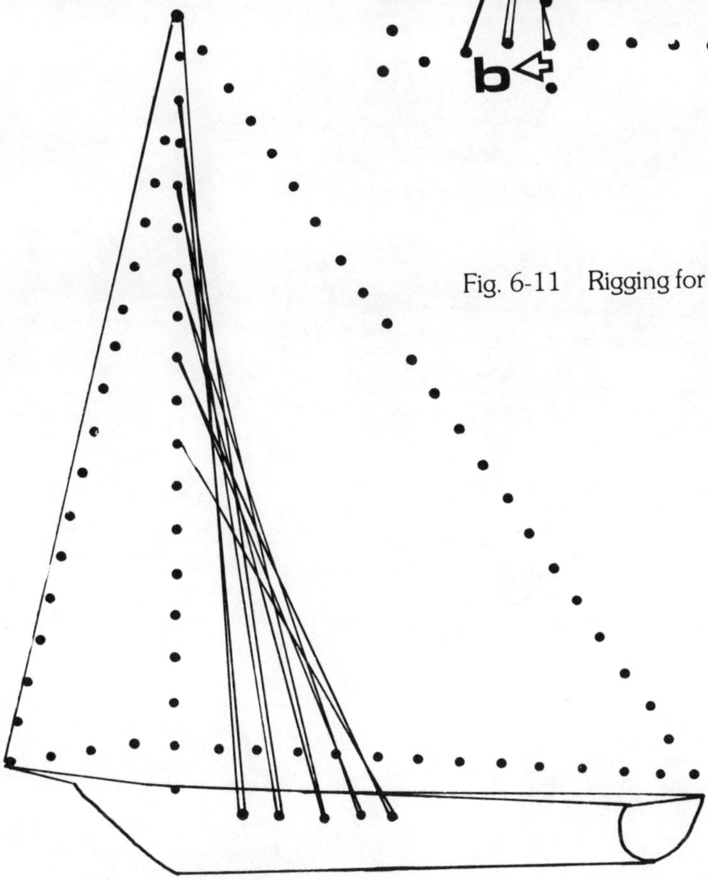

Fig. 6-11 Rigging for skipjack

Spinnaker

Base Layer

A billowing spinnaker looks lovely done in wire. The crisscross base looks very nice in this design.

Surface Layer

The surface of the spinnaker can be expanded by adding layers of wire to accentuate the curve.

Fig. 6-12 Spinnaker

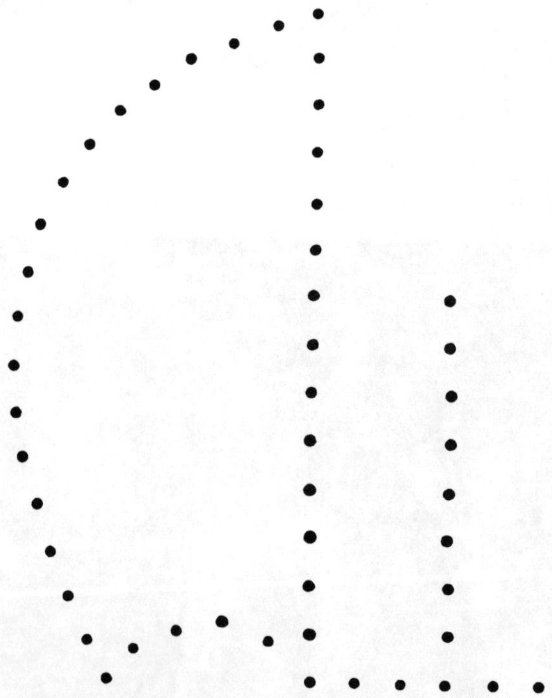

Fig. 6-13 Nailing pattern for spinnaker

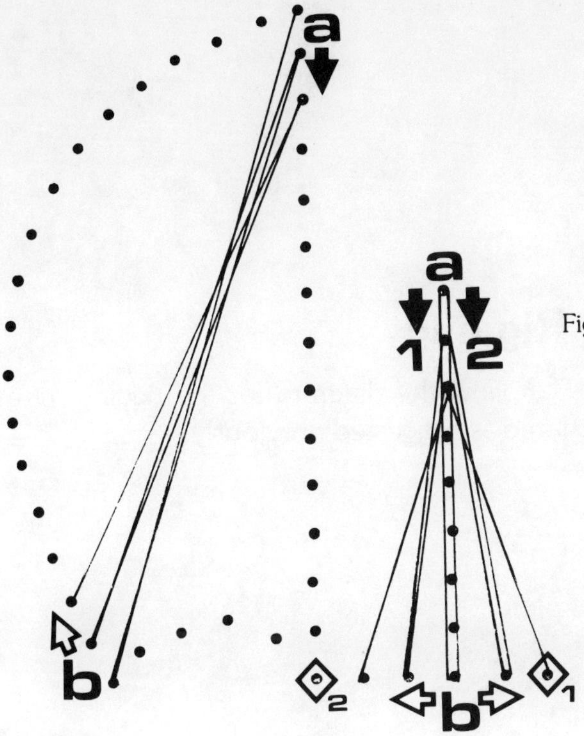

Fig. 6-14 Base layer of spinnaker

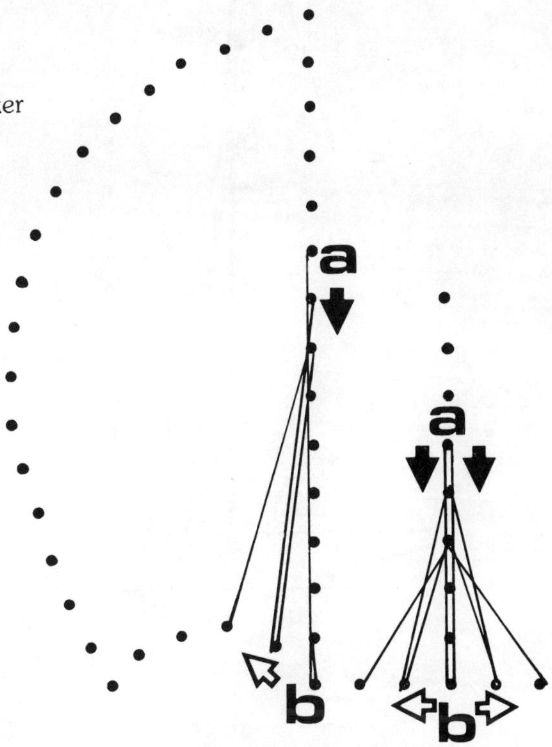

Fig. 6-15 Surface layer of spinnaker

Rigging

Follow the diagram for the rigging. Use lamé as suggested previously.

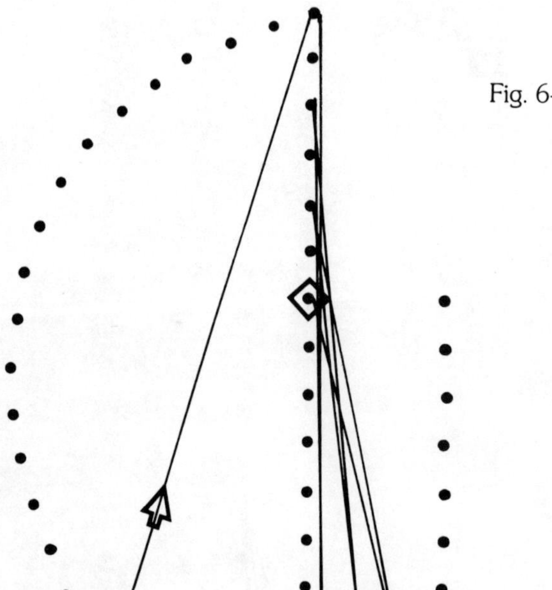

Fig. 6-16 Rigging for spinnaker

7 Advanced Projects

The advanced projects will present more of a challenge for those who have mastered the projects in the preceding chapters. These designs take more time, patience, and skill to complete.

The Crisscross Method

By working a double strand of wire between nails in a crisscross pattern, an "X" is formed. This method gives the row of nails a heavier look. Use this method anywhere a strong definition line is needed. Crisscrossing looks especially good done with lamé.

Clipper Ship

Base Layer

The crisscross pattern forms an "X" on each mast. These patterns will form the backs of the sails. Note that there are three different wiring sequences to follow in Fig. 7-4, Parts I, II and III.

Surface Layer

The arches are the same on each mast intersection, except they are wired in different directions. Be sure to check the direction of the arrows. Stop at the end of each vertical row of nails for wiring surface layer.

Rigging

Attach hull and rig according to the diagram shown in Fig. 7-6.

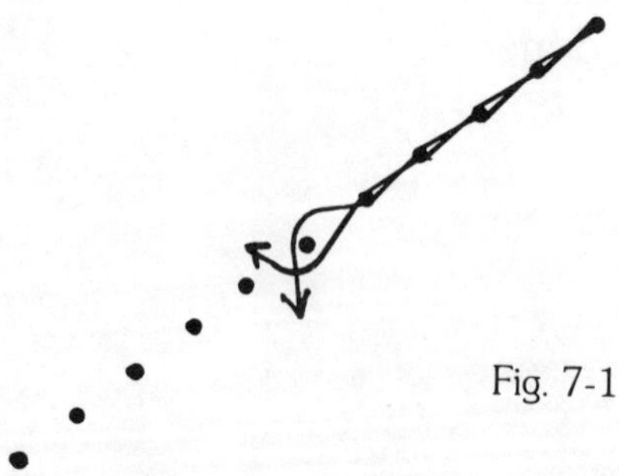

Fig. 7-1 Crisscross method

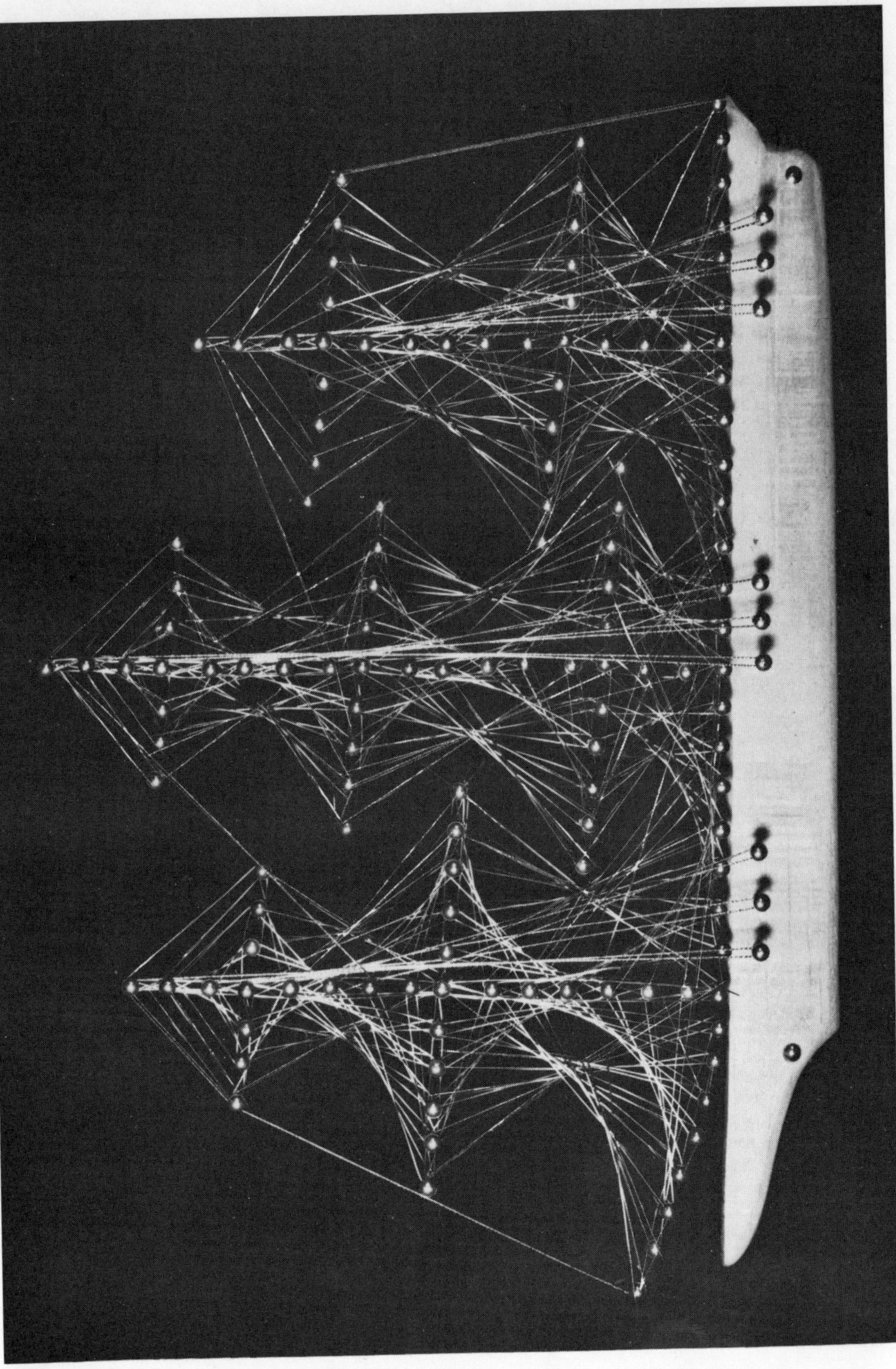

Fig. 7-2 Clipper ship

Fig. 7-3 Nailing pattern for clipper ship

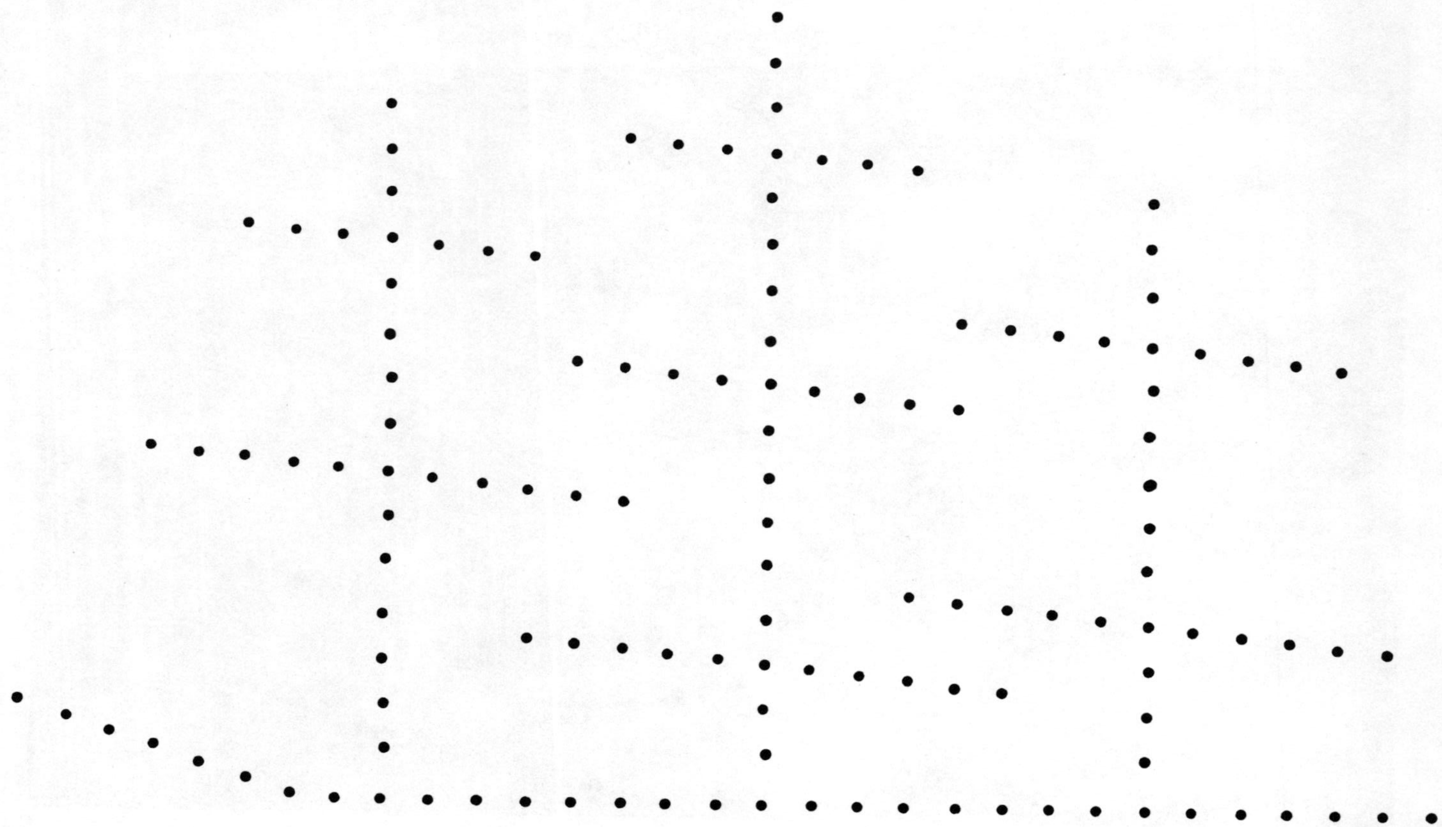

Fig. 7-4 Base layer of clipper ship

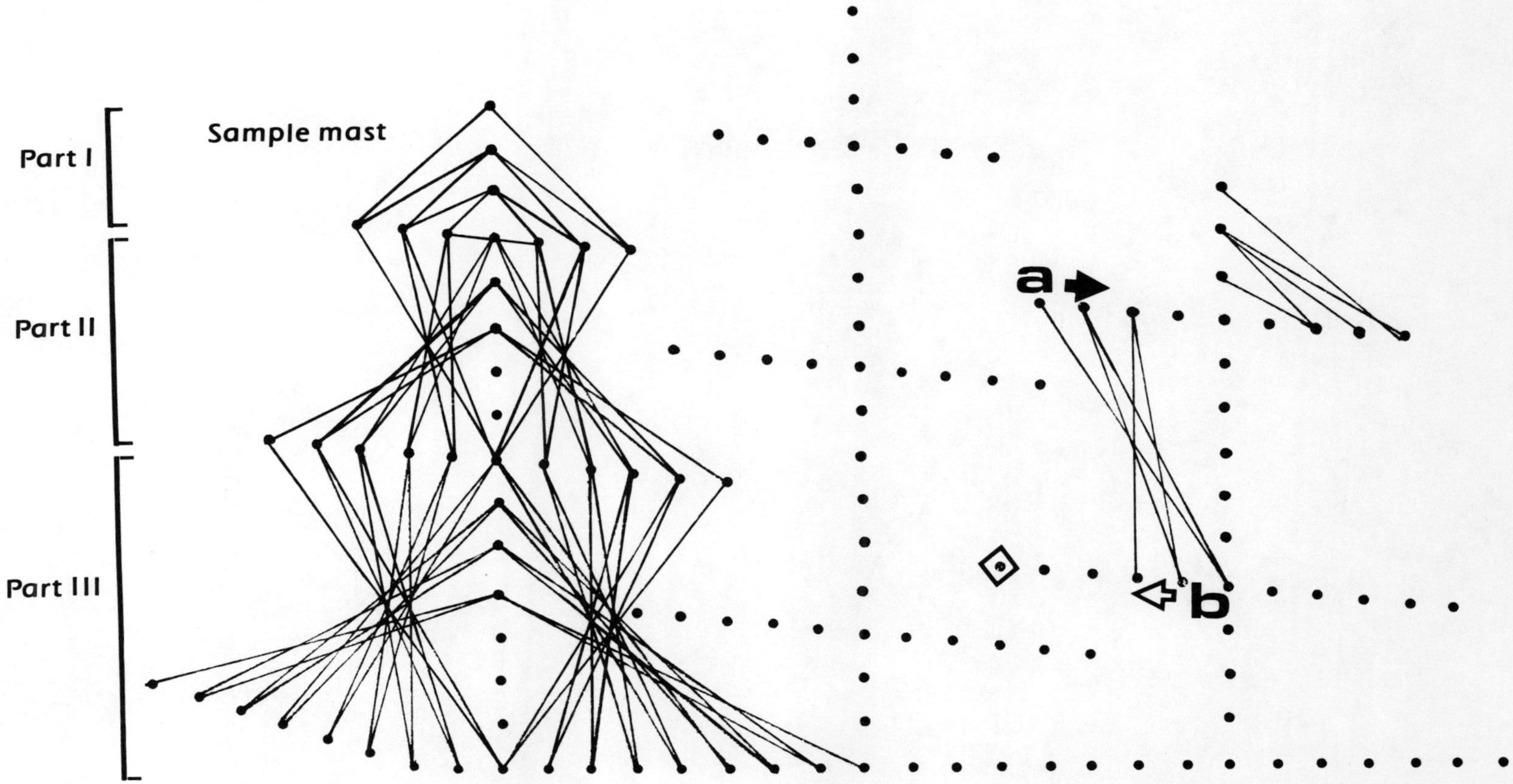

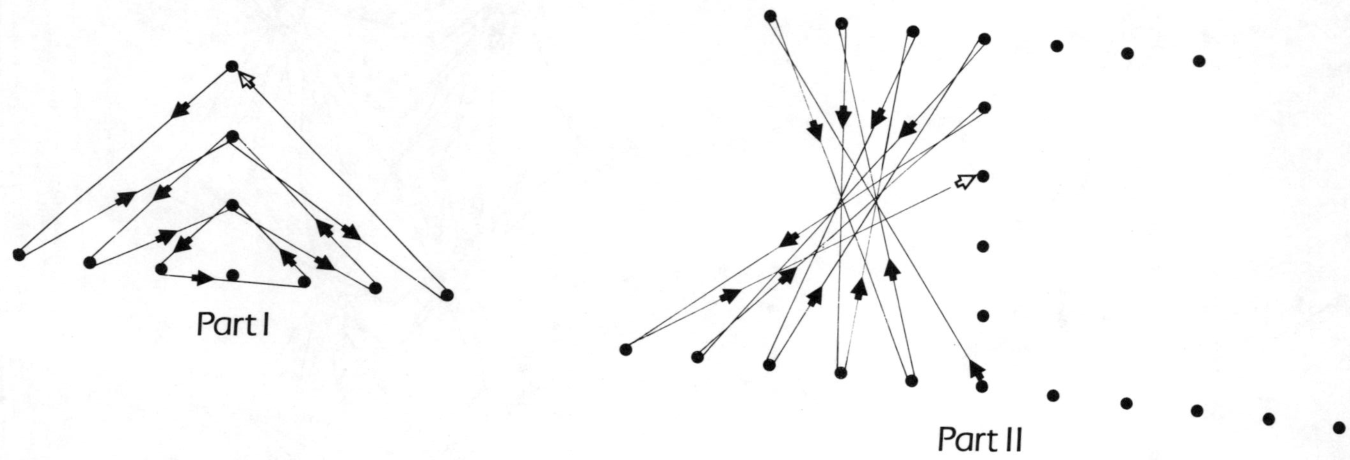

Fig. 7-4 Base layer of clipper ship (*continued*)

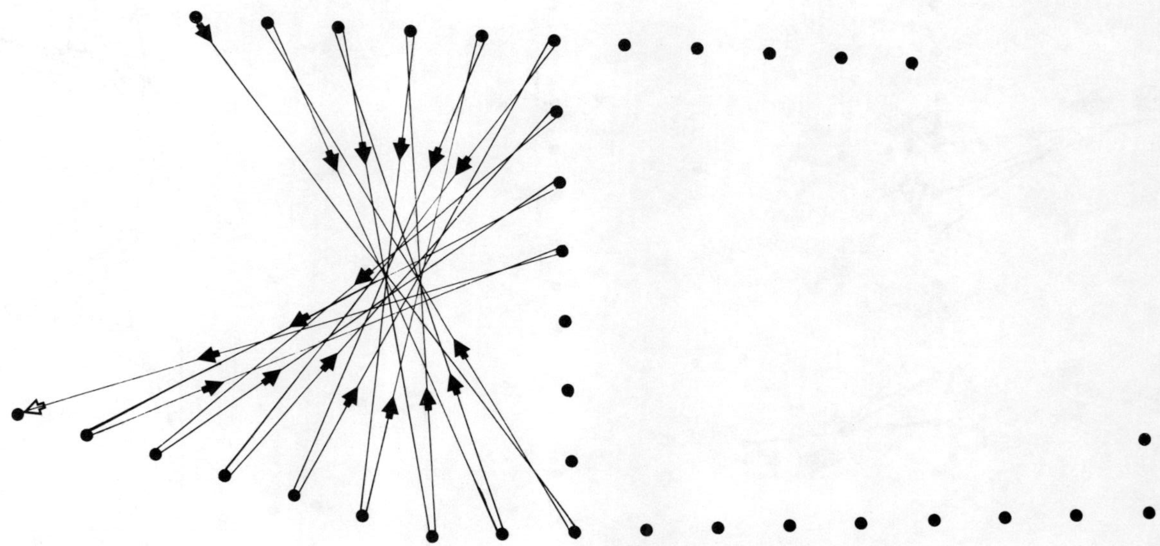

Fig. 7-4 Base layer of clipper ship (*continued*)

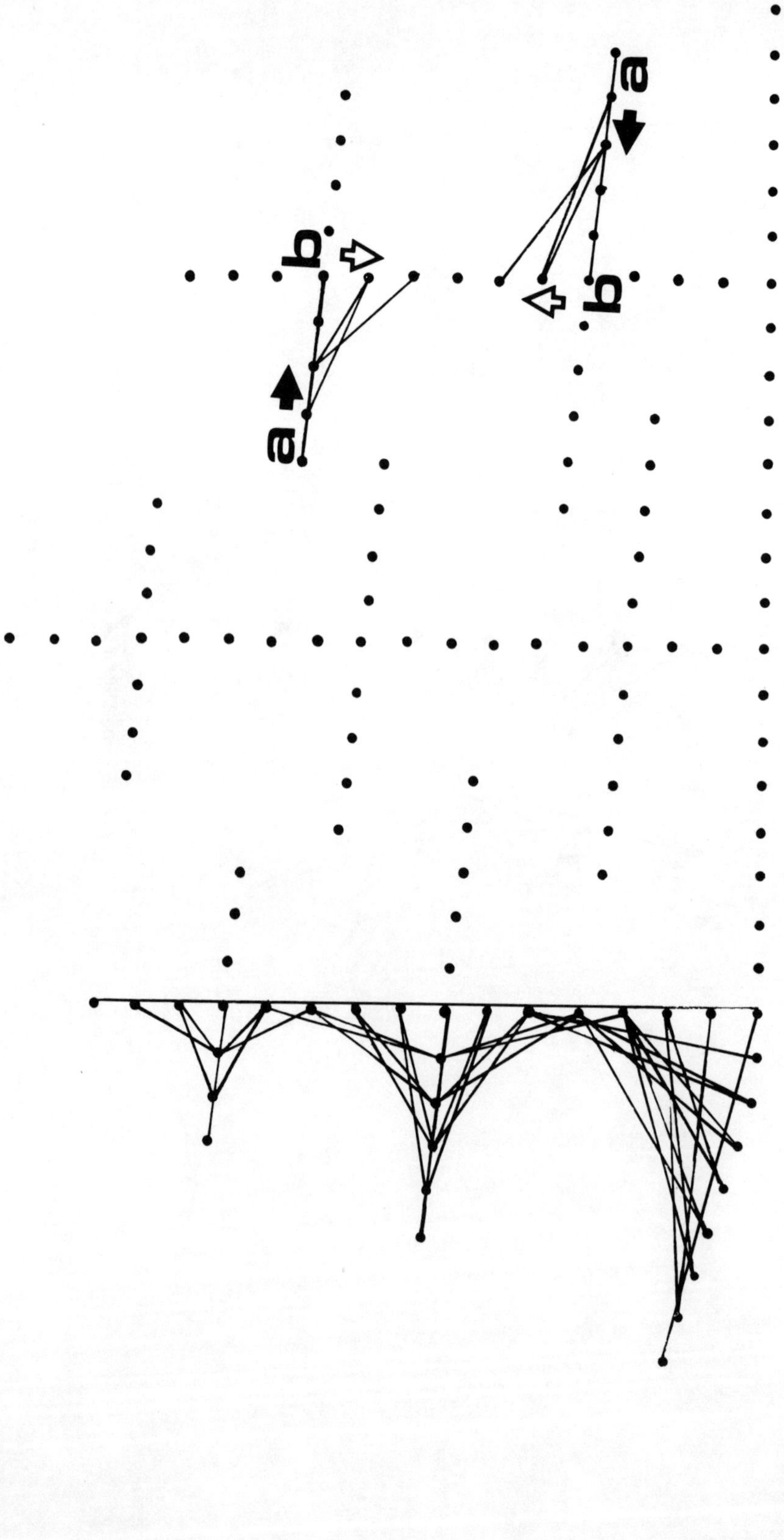

Fig. 7-5 Surface layer of clipper ship

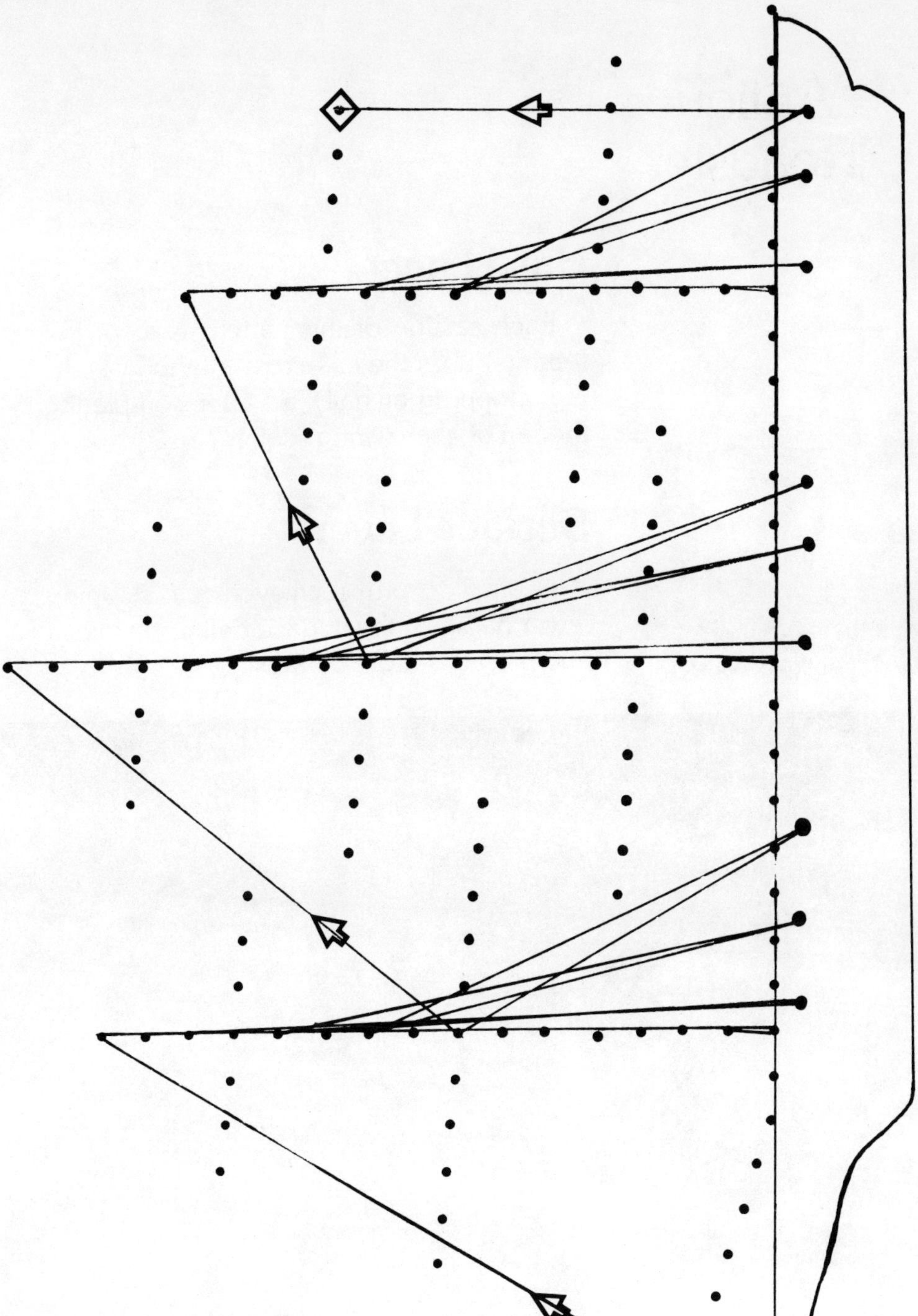

Fig. 7-6 Rigging for clipper ship

Antique Roadster

Base Layer

Each section of this pattern (except the fenders) uses the crisscross method of wiring, stopping at nail "a" after completing the rim of each wiring sequence.

Surface Layer

A smaller rim (achieved by skipping fewer nails) on the surface defines the lines and provides more contrast.

Fig. 7-7 Antique roadster

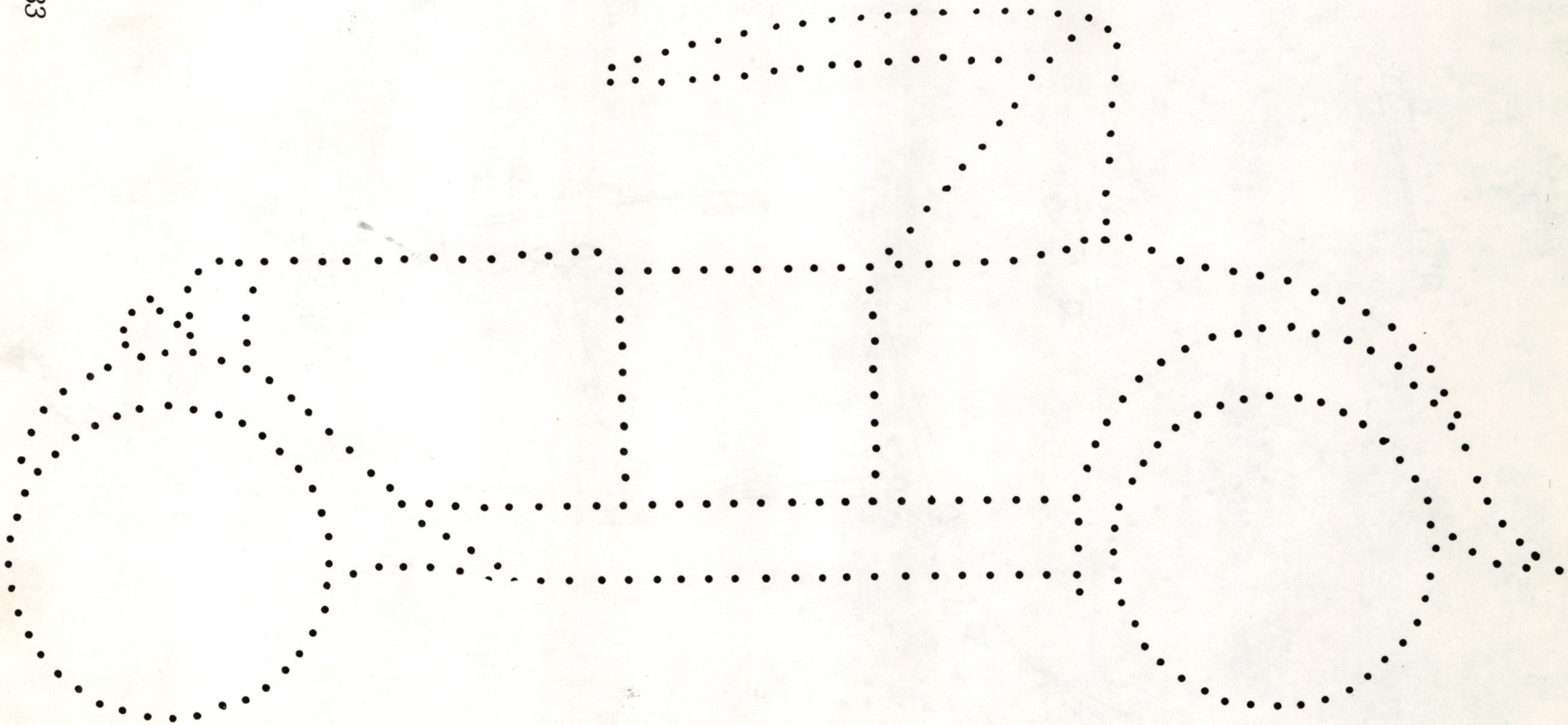

Fig. 7-8 Nailing pattern for roadster

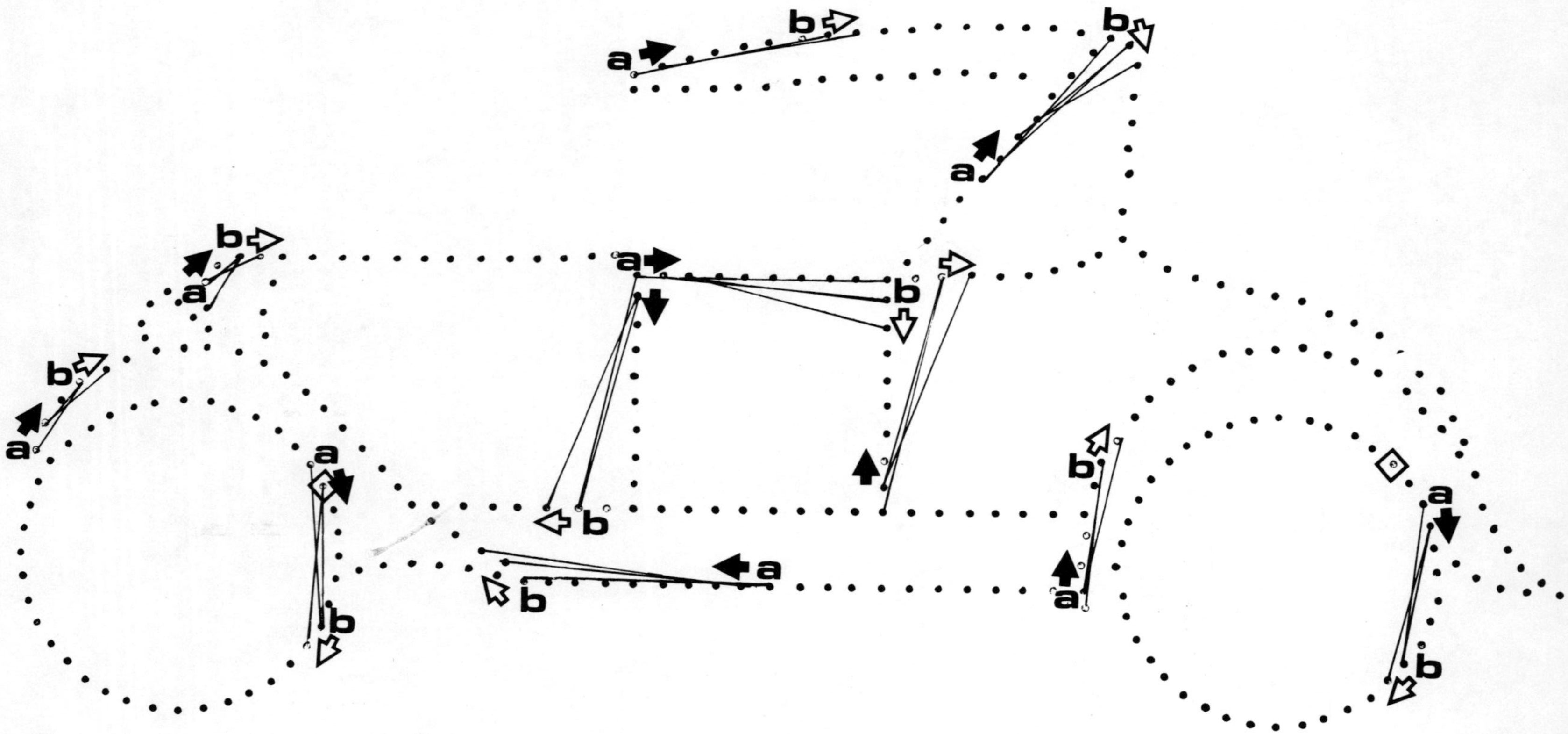

Fig. 7-9 Base layer of roadster

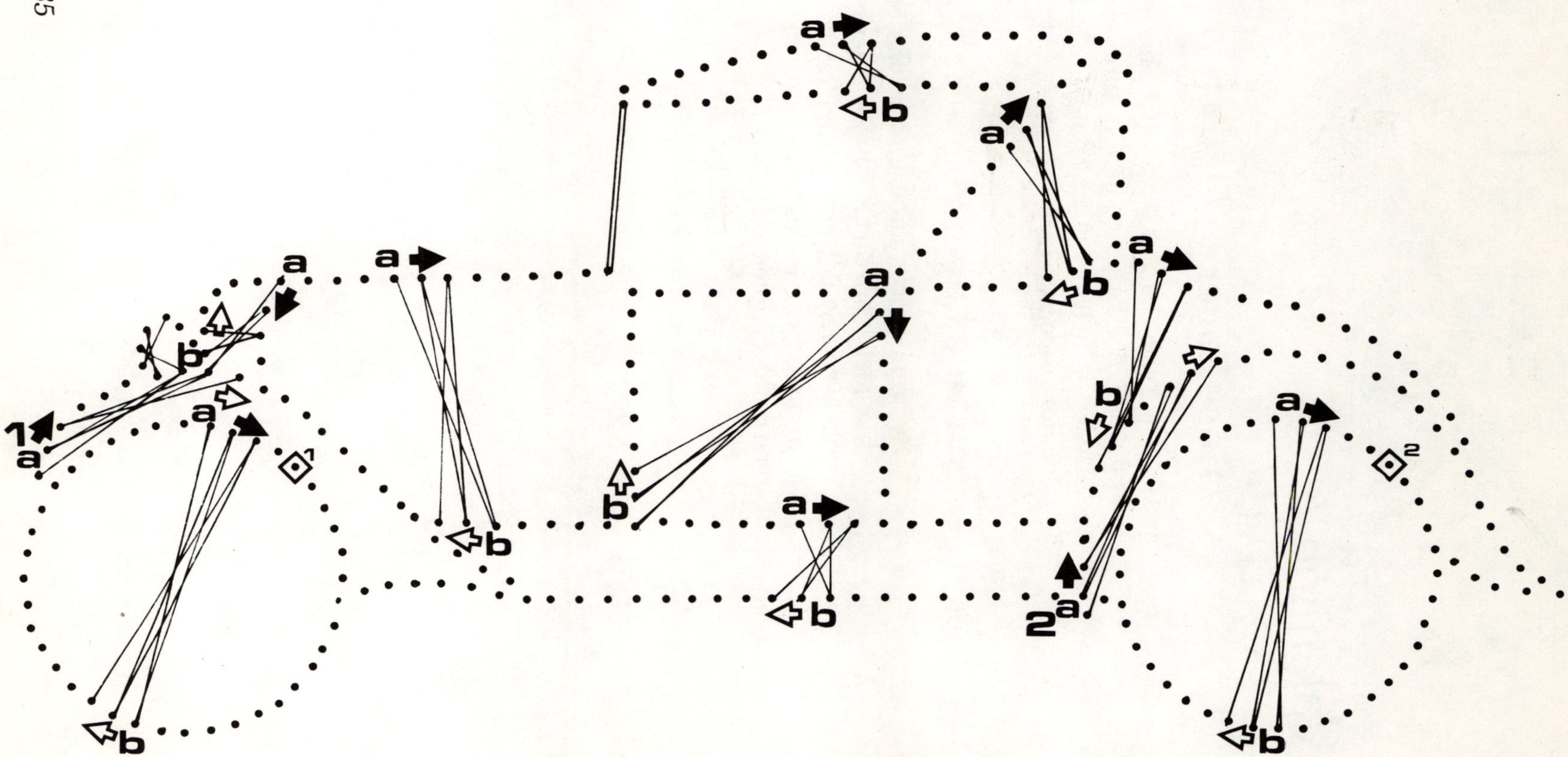

7-10 Surface layer of antique roadster

Valentine

Base Layer

The object of the base layer here is to make a rim larger than the surface rim usually is, while not covering the entire interior space with wire.

Surface Layer

By combining a larger rim on the base with a smaller rim on the surface, a sense of depth is achieved. Crisscrossing the wire to form a solid line is described at the beginning of this chapter.

Fig. 7-11 Valentine

Fig. 7-12 Nailing pattern for valentine

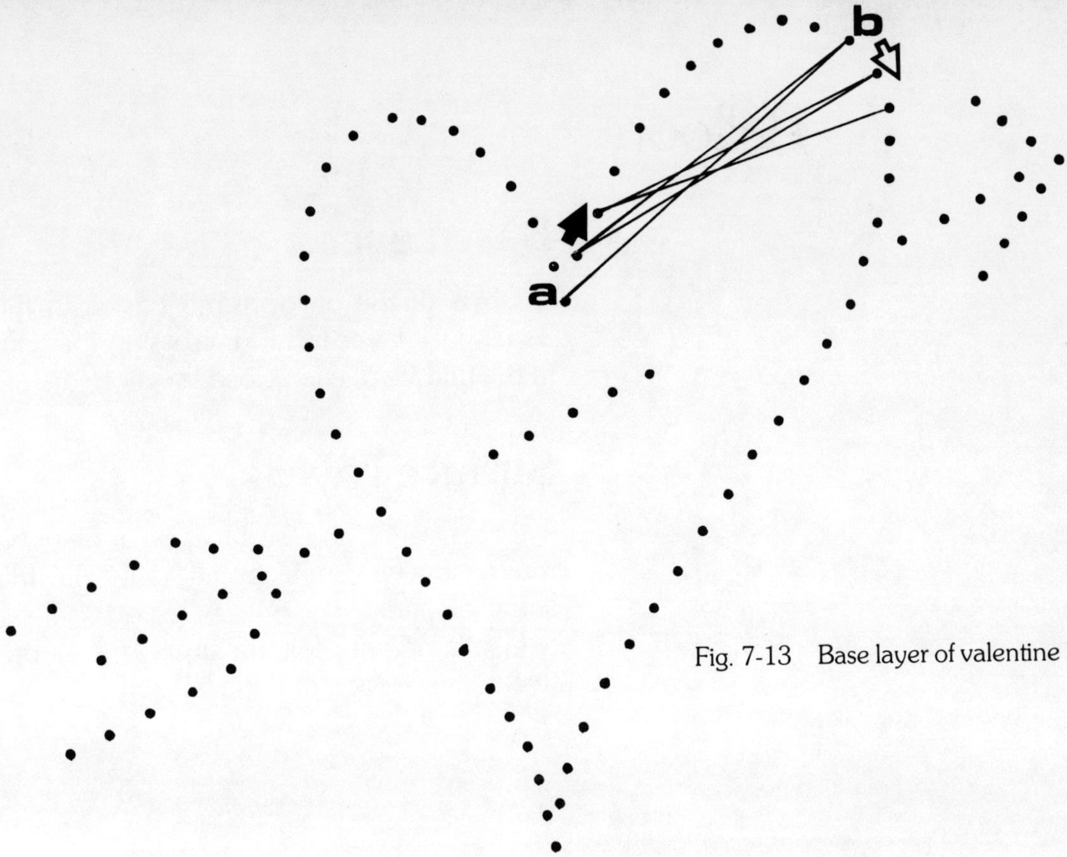

Fig. 7-13 Base layer of valentine

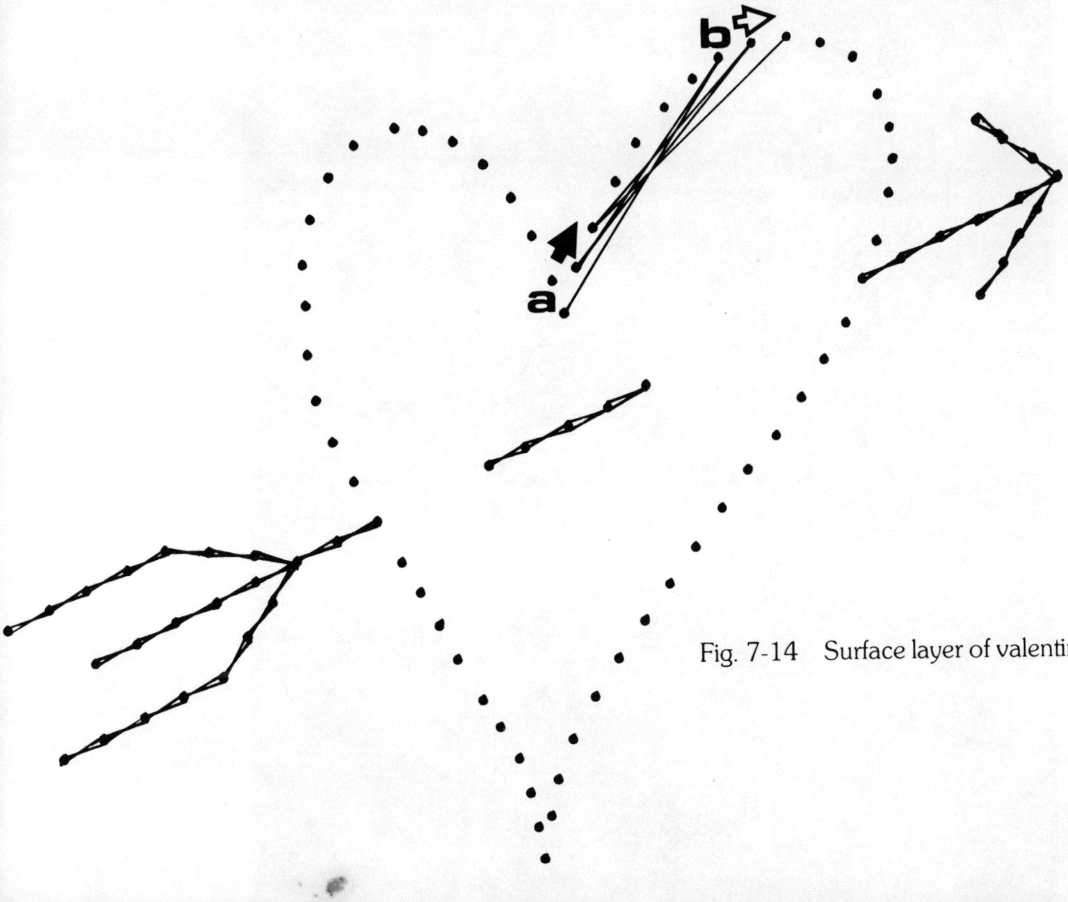

Fig. 7-14 Surface layer of valentine

Balloon

Base Layer

Do both the balloon and basket in the usual base layer fashion, crossing the wire in the middle of each closed section.

Surface Layer

The size of the surface rims may be made smaller by skipping nails on the surface layer.

Use lamé wire for the support lines between the balloon and the basket.

Fig. 7-15 Balloon

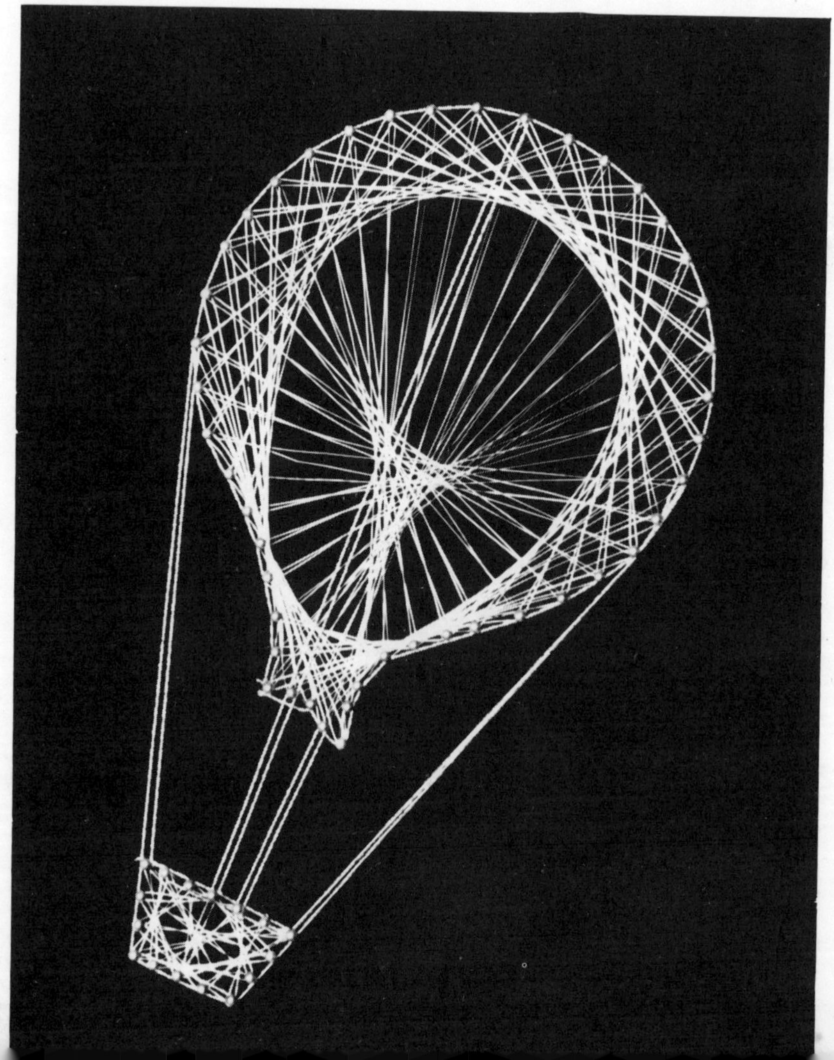

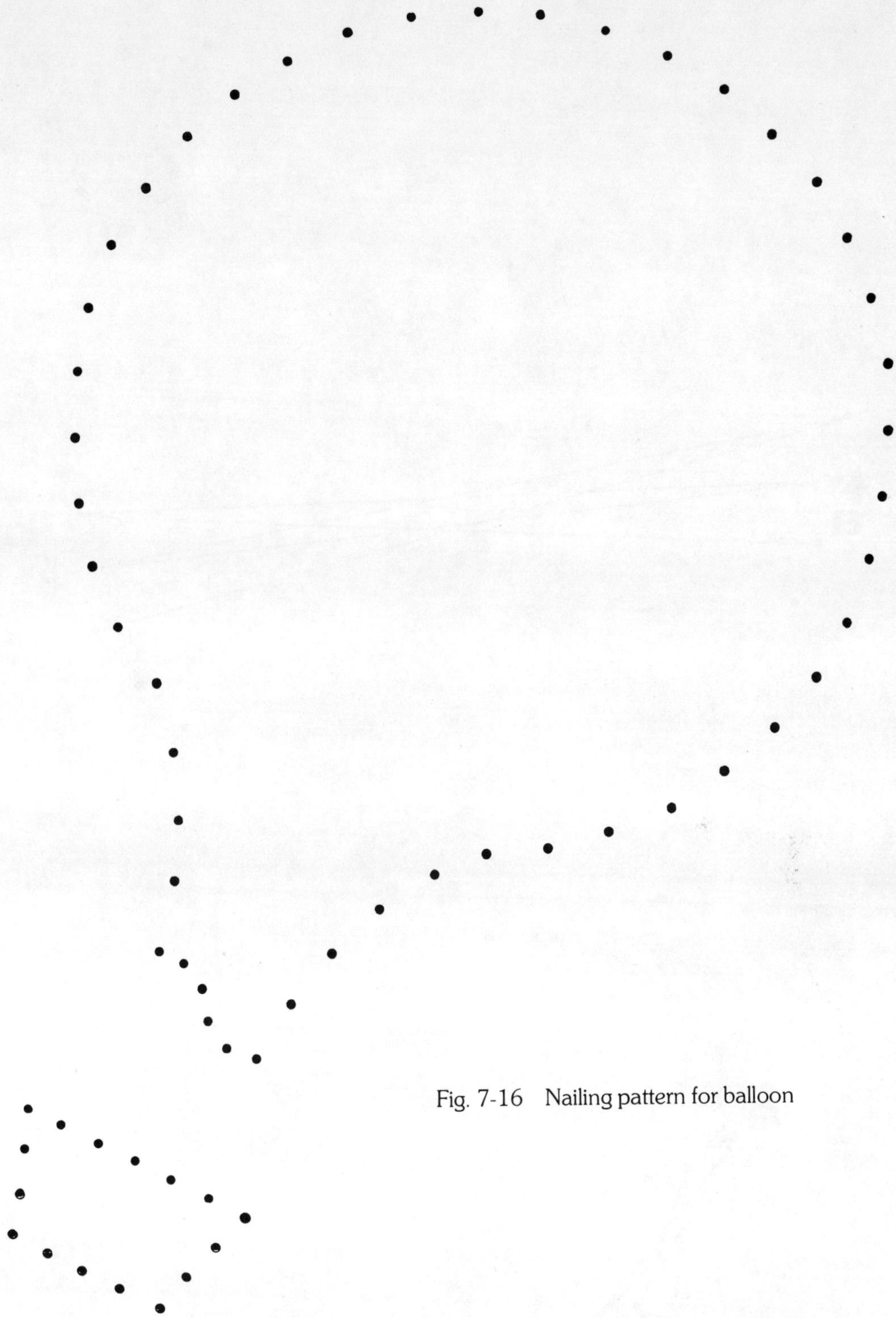

Fig. 7-16 Nailing pattern for balloon

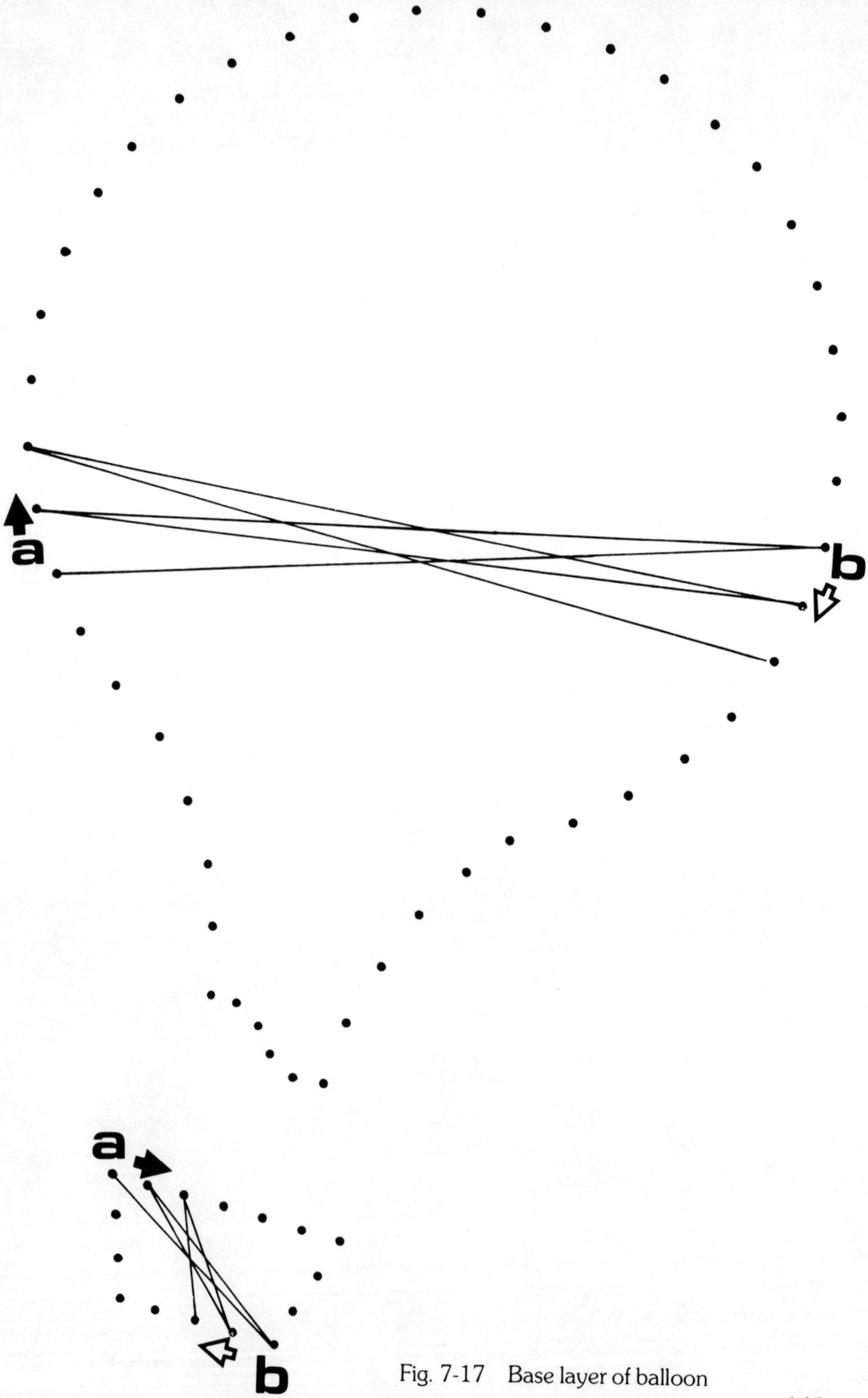

Fig. 7-17 Base layer of balloon

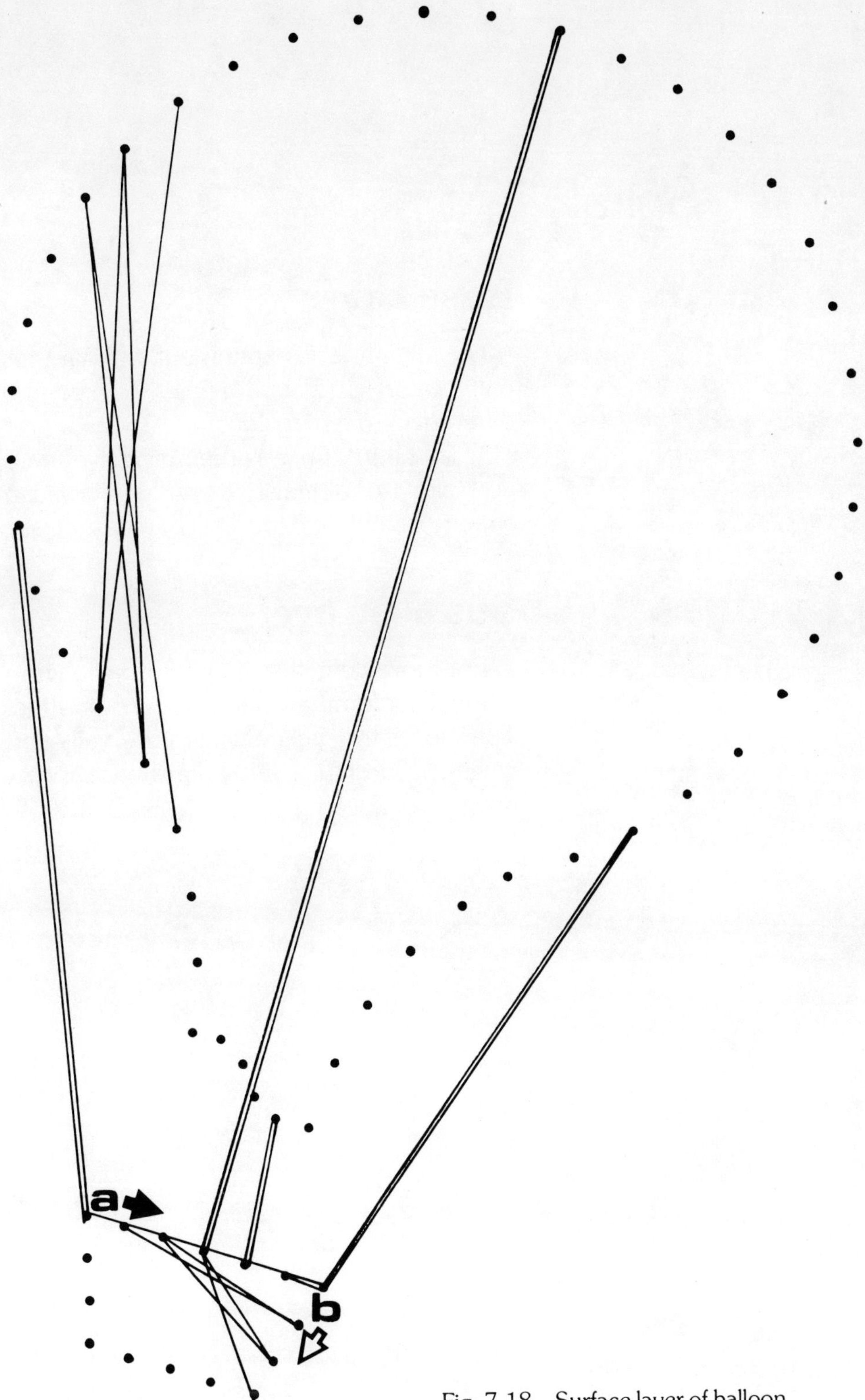

Fig. 7-18 Surface layer of balloon

Spiral

Base Layer

On this project, experiment with various nail counts and wire angles to see the differences in dimensions.

"Nail count" means the number of nails you skip to diminish a curve. This can change completely the look of a design.

Surface Layer

For more definition on any project, wrap a length of lamé around the outside edge. This closes the gaps between the nails and gives the design a more finished appearance.

Fig. 7-19 Spiral

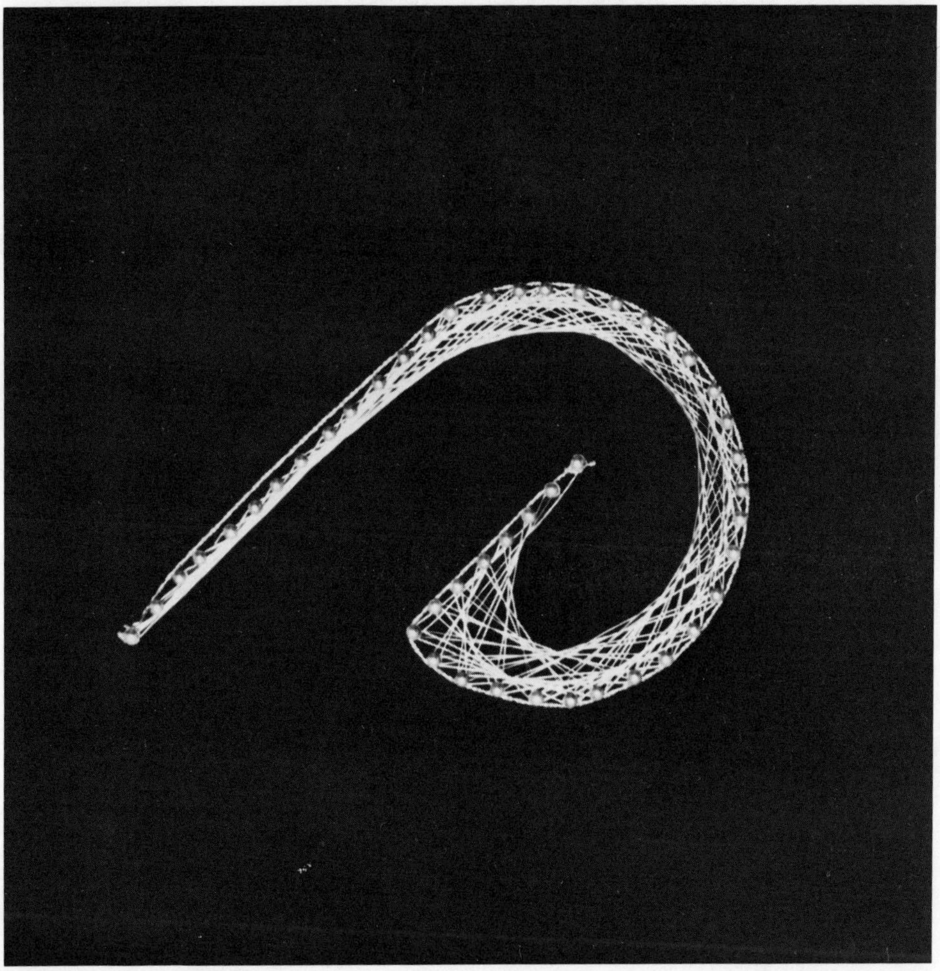

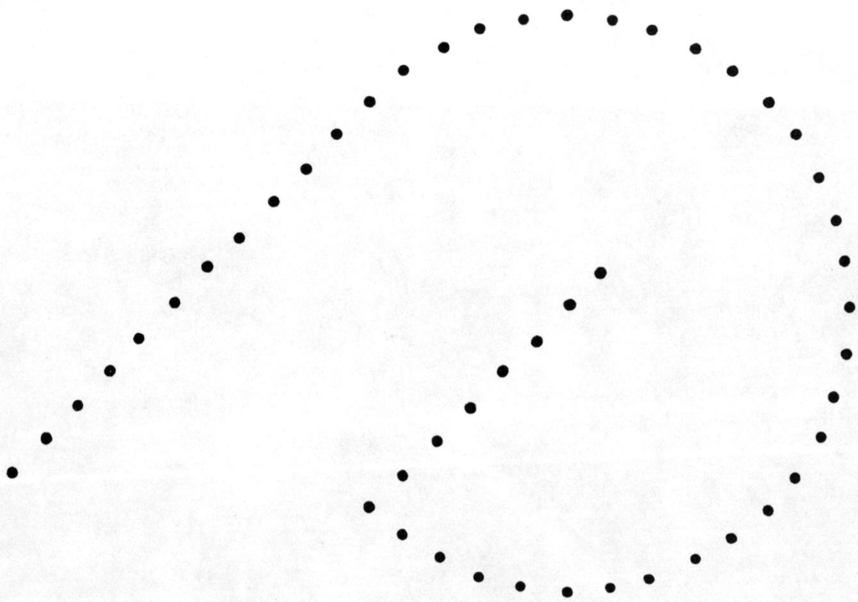

Fig. 7-20 Nailing pattern for spiral

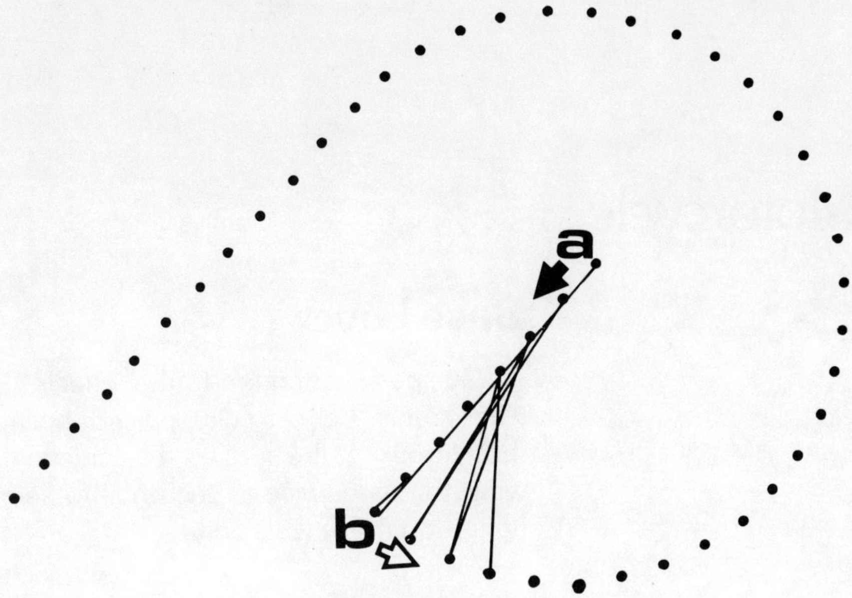

Fig. 7-21 Base layer of spiral

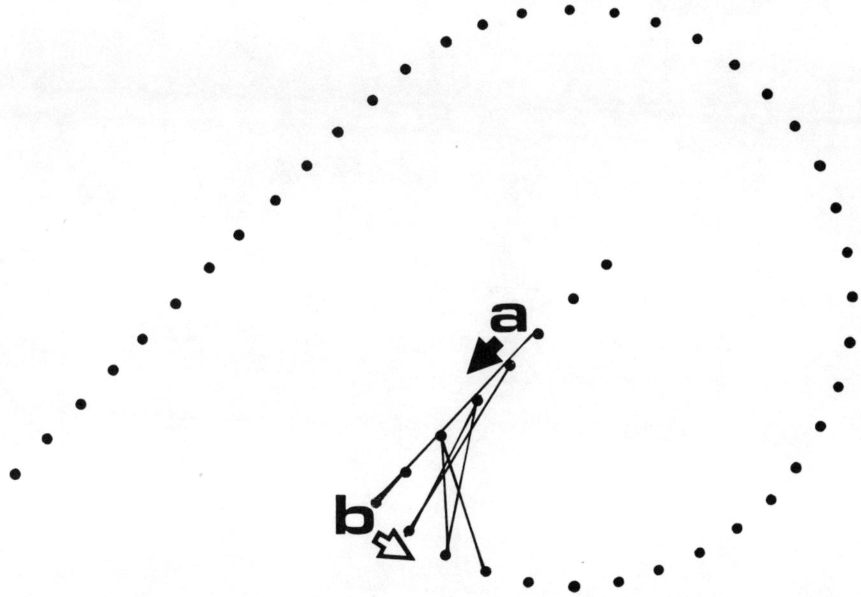

Fig. 7-22 Surface layer of spiral

Motorcycle

Base Layer

Pay special attention to the wheels. The wires must be carefully placed because they represent the spokes. To achieve this, wrap the wire twice at each nail to keep it tight—on the wheels only.

Surface Layer

Do all the accent lines in lamé. If you wish to dress up this design more, add some of your own lines. You can always remove them if you don't like them. Experimenting is the best way to improve your creative skills.

Fig. 7-23 Motorcycle

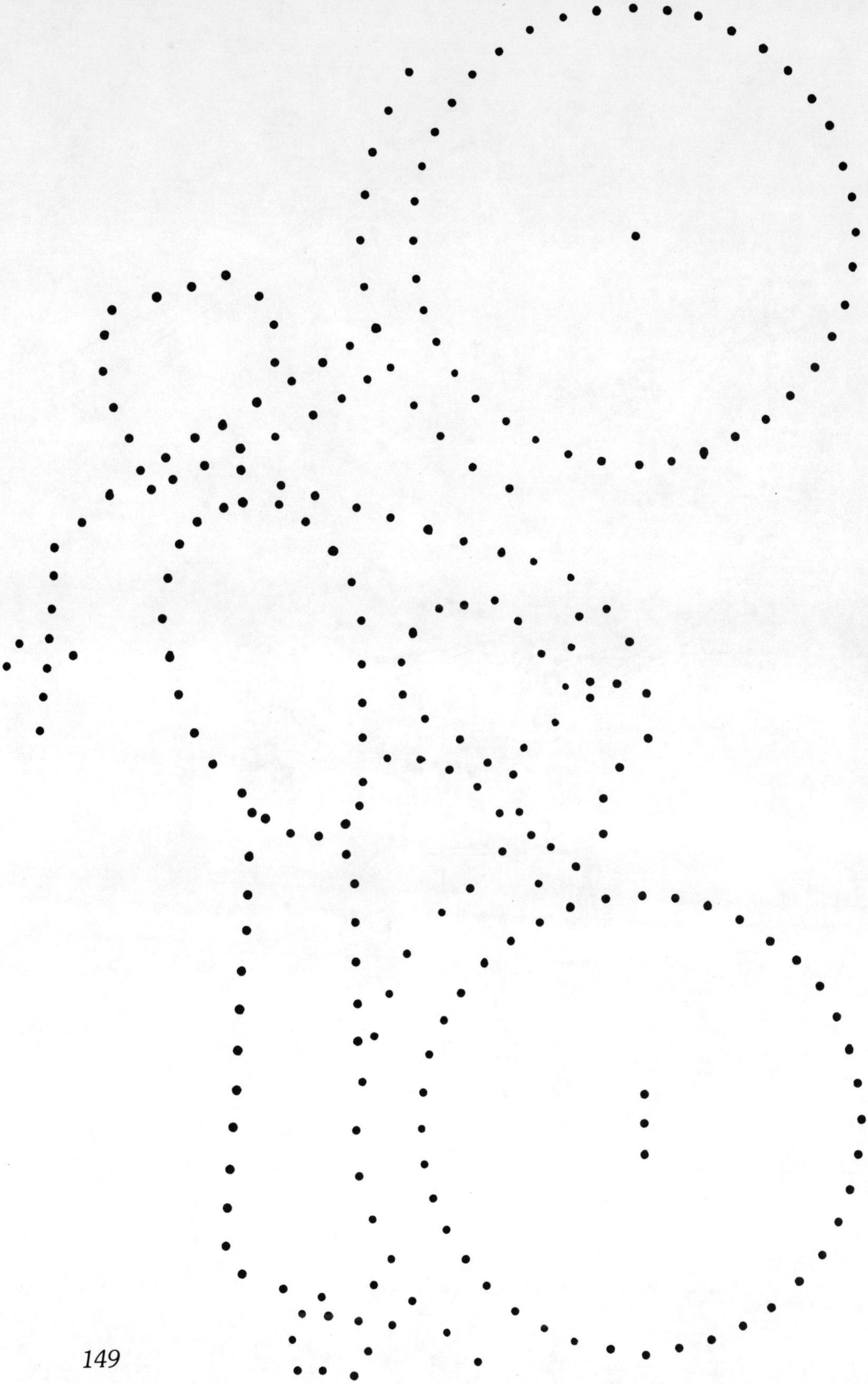

Fig. 7-24 Nailing pattern for motorcycle

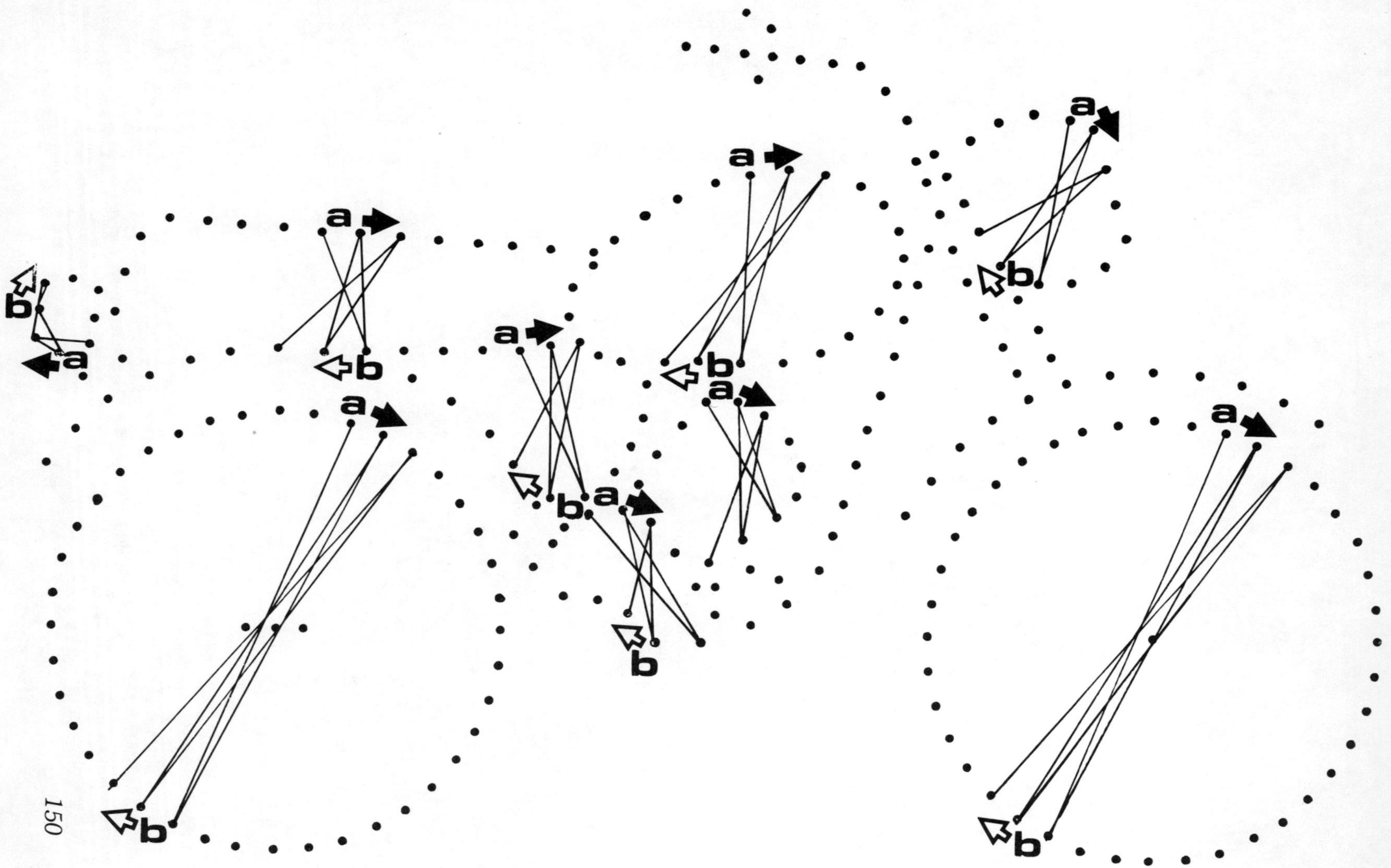

Fig. 7-25 Base layer of motorcycle

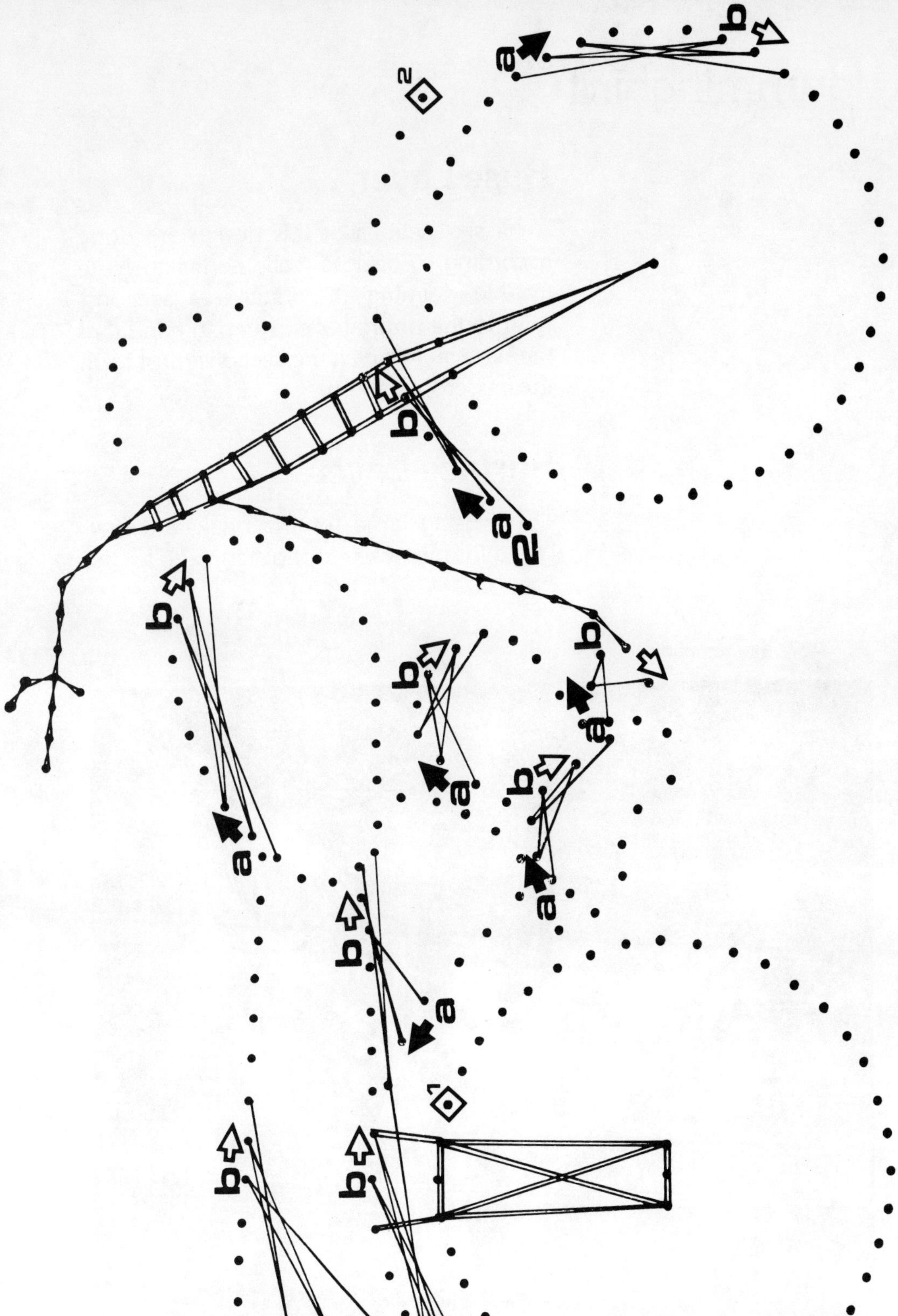

Fig. 7-26 Surface layer of motorcycle

Hummingbird

Base Layer

All six sections of this design are done according to basic directions. If you have trouble defining the individual sections, refer to the photograph. Keep in mind that the base layer on all the sections must form the crisscross pattern.

Surface Layer

Try using lamé for the beak and feet. Use a thumbtack or upholstery tack for the eye.

Fig. 7-27 Hummingbird

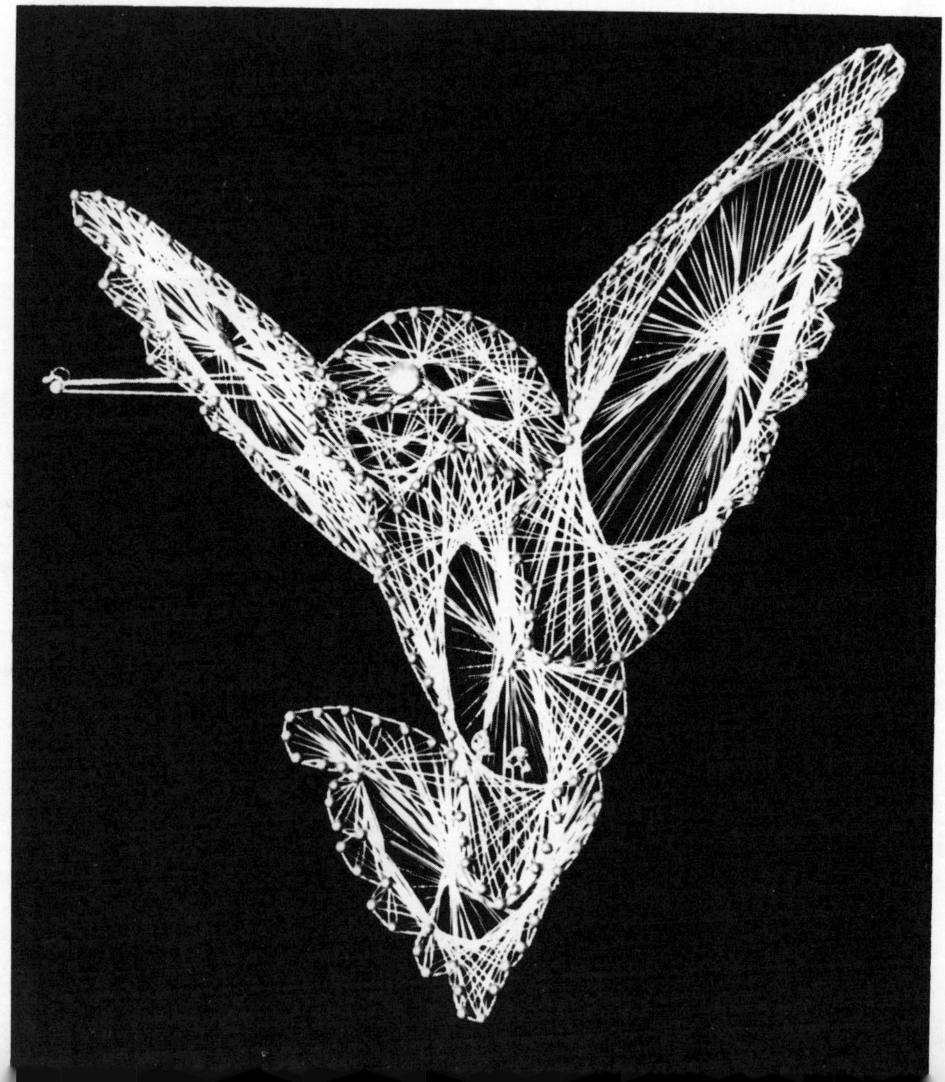

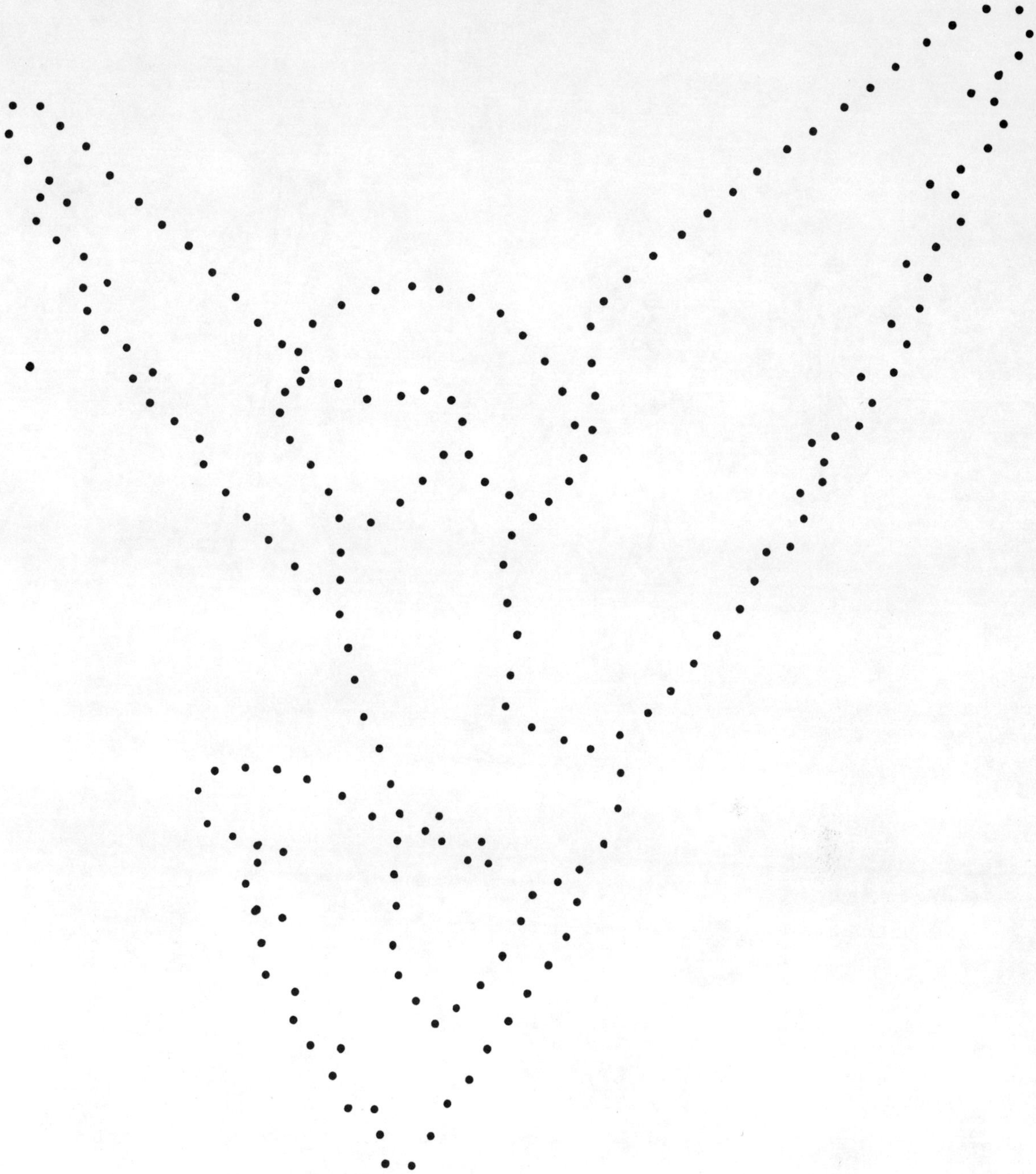

Fig. 7-28 Nailing pattern for hummingbird

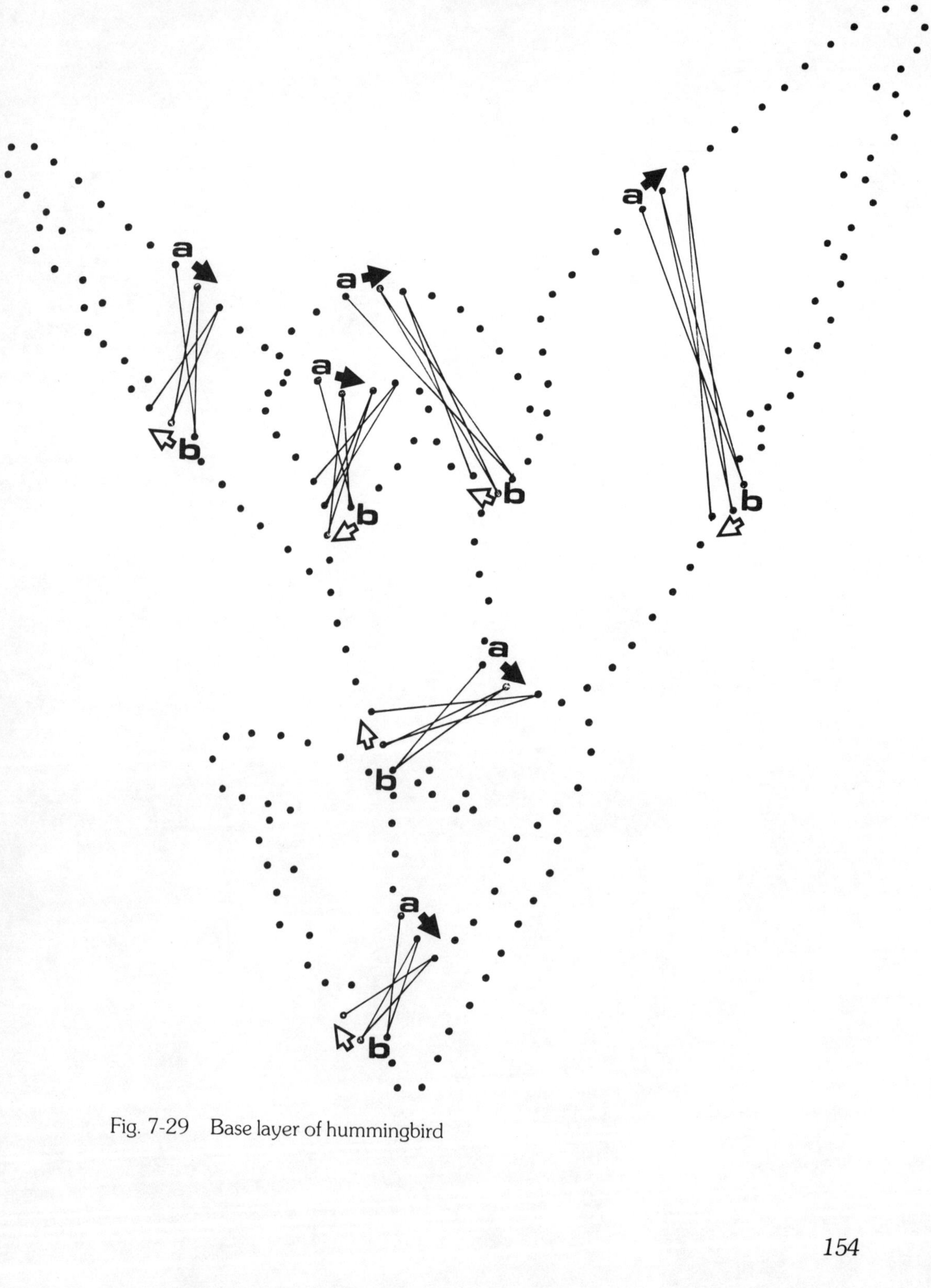

Fig. 7-29 Base layer of hummingbird

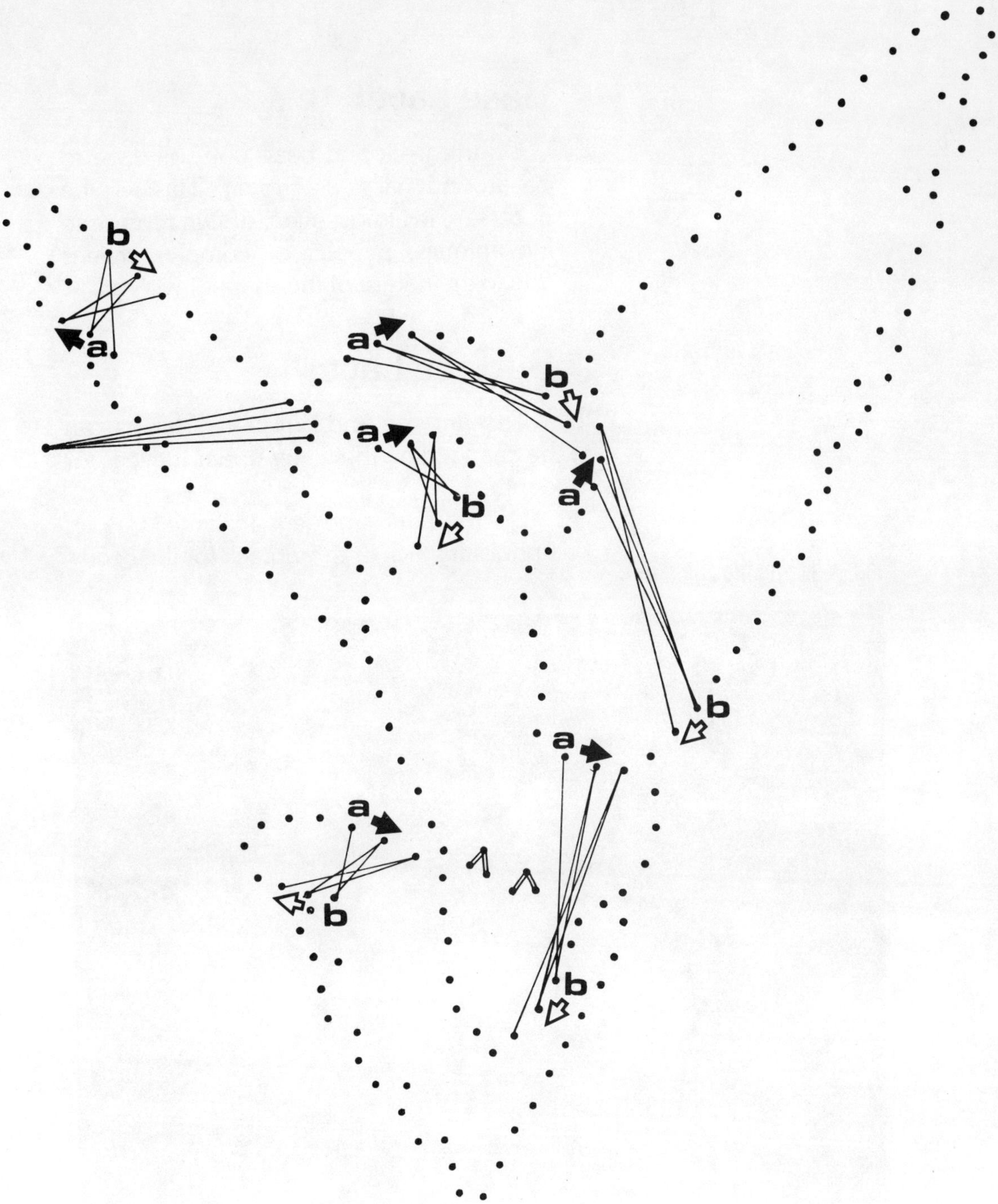

Fig. 7-30 Surface layer of hummingbird

Fluffy Egret

Base Layer

On the neck and head you will have to go around nails, as shown. This will be necessary in almost every design representing animals, people, or complex scenes due to the nature of the shapes involved.

Surface Layer

The rim size and number of layers can be changed on the water under the legs for depth.

Do the beak and legs in lamé. Use an upholstery tack or thumbtack for the eye.

Fig. 7-31 Fluffy egret

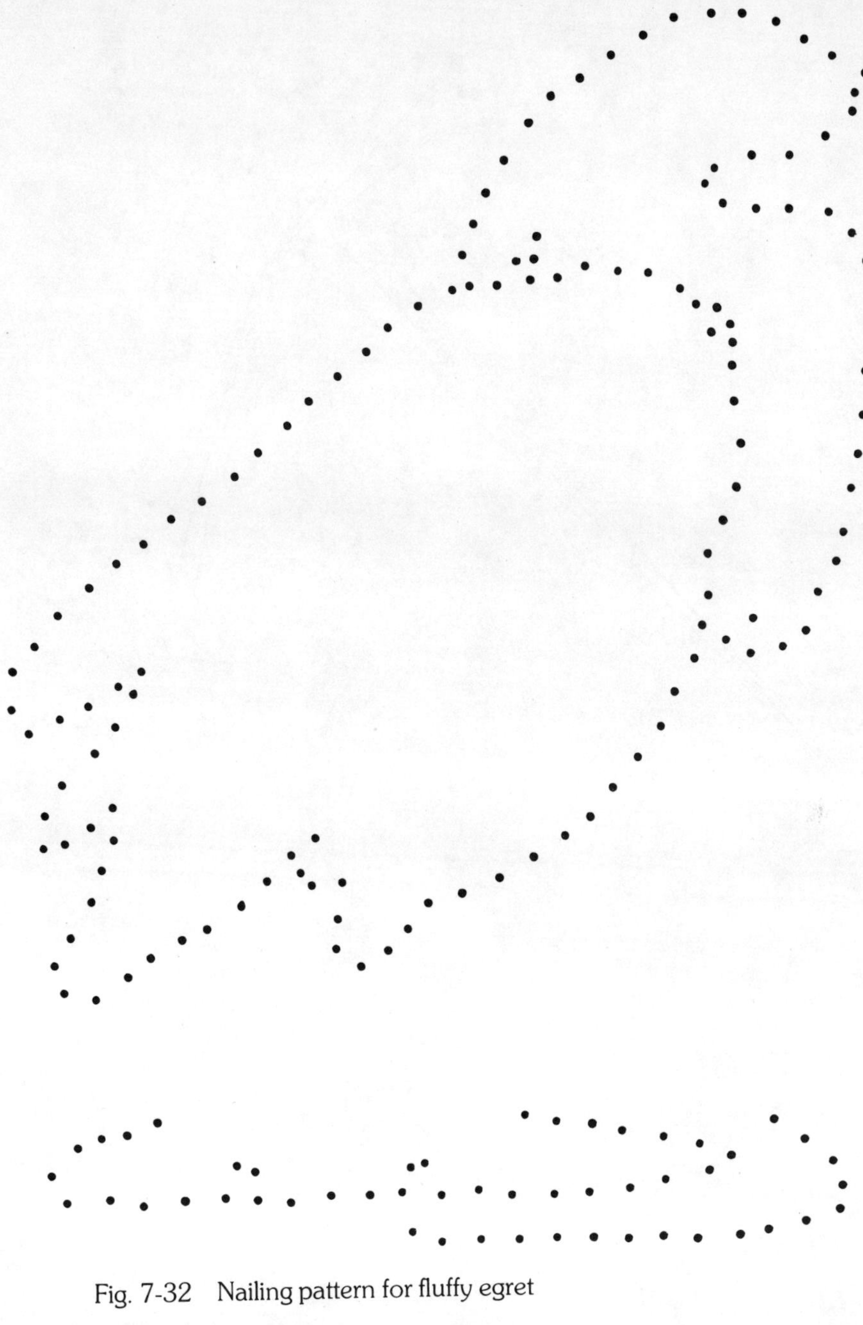

Fig. 7-32 Nailing pattern for fluffy egret

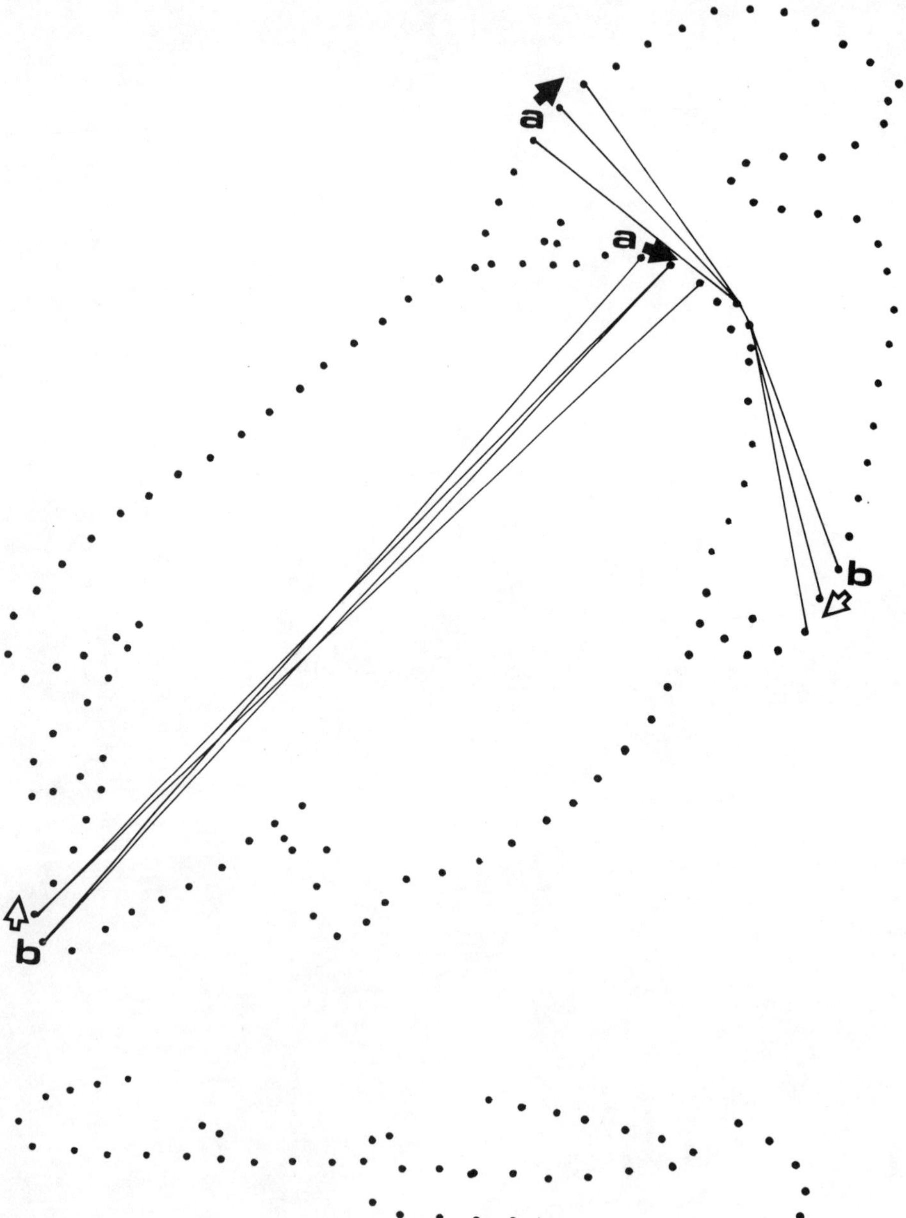

Fig. 7-33 Base layer of egret

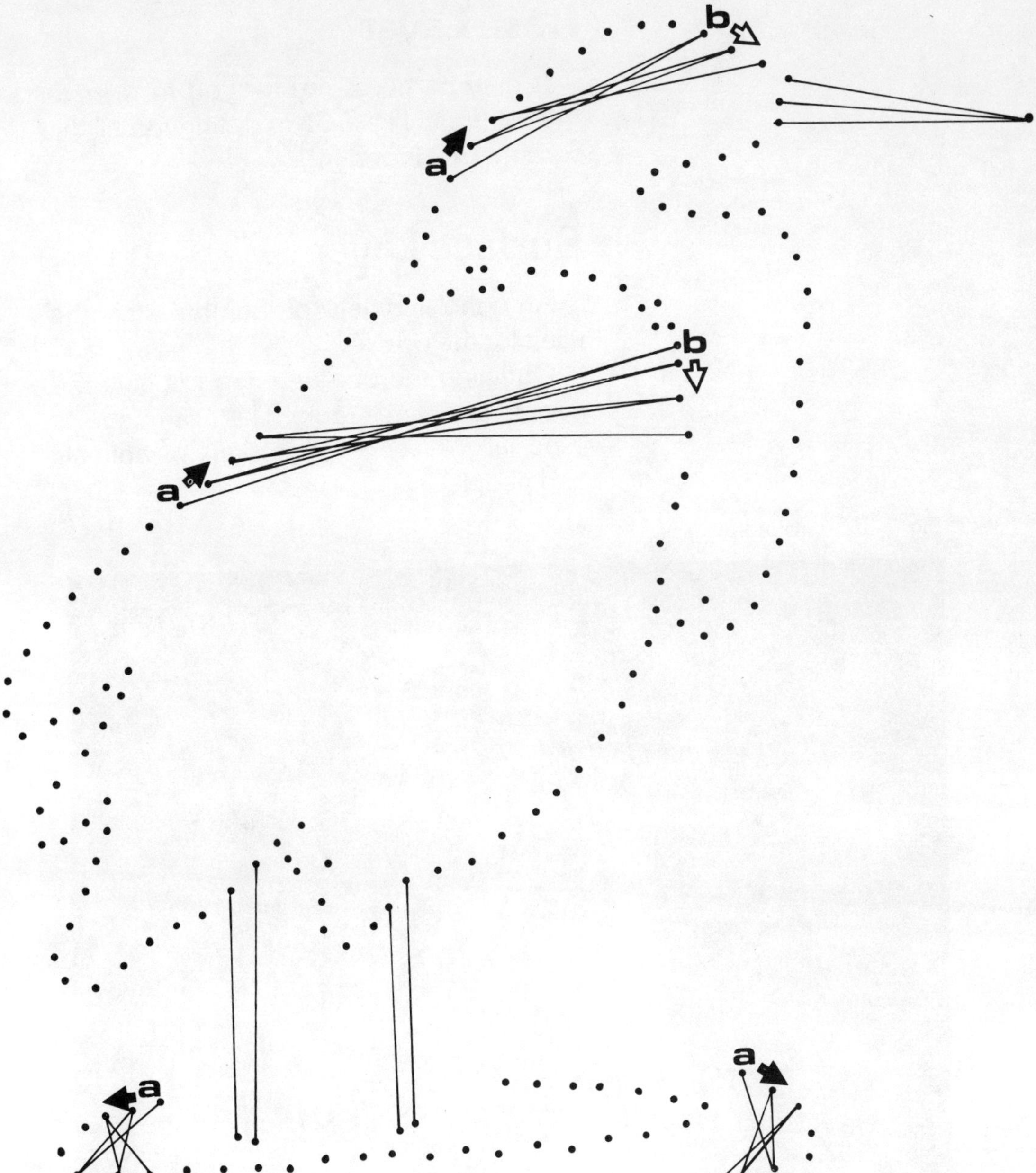

Fig. 7-34 Surface layer of egret

Groundhog

Base Layer

It may be necessary for you to refer to the picture in Fig. 7-35 to distinguish all the sections in this design.

Surface Layer

An upholstery tack or thumbtack can be used for the eye.

Outlining the outside edge will give the design a cleaner look. This technique is especially effective on designs of animals and people.

Fig. 7-35 Groundhog

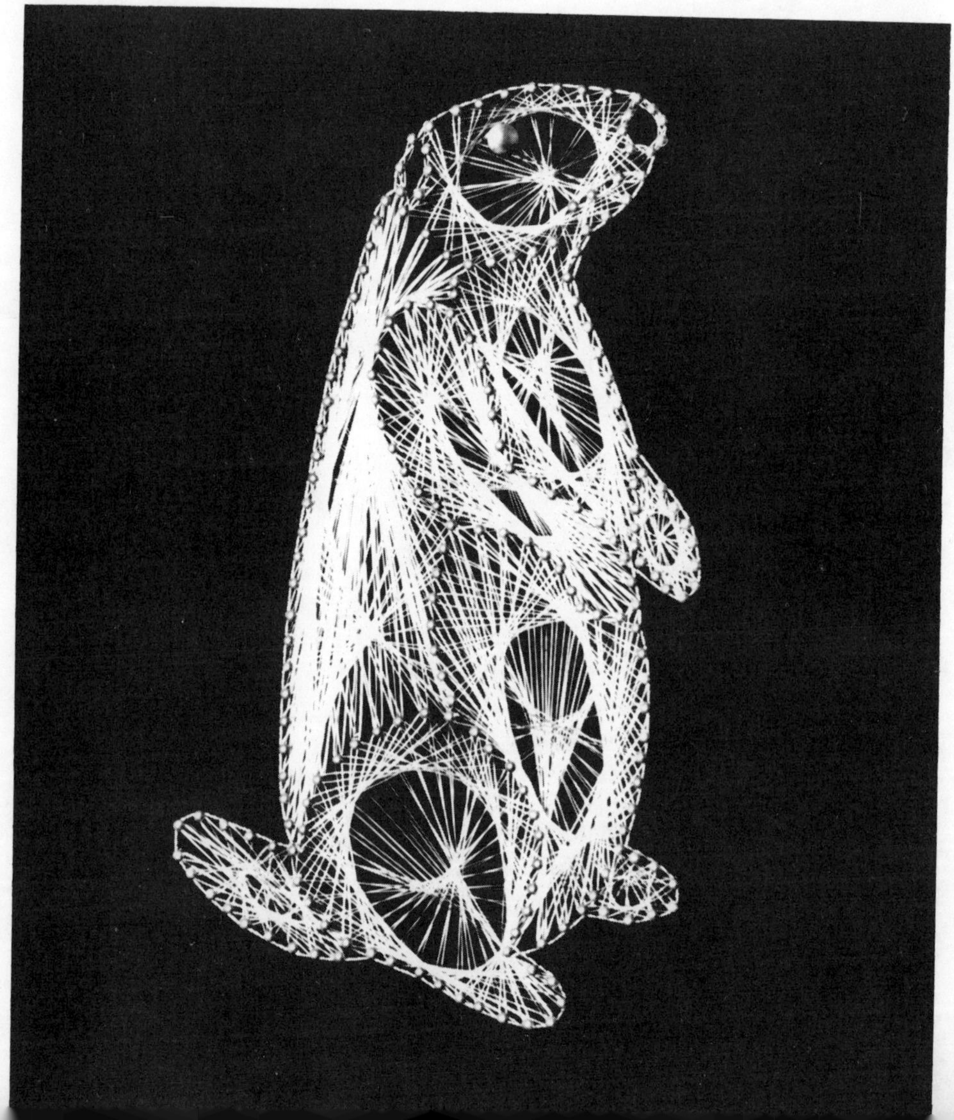

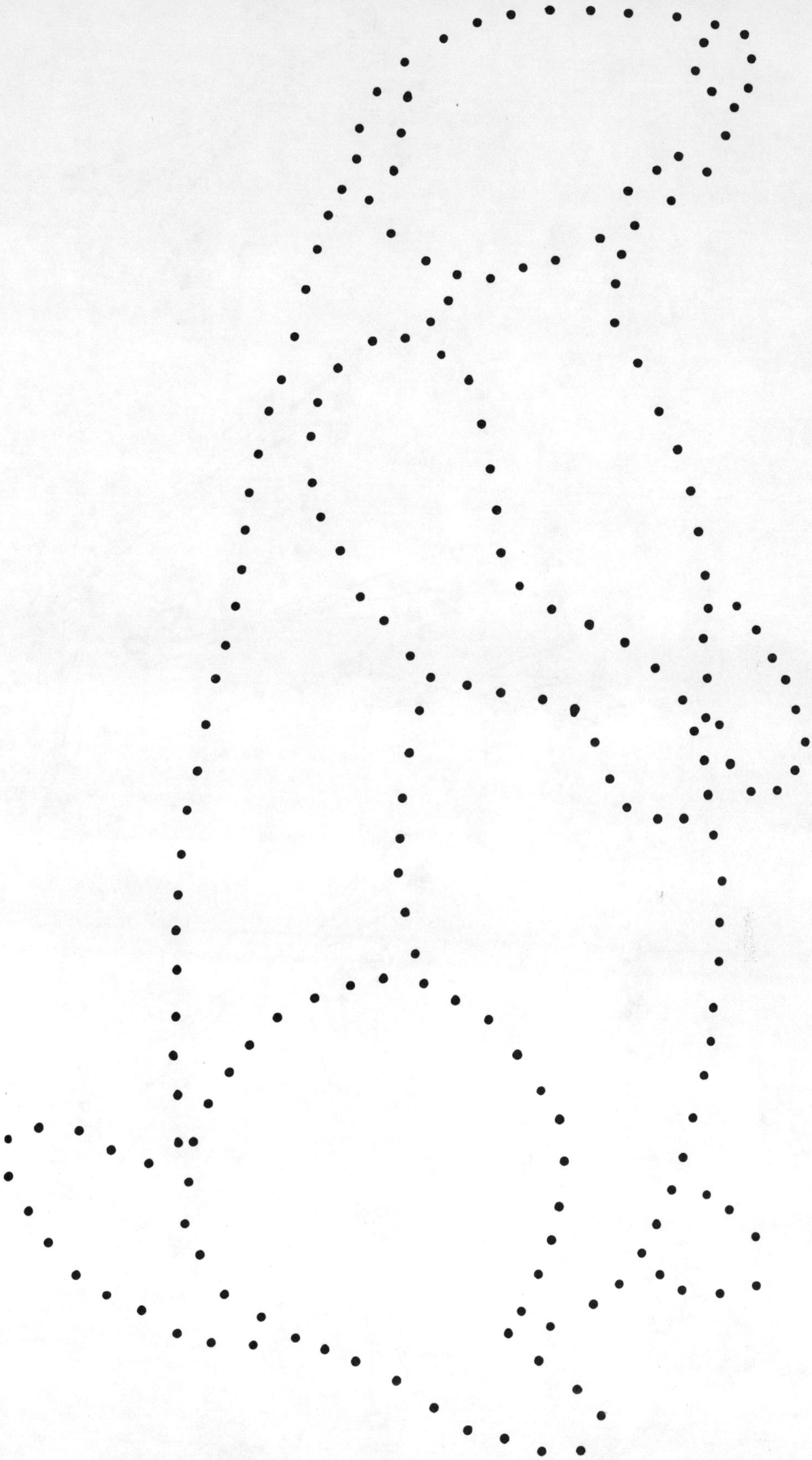

Fig. 7-36 Nailing pattern for groundhog

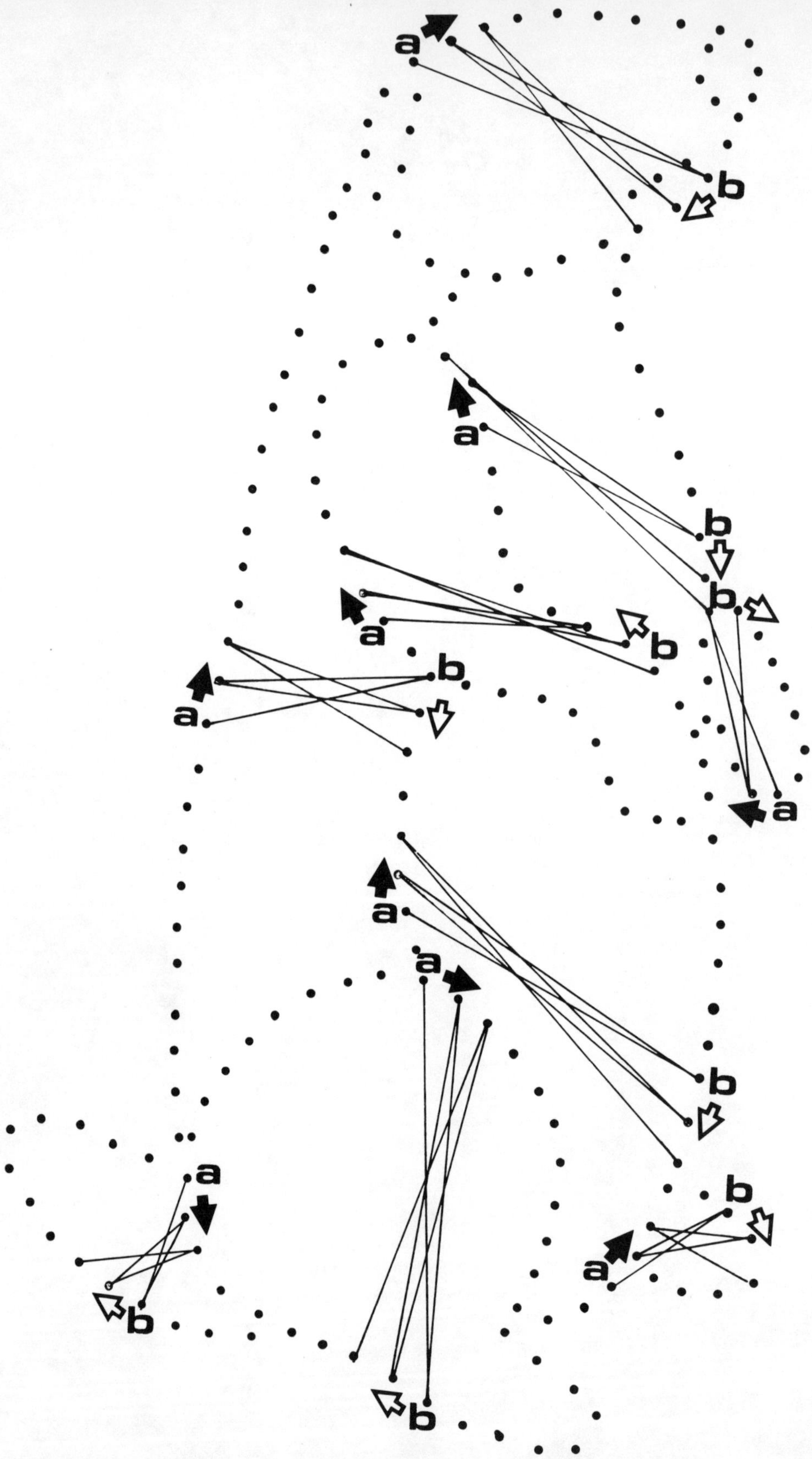

Fig. 7-37 Base layer of groundhog

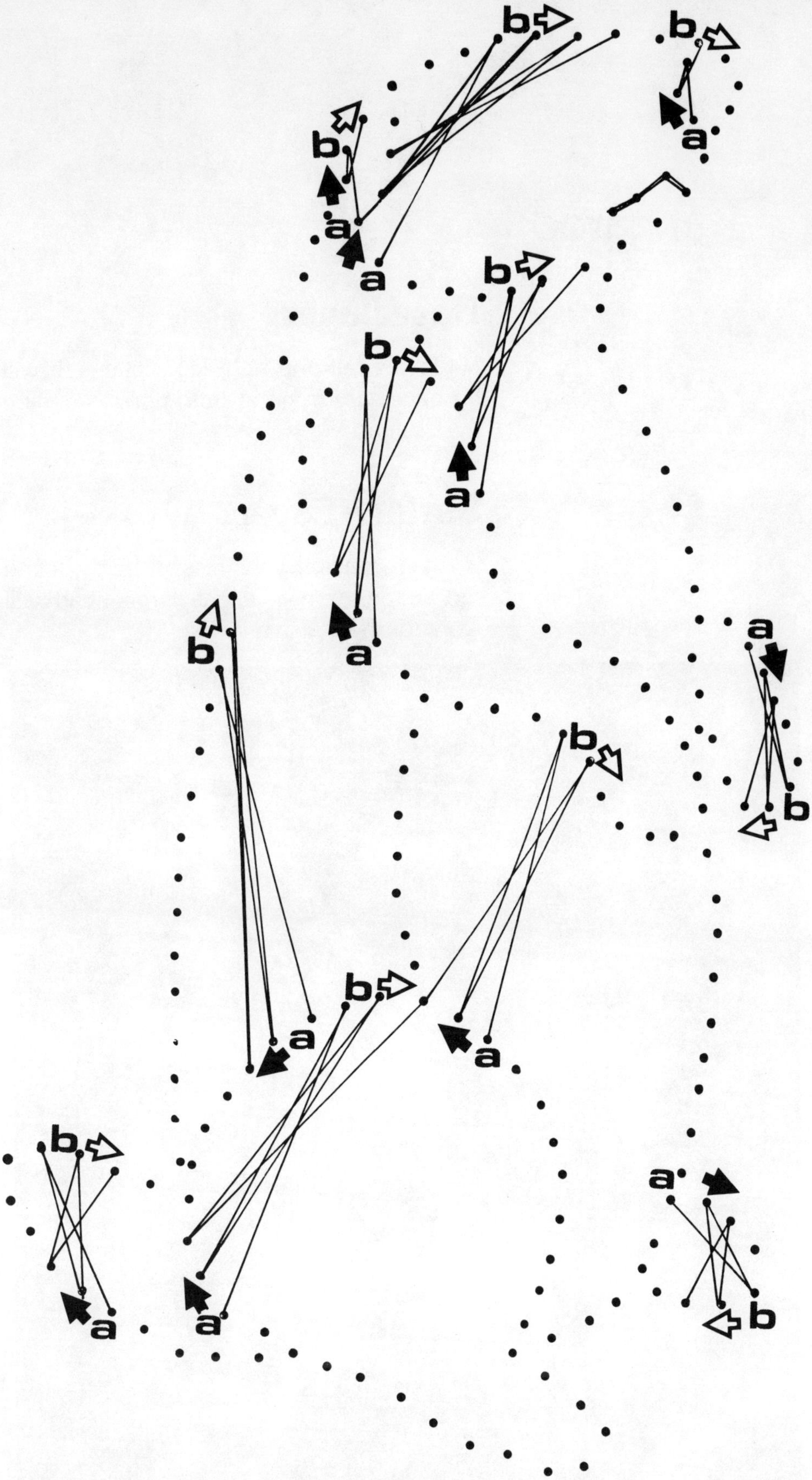

Fig. 7-38 Surface layer of groundhog

Kangaroo

Base Layer

On the tail and right leg sections, it will be necessary to go around nails to outline the design.

Surface Layer

Again, outlining this design helps define the shape. A nail with a large head will work for the eye in this case.

Fig. 7-39 Kangaroo

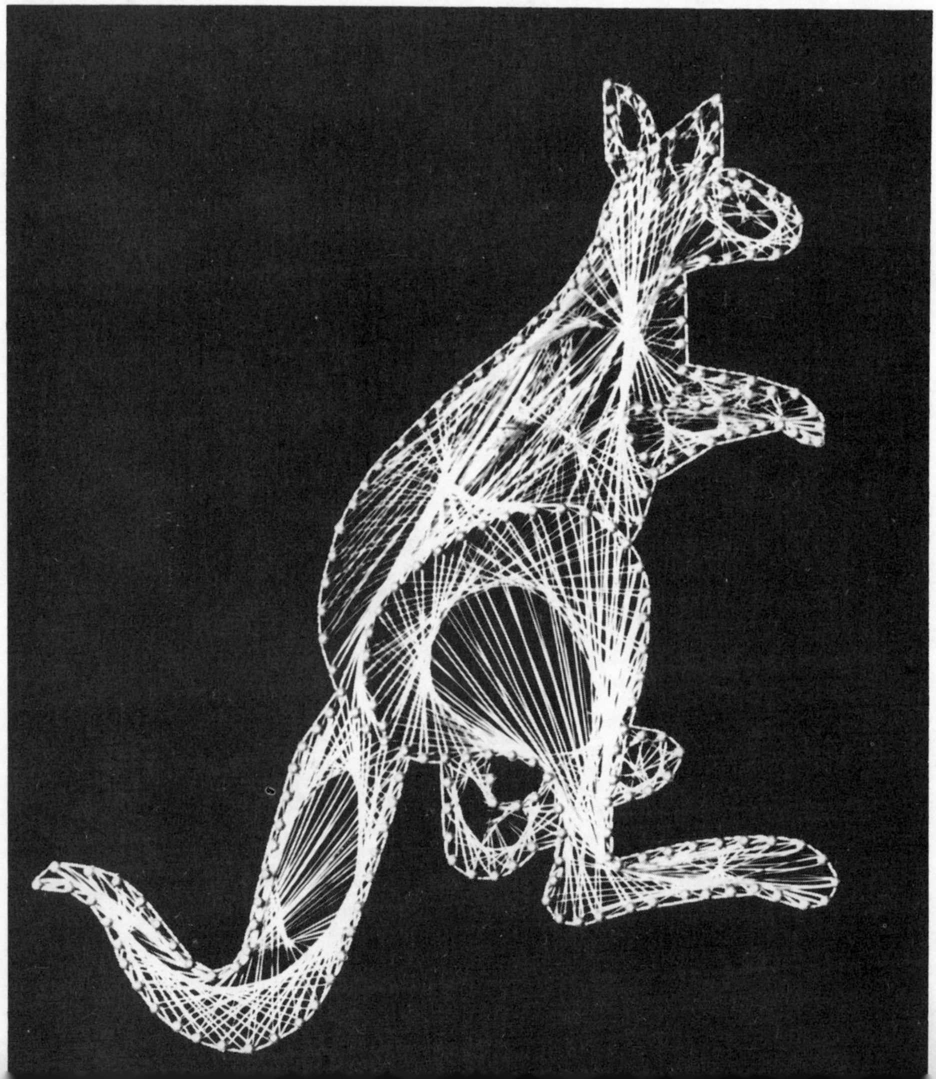

Fig. 7-40 Nailing pattern for kangaroo

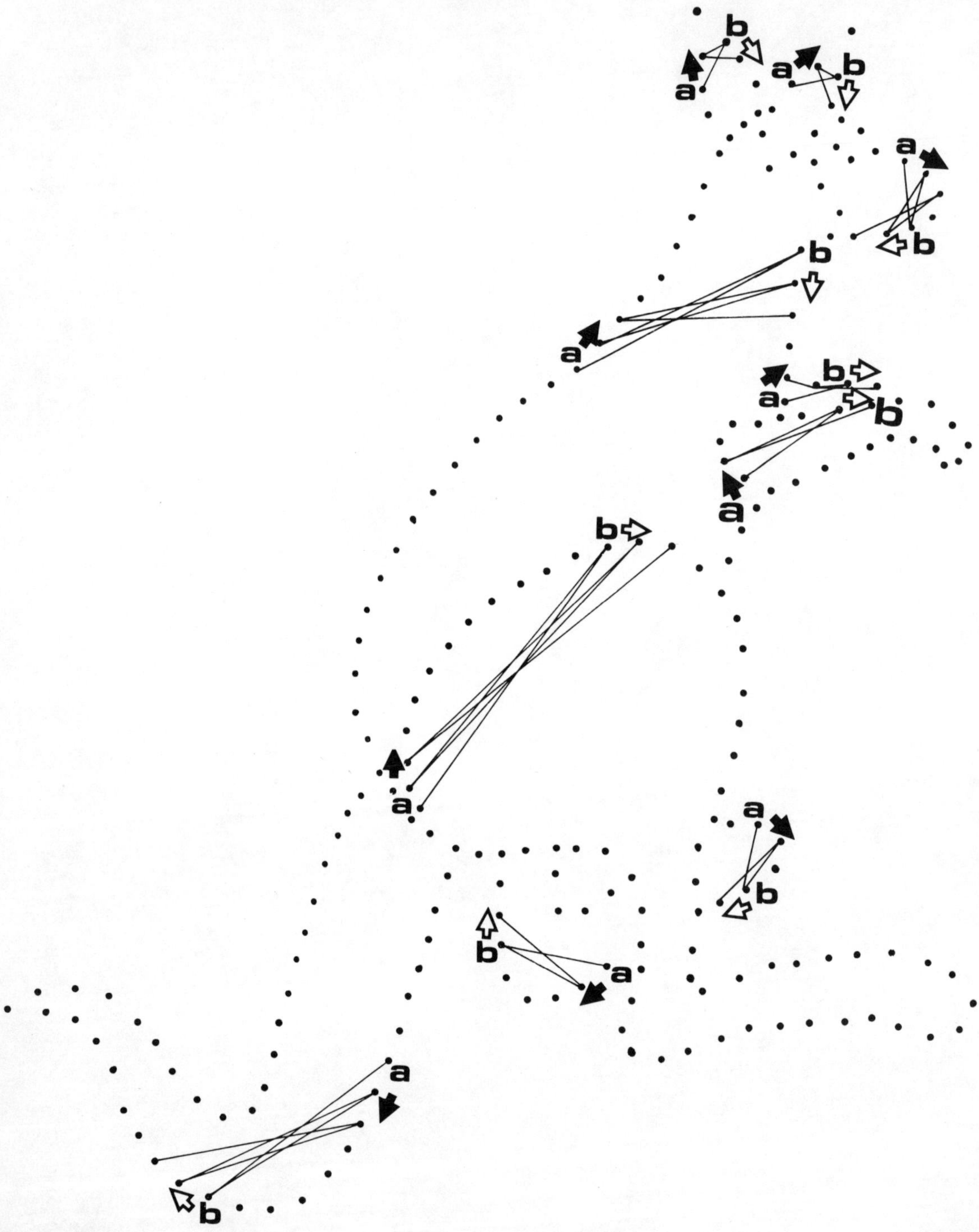

Fig. 7-41 Base layer of kangaroo

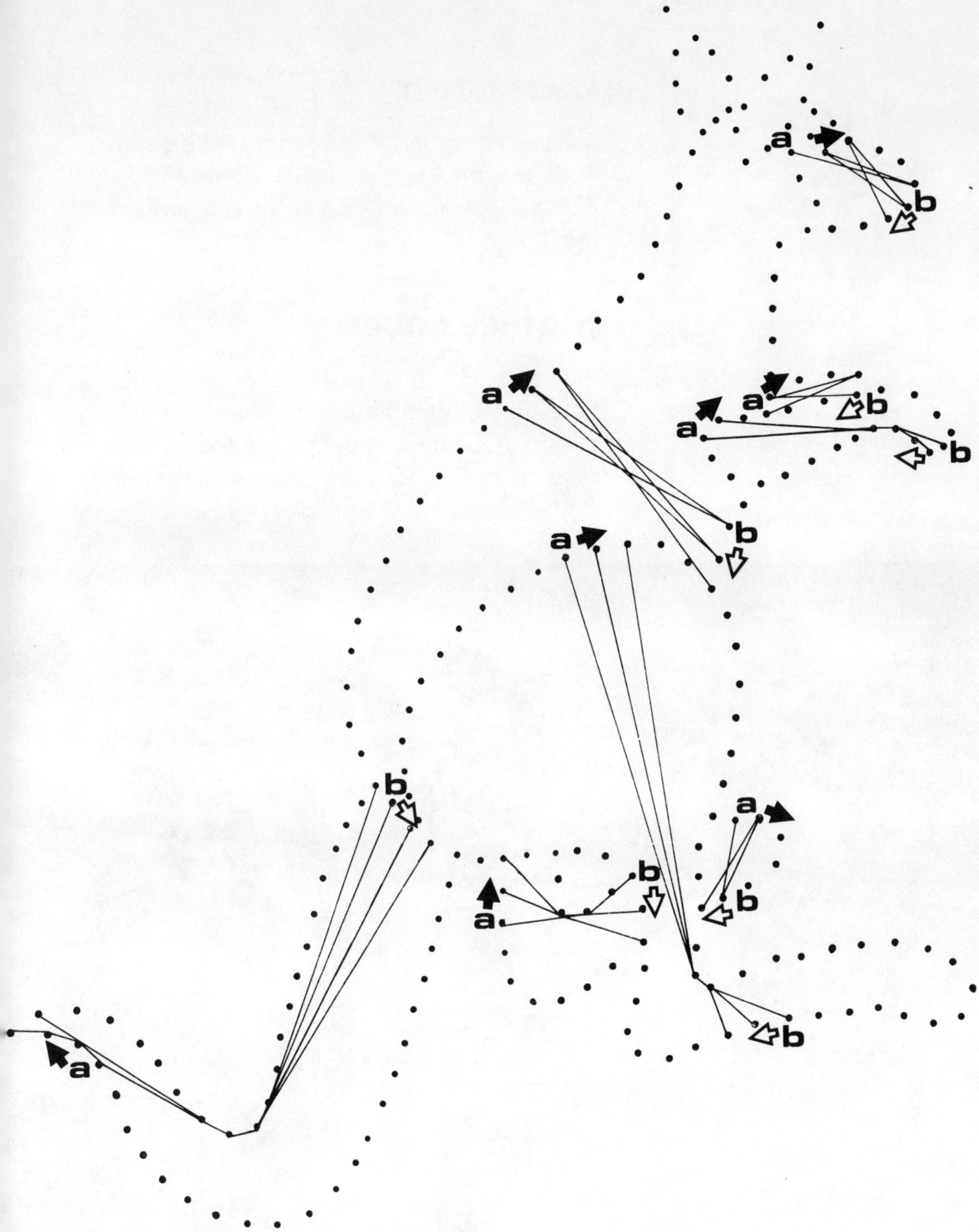

Fig. 7-42 Surface layer of kangaroo

Runner

Base Layer

It will be necessary to go around nails on both legs on the base layer of this design. This will create an outline or rim around the design.

Surface Layer

A nail with a large head or small upholstery tack can be used for the eye in this design. Outlining the outer edge is also recommended. All wiring sequences in Fig. 7-46 are circular, stopping at nail "a".

Fig. 7-43 Runner

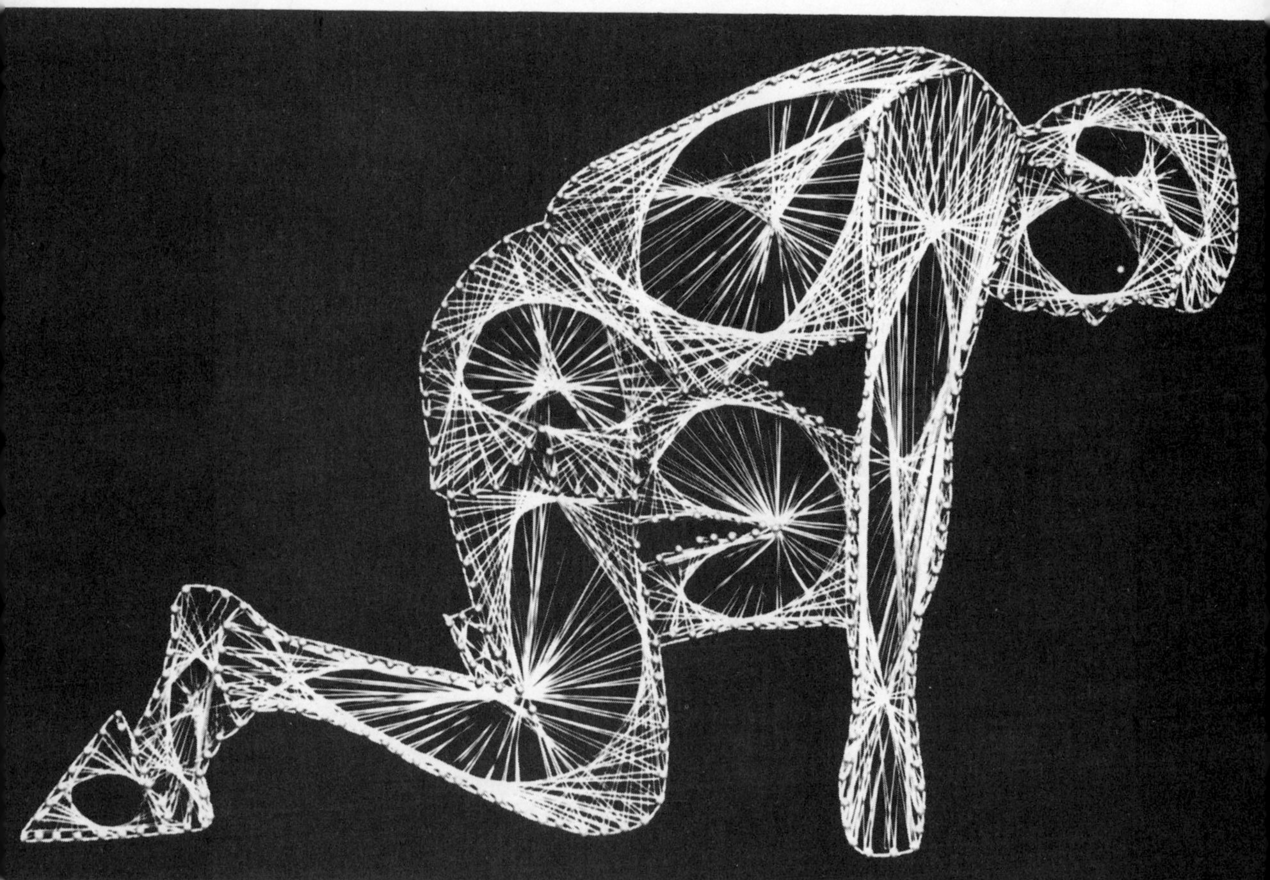

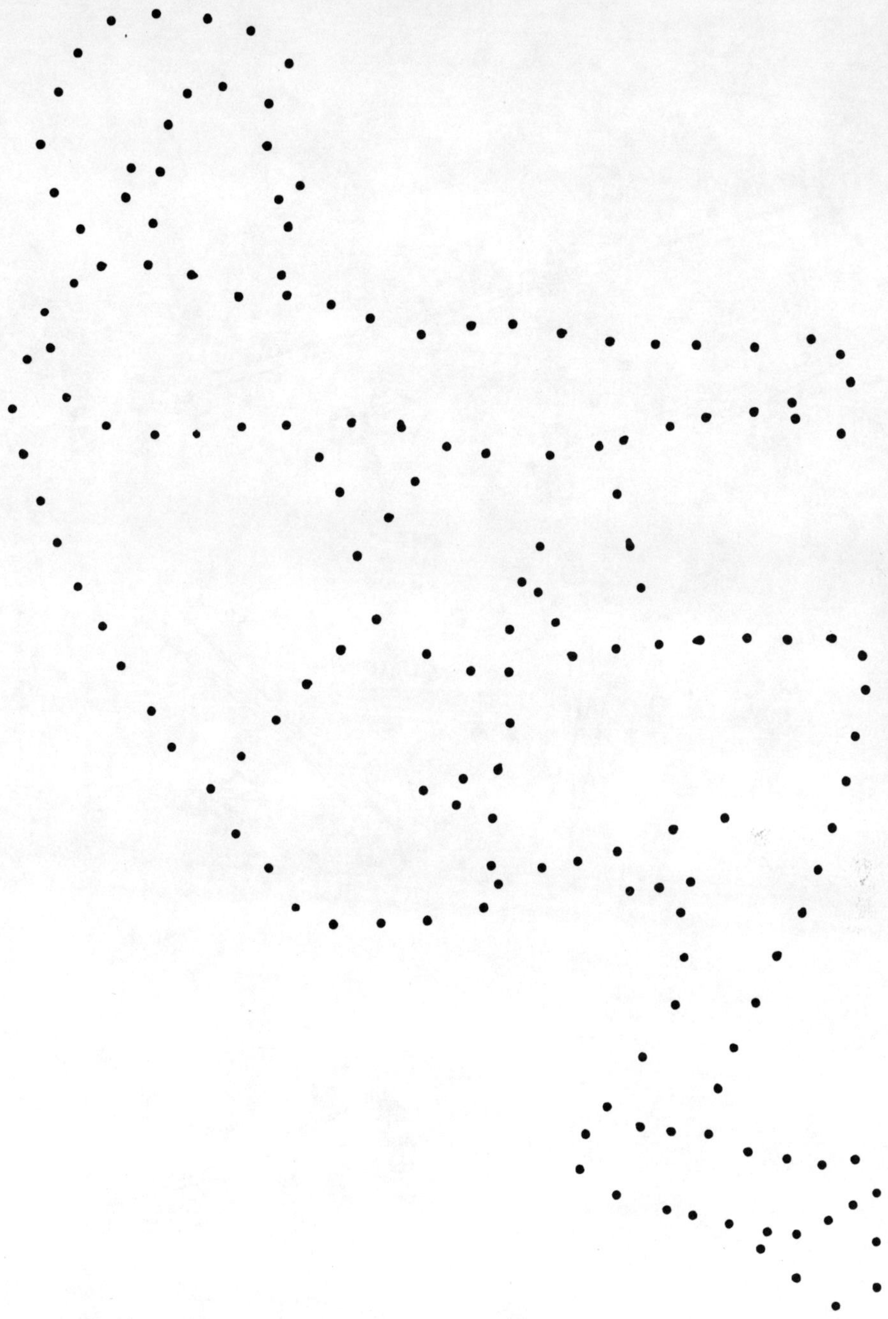

Fig. 7-44 Nailing pattern for runner

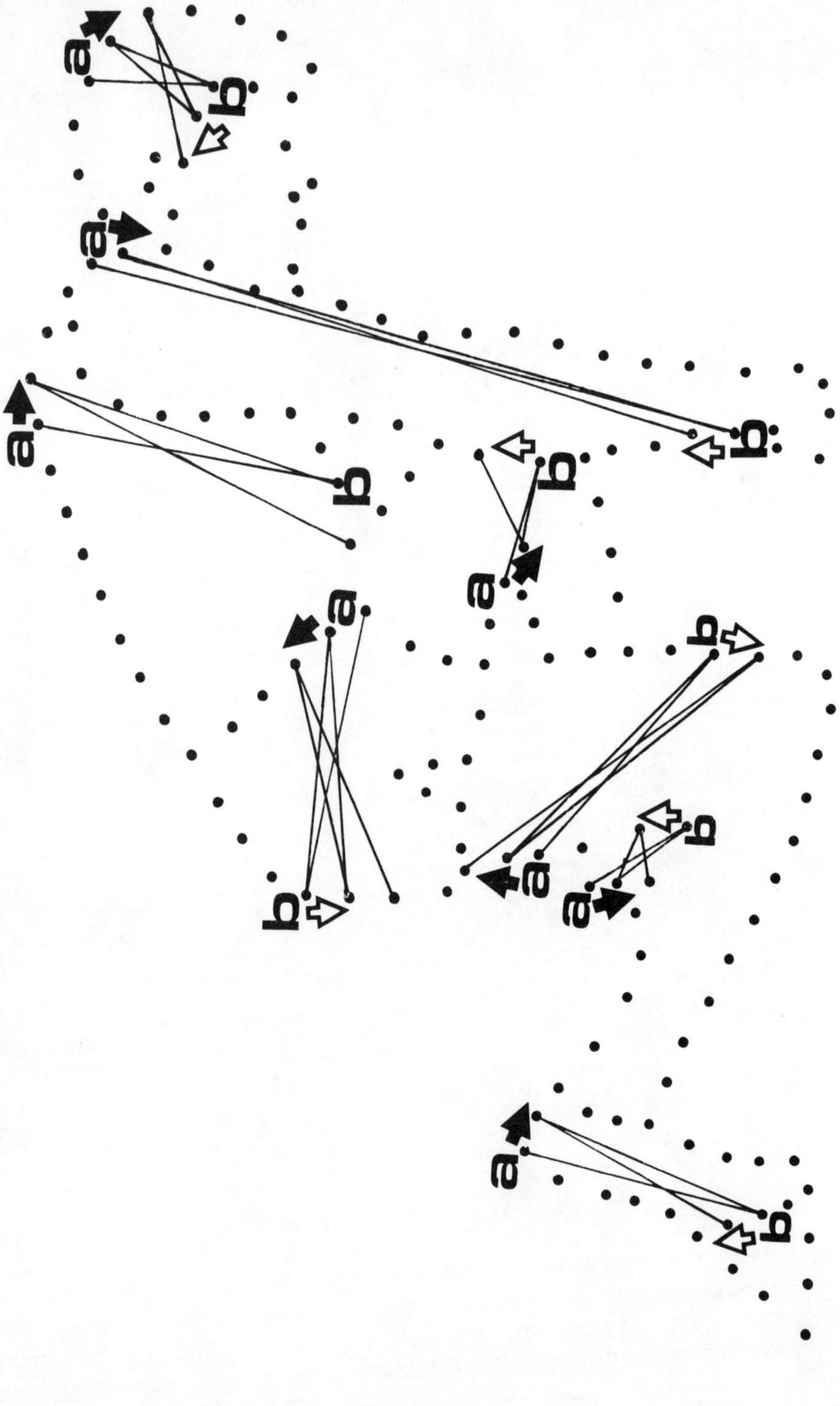

Fig. 7-45 Base layer of runner

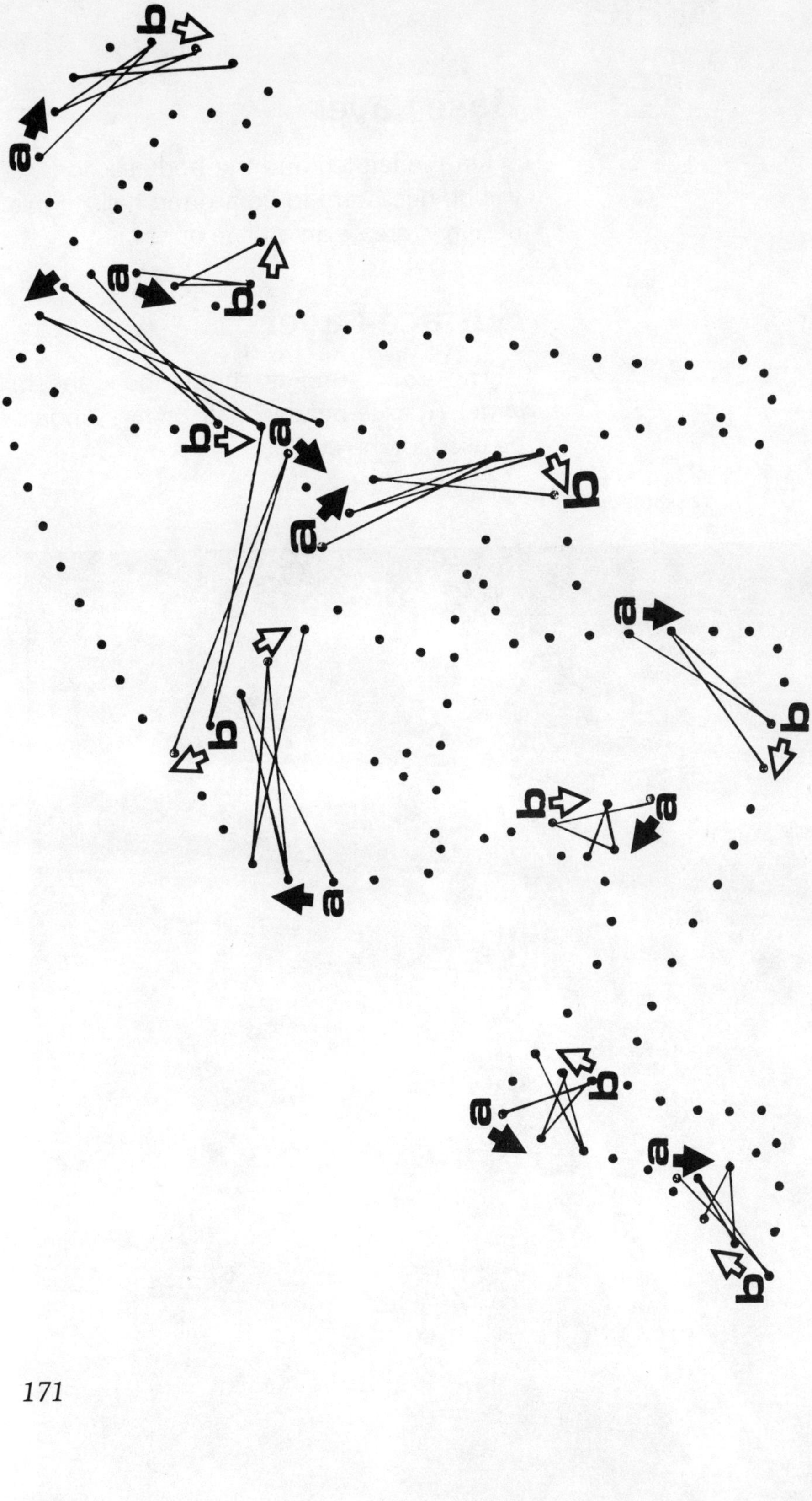

Fig. 7-46 Surface layer of runner

Figure Skater

Base Layer

On the left leg and the body sections, it will be necessary to go around nails in this design to create an outline or rim.

Surface Layer

The skate runners should be done in lamé. A large-headed nail or tack should be used for the eye.

Fig. 7-47 Figure skater

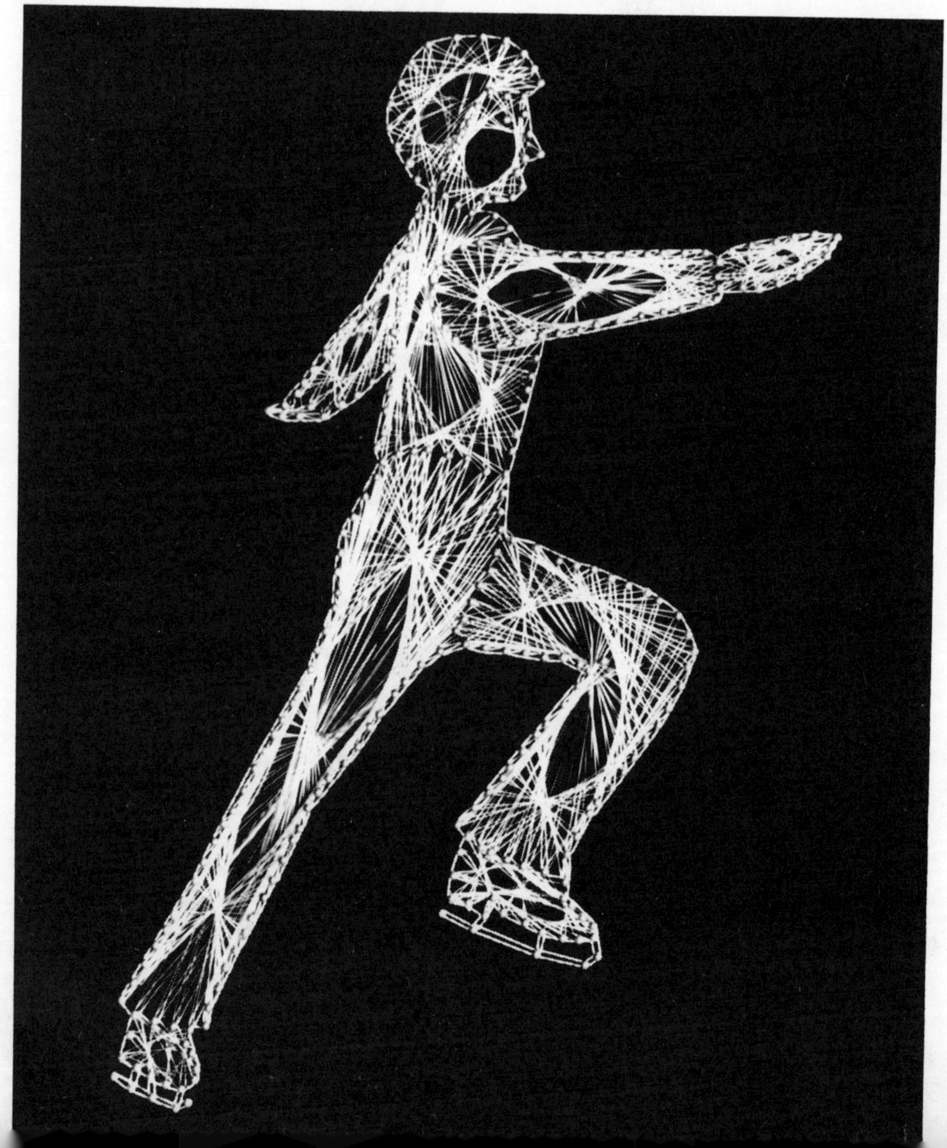

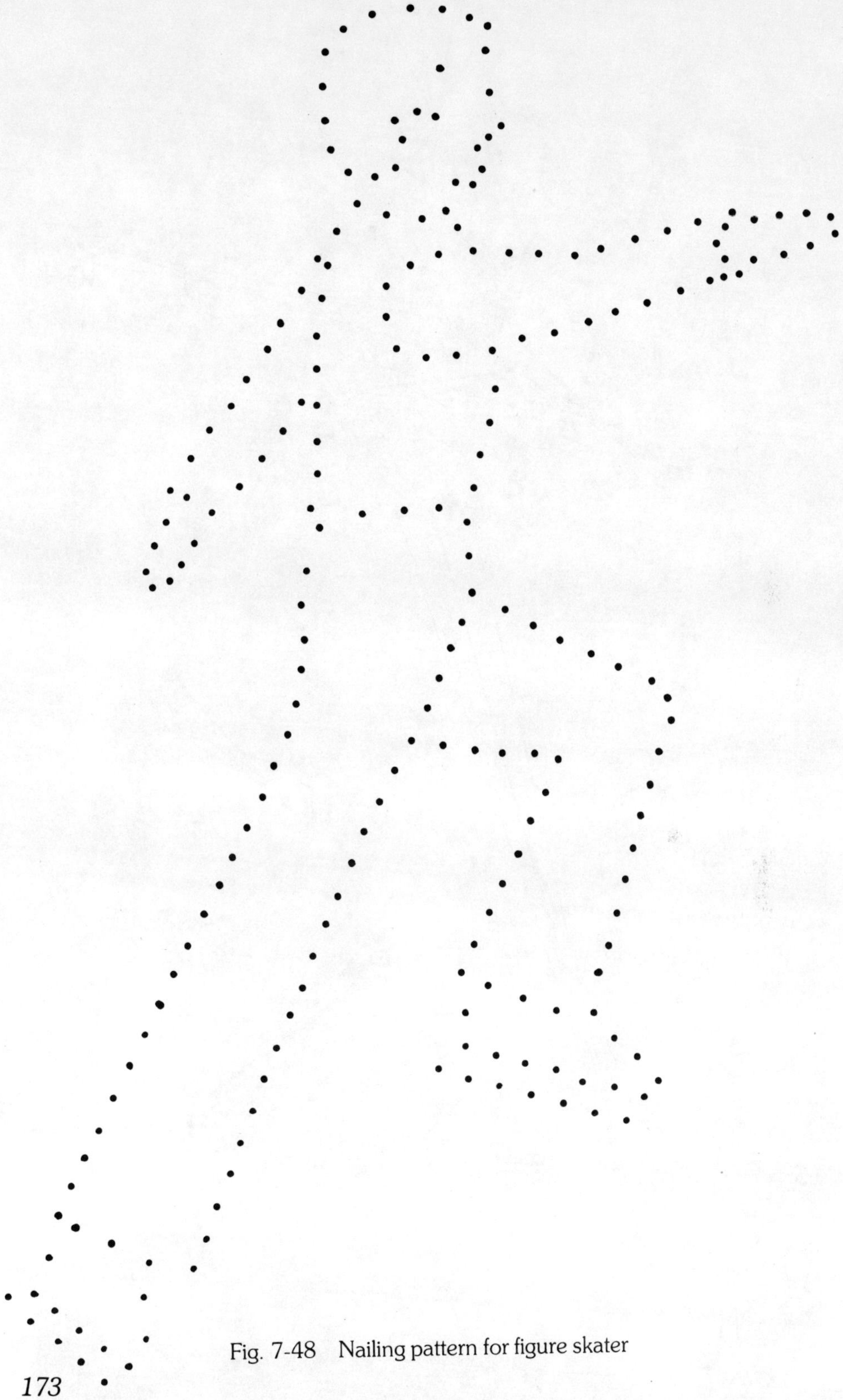

Fig. 7-48 Nailing pattern for figure skater

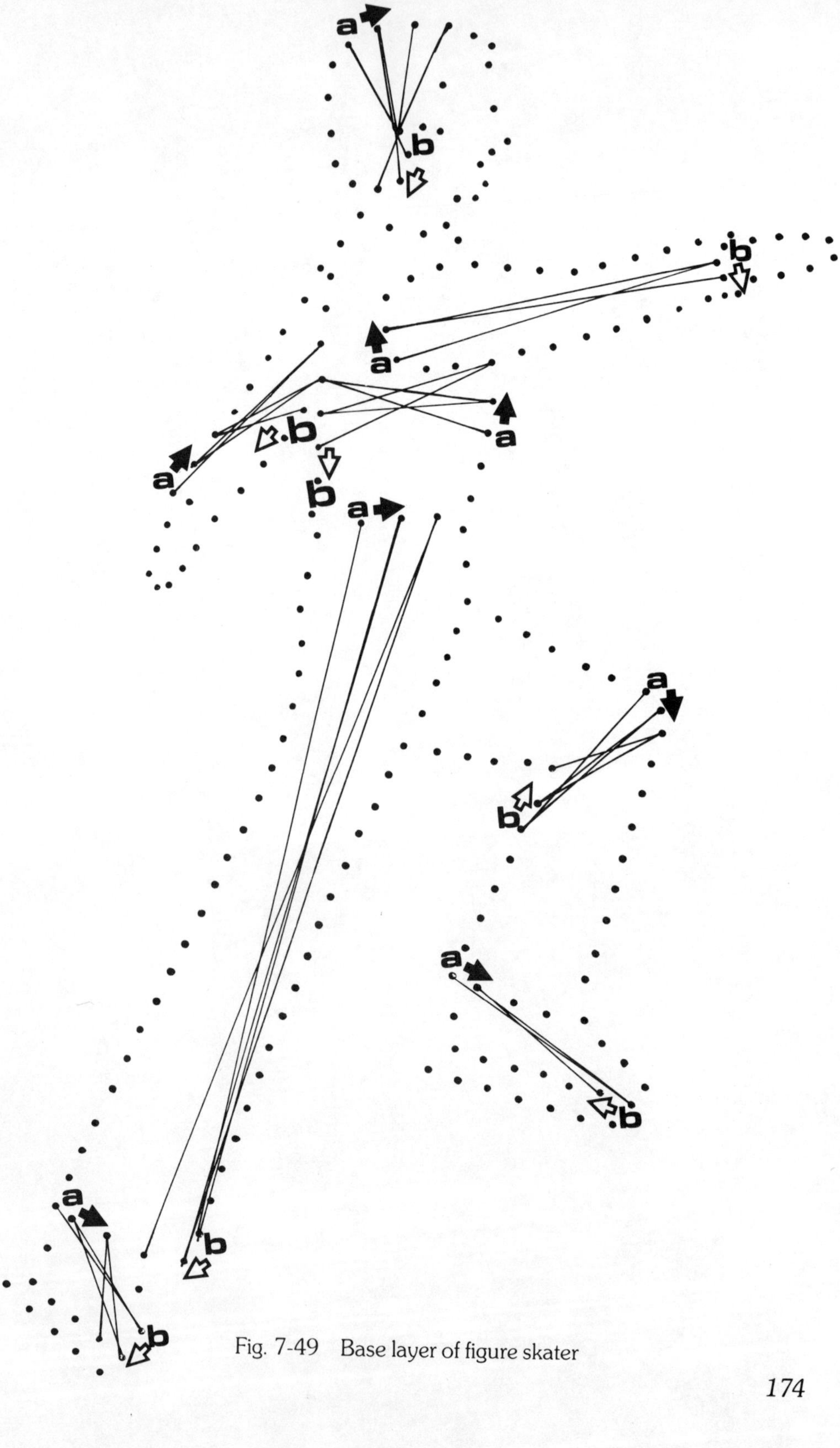

Fig. 7-49 Base layer of figure skater

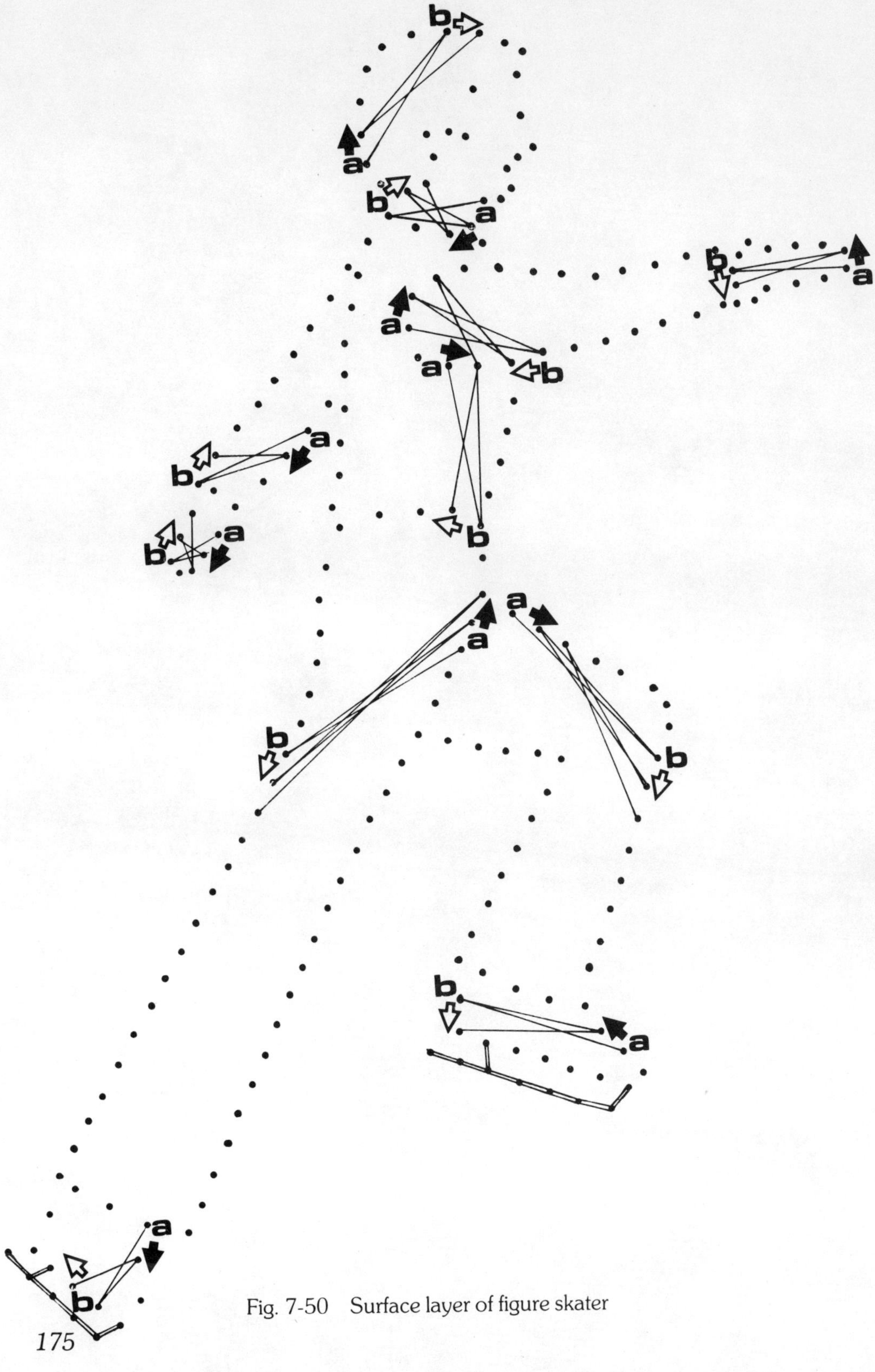

Fig. 7-50 Surface layer of figure skater